SECOND EDITION

Advanced Analytics with Spark

Patterns for Learning from Data at Scale

Sandy Ryza, Uri Laserson, Sean Owen, and Josh Wills

Beijing · Boston · Farnham · Sebastopol · Tokyo

Advanced Analytics with Spark

by Sandy Ryza, Uri Laserson, Sean Owen, and Josh Wills

Copyright © 2017 Sanford Ryza, Uri Laserson, Sean Owen, Joshua Wills. All rights reserved.

Printed in the United States of America.

Published by O'Reilly Media, Inc., 1005 Gravenstein Highway North, Sebastopol, CA 95472.

O'Reilly books may be purchased for educational, business, or sales promotional use. Online editions are also available for most titles (*http://oreilly.com/safari*). For more information, contact our corporate/institutional sales department: 800-998-9938 or *corporate@oreilly.com*.

Editor: Marie Beaugureau
Production Editor: Melanie Yarbrough
Copyeditor: Gillian McGarvey
Proofreader: Christina Edwards

Indexer: WordCo Indexing Services
Interior Designer: David Futato
Cover Designer: Karen Montgomery
Illustrator: Rebecca Demarest

June 2017:   Second Edition

Revision History for the Second Edition
2017-06-09:   First Release

The O'Reilly logo is a registered trademark of O'Reilly Media, Inc. *Advanced Analytics with Spark*, the cover image, and related trade dress are trademarks of O'Reilly Media, Inc.

While the publisher and the authors have used good faith efforts to ensure that the information and instructions contained in this work are accurate, the publisher and the authors disclaim all responsibility for errors or omissions, including without limitation responsibility for damages resulting from the use of or reliance on this work. Use of the information and instructions contained in this work is at your own risk. If any code samples or other technology this work contains or describes is subject to open source licenses or the intellectual property rights of others, it is your responsibility to ensure that your use thereof complies with such licenses and/or rights.

978-1-491-97295-3

[LSI]

Table of Contents

Foreword

Ever since we started the Spark project at Berkeley, I've been excited about not just building fast parallel systems, but helping more and more people make use of large-scale computing. This is why I'm very happy to see this book, written by four experts in data science, on advanced analytics with Spark. Sandy, Uri, Sean, and Josh have been working with Spark for a while, and have put together a great collection of content with equal parts explanations and examples.

The thing I like most about this book is its focus on examples, which are all drawn from real applications on real-world data sets. It's hard to find one, let alone 10, examples that cover big data and that you can run on your laptop, but the authors have managed to create such a collection and set everything up so you can run them in Spark. Moreover, the authors cover not just the core algorithms, but the intricacies of data preparation and model tuning that are needed to really get good results. You should be able to take the concepts in these examples and directly apply them to your own problems.

Big data processing is undoubtedly one of the most exciting areas in computing today, and remains an area of fast evolution and introduction of new ideas. I hope that this book helps you get started in this exciting new field.

— Matei Zaharia, CTO at Databricks
and Vice President, Apache Spark

Preface

Sandy Ryza

I don't like to think I have many regrets, but it's hard to believe anything good came out of a particular lazy moment in 2011 when I was looking into how to best distribute tough discrete optimization problems over clusters of computers. My advisor explained this newfangled Apache Spark thing he had heard of, and I basically wrote off the concept as too good to be true and promptly got back to writing my undergrad thesis in MapReduce. Since then, Spark and I have both matured a bit, but only one of us has seen a meteoric rise that's nearly impossible to avoid making "ignite" puns about. Cut to a few years later, and it has become crystal clear that Spark is something worth paying attention to.

Spark's long lineage of predecessors, from MPI to MapReduce, makes it possible to write programs that take advantage of massive resources while abstracting away the nitty-gritty details of distributed systems. As much as data processing needs have motivated the development of these frameworks, in a way the field of big data has become so related to these frameworks that its scope is defined by what these frameworks can handle. Spark's promise is to take this a little further—to make writing distributed programs feel like writing regular programs.

Spark is great at giving ETL pipelines huge boosts in performance and easing some of the pain that feeds the MapReduce programmer's daily chant of despair ("why? whyyyyy?") to the Apache Hadoop gods. But the exciting thing for me about it has always been what it opens up for complex analytics. With a paradigm that supports iterative algorithms and interactive exploration, Spark is finally an open source framework that allows a data scientist to be productive with large data sets.

I think the best way to teach data science is by example. To that end, my colleagues and I have put together a book of applications, trying to touch on the interactions between the most common algorithms, data sets, and design patterns in large-scale analytics. This book isn't meant to be read cover to cover. Page to a chapter that looks like something you're trying to accomplish, or that simply ignites your interest.

What's in This Book

The first chapter will place Spark within the wider context of data science and big data analytics. After that, each chapter will comprise a self-contained analysis using Spark. The second chapter will introduce the basics of data processing in Spark and Scala through a use case in data cleansing. The next few chapters will delve into the meat and potatoes of machine learning with Spark, applying some of the most common algorithms in canonical applications. The remaining chapters are a bit more of a grab bag and apply Spark in slightly more exotic applications—for example, querying Wikipedia through latent semantic relationships in the text or analyzing genomics data.

The Second Edition

Since the first edition, Spark has experienced a major version upgrade that instated an entirely new core API and sweeping changes in subcomponents like MLlib and Spark SQL. In the second edition, we've made major renovations to the example code and brought the materials up to date with Spark's new best practices.

Using Code Examples

Supplemental material (code examples, exercises, etc.) is available for download at *https://github.com/sryza/aas*.

This book is here to help you get your job done. In general, if example code is offered with this book, you may use it in your programs and documentation. You do not need to contact us for permission unless you're reproducing a significant portion of the code. For example, writing a program that uses several chunks of code from this book does not require permission. Selling or distributing a CD-ROM of examples from O'Reilly books does require permission. Answering a question by citing this book and quoting example code does not require permission. Incorporating a significant amount of example code from this book into your product's documentation does require permission.

We appreciate, but do not require, attribution. An attribution usually includes the title, author, publisher, and ISBN. For example: "*Advanced Analytics with Spark* by Sandy Ryza, Uri Laserson, Sean Owen, and Josh Wills (O'Reilly). Copyright 2015 Sandy Ryza, Uri Laserson, Sean Owen, and Josh Wills, 978-1-491-91276-8."

If you feel your use of code examples falls outside fair use or the permission given above, feel free to contact us at *permissions@oreilly.com*.

O'Reilly Safari

 *Safari* (formerly Safari Books Online) is a membership-based training and reference platform for enterprise, government, educators, and individuals.

Members have access to thousands of books, training videos, Learning Paths, interactive tutorials, and curated playlists from over 250 publishers, including O'Reilly Media, Harvard Business Review, Prentice Hall Professional, Addison-Wesley Professional, Microsoft Press, Sams, Que, Peachpit Press, Adobe, Focal Press, Cisco Press, John Wiley & Sons, Syngress, Morgan Kaufmann, IBM Redbooks, Packt, Adobe Press, FT Press, Apress, Manning, New Riders, McGraw-Hill, Jones & Bartlett, and Course Technology, among others.

For more information, please visit *http://oreilly.com/safari*.

How to Contact Us

Please address comments and questions concerning this book to the publisher:

O'Reilly Media, Inc.
1005 Gravenstein Highway North
Sebastopol, CA 95472
800-998-9938 (in the United States or Canada)
707-829-0515 (international or local)
707-829-0104 (fax)

To comment or ask technical questions about this book, send email to *bookquestions@oreilly.com*.

For more information about our books, courses, conferences, and news, see our website at *http://www.oreilly.com*.

Find us on Facebook: *https://facebook.com/oreilly*

Follow us on Twitter: *https://twitter.com/oreillymedia*

Watch us on YouTube: *https://www.youtube.com/oreillymedia*

Acknowledgments

It goes without saying that you wouldn't be reading this book if it were not for the existence of Apache Spark and MLlib. We all owe thanks to the team that has built and open sourced it, and the hundreds of contributors who have added to it.

We would like to thank everyone who spent a great deal of time reviewing the content of the book with expert eyes: Michael Bernico, Adam Breindel, Ian Buss, Parviz Deyhim, Jeremy Freeman, Chris Fregly, Debashish Ghosh, Juliet Hougland, Jonathan Keebler, Nisha Muktewar, Frank Nothaft, Nick Pentreath, Kostas Sakellis, Tom White, Marcelo Vanzin, and Juliet Hougland again. Thanks all! We owe you one. This has greatly improved the structure and quality of the result.

I (Sandy) also would like to thank Jordan Pinkus and Richard Wang for helping me with some of the theory behind the risk chapter.

Thanks to Marie Beaugureau and O'Reilly for the experience and great support in getting this book published and into your hands.

## CHAPTER 1

Analyzing Big Data

Sandy Ryza

[Data applications] are like sausages. It is better not to see them being made.
—Otto von Bismarck

- Build a model to detect credit card fraud using thousands of features and billions of transactions

- Intelligently recommend millions of products to millions of users

- Estimate financial risk through simulations of portfolios that include millions of instruments

- Easily manipulate data from thousands of human genomes to detect genetic associations with disease

These are tasks that simply could not have been accomplished 5 or 10 years ago. When people say that we live in an age of big data they mean that we have tools for collecting, storing, and processing information at a scale previously unheard of. Sitting behind these capabilities is an ecosystem of open source software that can leverage clusters of commodity computers to chug through massive amounts of data. Distributed systems like Apache Hadoop have found their way into the mainstream and have seen widespread deployment at organizations in nearly every field.

But just as a chisel and a block of stone do not make a statue, there is a gap between having access to these tools and all this data and doing something useful with it. This is where data science comes in. Just as sculpture is the practice of turning tools and raw material into something relevant to nonsculptors, data science is the practice of turning tools and raw data into something that non–data scientists might care about.

Often, "doing something useful" means placing a schema over it and using SQL to answer questions like "Of the gazillion users who made it to the third page in our registration process, how many are over 25?" The field of how to structure a data warehouse and organize information to make answering these kinds of questions easy is a rich one, but we will mostly avoid its intricacies in this book.

Sometimes, "doing something useful" takes a little extra. SQL still may be core to the approach, but in order to work around idiosyncrasies in the data or perform complex analysis, we need a programming paradigm that's a little bit more flexible and closer to the ground, and with richer functionality in areas like machine learning and statistics. These are the kinds of analyses we are going to talk about in this book.

For a long time, open source frameworks like R, the PyData stack, and Octave have made rapid analysis and model building viable over small data sets. With fewer than 10 lines of code, we can throw together a machine learning model on half a data set and use it to predict labels on the other half. With a little more effort, we can impute missing data, experiment with a few models to find the best one, or use the results of a model as inputs to fit another. What should an equivalent process look like that can leverage clusters of computers to achieve the same outcomes on huge data sets?

The right approach might be to simply extend these frameworks to run on multiple machines to retain their programming models and rewrite their guts to play well in distributed settings. However, the challenges of distributed computing require us to rethink many of the basic assumptions that we rely on in single-node systems. For example, because data must be partitioned across many nodes on a cluster, algorithms that have wide data dependencies will suffer from the fact that network transfer rates are orders of magnitude slower than memory accesses. As the number of machines working on a problem increases, the probability of a failure increases. These facts require a programming paradigm that is sensitive to the characteristics of the underlying system: one that discourages poor choices and makes it easy to write code that will execute in a highly parallel manner.

Of course, single-machine tools like PyData and R that have come to recent prominence in the software community are not the only tools used for data analysis. Scientific fields like genomics that deal with large data sets have been leveraging parallel computing frameworks for decades. Most people processing data in these fields today are familiar with a cluster-computing environment called HPC (high-performance computing). Where the difficulties with PyData and R lie in their inability to scale, the difficulties with HPC lie in its relatively low level of abstraction and difficulty of use. For example, to process a large file full of DNA-sequencing reads in parallel, we must manually split it up into smaller files and submit a job for each of those files to the cluster scheduler. If some of these fail, the user must detect the failure and take care of manually resubmitting them. If the analysis requires all-to-all operations like sorting the entire data set, the large data set must be streamed through a single node, or the scientist must resort to lower-level distributed frameworks like MPI, which are difficult to program without extensive knowledge of C and distributed/networked systems.

Tools written for HPC environments often fail to decouple the in-memory data models from the lower-level storage models. For example, many tools only know how to read data from a POSIX filesystem in a single stream, making it difficult to make tools naturally parallelize, or to use other storage backends, like databases. Recent systems in the Hadoop ecosystem provide abstractions that allow users to treat a cluster of computers more like a single computer—to automatically split up files and distribute storage over many machines, divide work into smaller tasks and execute them in a distributed manner, and recover from failures. The Hadoop ecosystem can automate a lot of the hassle of working with large data sets, and is far cheaper than HPC.

The Challenges of Data Science

A few hard truths come up so often in the practice of data science that evangelizing these truths has become a large role of the data science team at Cloudera. For a system that seeks to enable complex analytics on huge data to be successful, it needs to be informed by—or at least not conflict with—these truths.

First, the vast majority of work that goes into conducting successful analyses lies in preprocessing data. Data is messy, and cleansing, munging, fusing, mushing, and many other verbs are prerequisites to doing anything useful with it. Large data sets in particular, because they are not amenable to direct examination by humans, can require computational methods to even discover what preprocessing steps are required. Even when it comes time to optimize model performance, a typical data pipeline requires spending far more time in feature engineering and selection than in choosing and writing algorithms.

For example, when building a model that attempts to detect fraudulent purchases on a website, the data scientist must choose from a wide variety of potential features: fields that users are required to fill out, IP location info, login times, and click logs as users navigate the site. Each of these comes with its own challenges when converting to vectors fit for machine learning algorithms. A system needs to support more flexible transformations than turning a 2D array of doubles into a mathematical model.

Second, *iteration* is a fundamental part of data science. Modeling and analysis typically require multiple passes over the same data. One aspect of this lies within machine learning algorithms and statistical procedures. Popular optimization procedures like stochastic gradient descent and expectation maximization involve repeated scans over their inputs to reach convergence. Iteration also matters within the data scientist's own workflow. When data scientists are initially investigating and trying to get a feel for a data set, usually the results of a query inform the next query that should run. When building models, data scientists do not try to get it right in one try.

Choosing the right features, picking the right algorithms, running the right significance tests, and finding the right hyperparameters all require experimentation. A framework that requires reading the same data set from disk each time it is accessed adds delay that can slow down the process of exploration and limit the number of things we get to try.

Third, the task isn't over when a well-performing model has been built. If the point of data science is to make data useful to non–data scientists, then a model stored as a list of regression weights in a text file on the data scientist's computer has not really accomplished this goal. Uses of data recommendation engines and real-time fraud detection systems culminate in data applications. In these, models become part of a production service and may need to be rebuilt periodically or even in real time.

For these situations, it is helpful to make a distinction between analytics in the lab and analytics in the factory. In the lab, data scientists engage in exploratory analytics. They try to understand the nature of the data they are working with. They visualize it and test wild theories. They experiment with different classes of features and auxiliary sources they can use to augment it. They cast a wide net of algorithms in the hopes that one or two will work. In the factory, in building a data application, data scientists engage in operational analytics. They package their models into services that can inform real-world decisions. They track their models' performance over time and obsess about how they can make small tweaks to squeeze out another percentage point of accuracy. They care about SLAs and uptime. Historically, exploratory analytics typically occurs in languages like R, and when it comes time to build production applications, the data pipelines are rewritten entirely in Java or C++.

Of course, everybody could save time if the original modeling code could be actually used in the app for which it is written, but languages like R are slow and lack integration with most planes of the production infrastructure stack, and languages like Java and C++ are just poor tools for exploratory analytics. They lack read-evaluate-print loop (REPL) environments to play with data interactively and require large amounts of code to express simple transformations. A framework that makes modeling easy but is also a good fit for production systems is a huge win.

Introducing Apache Spark

Enter Apache Spark, an open source framework that combines an engine for distributing programs across clusters of machines with an elegant model for writing programs atop it. Spark, which originated at the UC Berkeley AMPLab and has since been contributed to the Apache Software Foundation, is arguably the first open source software that makes distributed programming truly accessible to data scientists.

One illuminating way to understand Spark is in terms of its advances over its predecessor, Apache Hadoop's MapReduce. MapReduce revolutionized computation over huge data sets by offering a simple model for writing programs that could execute in parallel across hundreds to thousands of machines. The MapReduce engine achieves near linear scalability—as the data size increases, we can throw more computers at it and see jobs complete in the same amount of time—and is resilient to the fact that failures that occur rarely on a single machine occur all the time on clusters of thousands of machines. It breaks up work into small *tasks* and can gracefully accommodate task failures without compromising the job to which they belong.

Spark maintains MapReduce's linear scalability and fault tolerance, but extends it in three important ways. First, rather than relying on a rigid map-then-reduce format, its engine can execute a more general directed acyclic graph (DAG) of operators. This means that in situations where MapReduce must write out intermediate results to the distributed filesystem, Spark can pass them directly to the next step in the pipeline. In this way, it is similar to *Dryad* (*http://bit.ly/2r3TRpE*), a descendant of MapReduce that originated at Microsoft Research. Second, it complements this capability with a rich set of transformations that enable users to express computation more naturally. It has a strong developer focus and streamlined API that can represent complex pipelines in a few lines of code.

Third, Spark extends its predecessors with in-memory processing. Its Dataset and DataFrame abstractions enable developers to materialize any point in a processing pipeline into memory across the cluster, meaning that future steps that want to deal with the same data set need not recompute it or reload it from disk. This capability opens up use cases that distributed processing engines could not previously approach. Spark is well suited for highly iterative algorithms that require multiple passes over a data set, as well as reactive applications that quickly respond to user queries by scanning large in-memory data sets.

Perhaps most importantly, Spark fits well with the aforementioned hard truths of data science, acknowledging that the biggest bottleneck in building data applications is not CPU, disk, or network, but analyst productivity. It perhaps cannot be overstated how much collapsing the full pipeline, from preprocessing to model evaluation, into a single programming environment can speed up development. By packaging an expressive programming model with a set of analytic libraries under a REPL, Spark avoids the roundtrips to IDEs required by frameworks like MapReduce and the challenges of subsampling and moving data back and forth from the Hadoop distributed file system (HDFS) required by frameworks like R. The more quickly analysts can experiment with their data, the higher likelihood they have of doing something useful with it.

With respect to the pertinence of munging and ETL, Spark strives to be something closer to the Python of big data than the MATLAB of big data. As a general-purpose computation engine, its core APIs provide a strong foundation for data transformation independent of any functionality in statistics, machine learning, or matrix algebra. Its Scala and Python APIs allow programming in expressive general-purpose languages, as well as access to existing libraries.

Spark's in-memory caching makes it ideal for iteration both at the micro- and macro-level. Machine learning algorithms that make multiple passes over their training set can cache it in memory. When exploring and getting a feel for a data set, data scientists can keep it in memory while they run queries, and easily cache transformed versions of it as well without suffering a trip to disk.

Last, Spark spans the gap between systems designed for exploratory analytics and systems designed for operational analytics. It is often quoted that a data scientist is someone who is better at engineering than most statisticians, and better at statistics than most engineers. At the very least, Spark is better at being an operational system than most exploratory systems and better for data exploration than the technologies commonly used in operational systems. It is built for performance and reliability from the ground up. Sitting atop the JVM, it can take advantage of many of the operational and debugging tools built for the Java stack.

Spark boasts strong integration with the variety of tools in the Hadoop ecosystem. It can read and write data in all of the data formats supported by MapReduce, allowing it to interact with formats commonly used to store data on Hadoop, like Apache Avro and Apache Parquet (and good old CSV). It can read from and write to NoSQL databases like Apache HBase and Apache Cassandra. Its stream-processing library, Spark Streaming, can ingest data continuously from systems like Apache Flume and Apache Kafka. Its SQL library, SparkSQL, can interact with the Apache Hive Metastore, and the Hive on Spark initiative enabled Spark to be used as an underlying execution engine for Hive, as an alternative to MapReduce. It can run inside YARN, Hadoop's scheduler and resource manager, allowing it to share cluster resources dynamically and to be managed with the same policies as other processing engines, like MapReduce and Apache Impala.

About This Book

The rest of this book is not going to be about Spark's merits and disadvantages. There are a few other things that it will not be about either. It will introduce the Spark programming model and Scala basics, but it will not attempt to be a Spark reference or provide a comprehensive guide to all its nooks and crannies. It will not try to be a machine learning, statistics, or linear algebra reference, although many of the chapters will provide some background on these before using them.

Instead, it will try to help the reader get a feel for what it's like to use Spark for complex analytics on large data sets. It will cover the entire pipeline: not just building and evaluating models, but also cleansing, preprocessing, and exploring data, with attention paid to turning results into production applications. We believe that the best way to teach this is by example, so after a quick chapter describing Spark and its ecosystem, the rest of the chapters will be self-contained illustrations of what it looks like to use Spark for analyzing data from different domains.

When possible, we will attempt not to just provide a "solution," but to demonstrate the full data science workflow, with all of its iterations, dead ends, and restarts. This book will be useful for getting more comfortable with Scala, Spark, and machine learning and data analysis. However, these are in service of a larger goal, and we hope that most of all, this book will teach you how to approach tasks like those described at the beginning of this chapter. Each chapter, in about 20 measly pages, will try to get as close as possible to demonstrating how to build one of these pieces of data applications.

The Second Edition

The years 2015 and 2016 saw seismic changes in Spark, culminating in the release of Spark 2.0 in July of 2016. The most salient of these changes are the modifications to Spark's core API. In versions prior to Spark 2.0, Spark's API centered around *Resilient Distributed Datasets* (RDDs), which are lazily instantiated collections of objects, partitioned across a cluster of computers.

Although RDDs enabled a powerful and expressive API, they suffered two main problems. First, they didn't lend themselves well to performant, stable execution. By relying on Java and Python objects, RDDs used memory inefficiently and exposed Spark programs to long garbage-collection pauses. They also tied the execution plan into the API, which put a heavy burden on the user to optimize the execution of their program. For example, where a traditional RDBMS might be able to pick the best join strategy based on the size of the tables being joined, Spark required users to make this choice on their own. Second, Spark's API ignored the fact that data often fits into a structured relational form, and when it does, an API can supply primitives that makes the data much easier to manipulate, such as by allowing users to refer to column names instead of ordinal positions in a tuple.

Spark 2.0 addressed these problems by replacing RDDs with Datasets and DataFrames. *Datasets* are similar to RDDs but map the objects they represent to *encoders*, which enable a much more efficient in-memory representation. This means that Spark programs execute faster, use less memory, and run more predictably. Spark also places an optimizer between data sets and their execution plan, which means that it can make more intelligent decisions about how to execute them. *DataFrame* is a subclass of Dataset that is specialized to model relational data (i.e., data with rows and fixed sets of columns). By understanding the notion of a column, Spark can offer a cleaner, expressive API, as well as enable a number of performance optimizations. For example, if Spark knows that only a subset of the columns are needed to produce a result, it can avoid materializing those columns into memory. And many transformations that previously needed to be expressed as user-defined functions (UDFs) are now expressible directly in the API. This is especially advantageous when using Python, because Spark's internal machinery can execute transformations much faster than functions defined in Python. DataFrames also offer interoperability with Spark SQL, meaning that users can write a SQL query that returns a data frame and then use that DataFrame programmatically in the Spark-supported language of their choice. Although the new API looks very similar to the old API, enough details have changed that nearly all Spark programs need to be updated.

In addition to the code API changes, Spark 2.0 saw big changes to the APIs used for machine learning and statistical analysis. In prior versions, each machine learning algorithm had its own API. Users who wanted to prepare data for input into algorithms or to feed the output of one algorithm into another needed to write their own custom orchestration code. Spark 2.0 contains the *Spark ML* API, which introduces a framework for composing pipelines of machine learning algorithms and feature transformation steps. The API, inspired by Python's popular Scikit-Learn API, revolves around *estimators* and *transformers*, objects that learn parameters from the data and then use those parameters to transform data. The Spark ML API is heavily integrated with the DataFrames API, which makes it easy to train machine learning models on relational data. For example, users can refer to features by name instead of by ordinal position in a feature vector.

Taken together, all these changes to Spark have rendered much of the first edition obsolete. This second edition updates all of the chapters to use the new Spark APIs when possible. Additionally, we've cut some bits that are no longer relevant. For example, we've removed a full appendix that dealt with some of the intricacies of the API, in part because Spark now handles these situations intelligently without user intervention. With Spark in a new era of maturity and stability, we hope that these changes will preserve the book as an useful resource on analytics with Spark for years to come.

## CHAPTER 2

Introduction to Data Analysis with Scala and Spark

Josh Wills

If you are immune to boredom, there is literally nothing you cannot accomplish.
—David Foster Wallace

Data cleansing is the first step in any data science project, and often the most important. Many clever analyses have been undone because the data analyzed had fundamental quality problems or underlying artifacts that biased the analysis or led the data scientist to see things that weren't really there.

Despite its importance, most textbooks and classes on data science either don't cover data cleansing or only give it a passing mention. The explanation for this is simple: cleansing data is really boring. It is the tedious, dull work that you have to do before you can get to the really cool machine learning algorithm that you've been dying to apply to a new problem. Many new data scientists tend to rush past it to get their data into a minimally acceptable state, only to discover that the data has major quality issues after they apply their (potentially computationally intensive) algorithm and end up with a nonsense answer as output.

Everyone has heard the saying "garbage in, garbage out." But there is something even more pernicious: getting reasonable-looking answers from a reasonable-looking data set that has major (but not obvious at first glance) quality issues. Drawing significant conclusions based on this kind of mistake is the sort of thing that gets data scientists fired.

One of the most important talents that you can develop as a data scientist is the ability to discover interesting and worthwhile problems in every phase of the data analytics lifecycle. The more skill and brainpower that you can apply early on in an analysis project, the stronger your confidence will be in your final product.

Of course, it's easy to say all that—it's the data science equivalent of telling children to eat their vegetables—but it's much more fun to play with a new tool like Spark that lets us build fancy machine learning algorithms, develop streaming data processing engines, and analyze web-scale graphs. And what better way to introduce you to working with data using Spark and Scala than a data cleansing exercise?

Scala for Data Scientists

Most data scientists have a favorite tool, like R or Python, for interactive data munging and analysis. Although they're willing to work in other environments when they have to, data scientists tend to get very attached to their favorite tool, and are always looking to find a way to use it. Introducing a data scientist to a new tool that has a new syntax and set of patterns to learn can be challenging under the best of circumstances.

There are libraries and wrappers for Spark that allow you to use it from R or Python. The Python wrapper, which is called PySpark, is actually quite good; we'll cover some examples that involve using it in Chapter 11. But the vast majority of our examples will be written in Scala, because we think that learning how to work with Spark in the same language in which the underlying framework is written has a number of advantages, such as the following:

It reduces performance overhead.
> Whenever we're running an algorithm in R or Python on top of a JVM-based language like Scala, we have to do some work to pass code and data across the different environments, and oftentimes, things can get lost in translation. When you're writing data analysis algorithms in Spark with the Scala API, you can be far more confident that your program will run as intended.

It gives you access to the latest and greatest.
> All of Spark's machine learning, stream processing, and graph analytics libraries are written in Scala, and the Python and R bindings tend to get support this new functionality much later. If you want to take advantage of all the features that Spark has to offer (without waiting for a port to other language bindings), you will need to learn at least a little bit of Scala; and if you want to be able to extend those functions to solve new problems you encounter, you'll need to learn a little bit more.

It will help you understand the Spark philosophy.
> Even when you're using Spark from Python or R, the APIs reflect the underlying computation philosophy that Spark inherited from the language in which it was developed—Scala. If you know how to use Spark in Scala—even if you primarily use it from other languages—you'll have a better understanding of the system and will be in a better position to "think in Spark."

There is another advantage of learning how to use Spark from Scala, but it's a bit more difficult to explain because of how different Spark is from any other data analysis tool. If you've ever analyzed data pulled from a database in R or Python, you're used to working with languages like SQL to retrieve the information you want, and then switching into R or Python to manipulate and visualize that data. You're used to using one language (SQL) for retrieving and manipulating lots of data stored in a remote cluster, and another language (Python/R) for manipulating and visualizing information stored on your own machine. And if you wanted to move some of your computation into the database engine via a SQL UDF, you needed to move to yet another programming environment like C++ or Java and learn a bit about the internals of the database. If you've been doing this for long enough, you probably don't even think about it anymore.

With Spark and Scala, the experience is different, because you have the option of using the same language for *everything*. You're writing Scala to retrieve data from the cluster via Spark. You're writing Scala to manipulate that data locally on your machine. And then—and this is the really neat part—you can send Scala code into the cluster so that you can perform the exact same transformations that you performed locally on data that is still stored in the cluster. Even when you're working in a higher-level language like Spark SQL, you can write your UDFs inline, register them with the Spark SQL engine, and use them right away—no context switching required.

It's difficult to express how transformative it is to do all of your data munging and analysis in a single environment, regardless of where the data itself is stored and processed. It's the sort of thing that you have to experience to understand, and we wanted to be sure that our examples captured some of that magic feeling we experienced when we first started using Spark.

The Spark Programming Model

Spark programming starts with a data set, usually residing in some form of distributed, persistent storage like HDFS. Writing a Spark program typically consists of a few related steps:

1. Define a set of transformations on the input data set.
2. Invoke actions that output the transformed data sets to persistent storage or return results to the driver's local memory.
3. Run local computations that operate on the results computed in a distributed fashion. These can help you decide what transformations and actions to undertake next.

As Spark has matured from version 1.2 to version 2.1, the number and quality of tools available for performing these steps have increased. You can mix and match complex SQL queries, machine learning libraries, and custom code as you carry out your analysis, and you can leverage all of the higher-level abstractions that the Spark community has developed over the past few years in order to answer more questions in less time. At the same time, it's important to remember that all of these higher-level abstractions still rely on the same philosophy that has been present in Spark since the very beginning: the interplay between storage and execution. Spark pairs these abstractions in an elegant way that essentially allows any intermediate step in a data processing pipeline to be cached in memory for later use. Understanding these principles will help you make better use of Spark for data analysis.

Record Linkage

The problem that we're going to study in this chapter goes by a lot of different names in the literature and in practice: entity resolution, record deduplication, merge-and-purge, and list washing. Ironically, this makes it difficult to find all of the research papers on this topic in order to get a good overview of solution techniques; we need a data scientist to deduplicate the references to this data cleansing problem! For our purposes in the rest of this chapter, we're going to refer to this problem as *record linkage*.

The general structure of the problem is something like this: we have a large collection of records from one or more source systems, and it is likely that multiple records refer to the same underlying entity, such as a customer, a patient, or the location of a business or an event. Each entity has a number of attributes, such as a name, an address, or a birthday, and we will need to use these attributes to find the records that refer to the same entity. Unfortunately, the values of these attributes aren't perfect: values might have different formatting, typos, or missing information that means that a simple equality test on the values of the attributes will cause us to miss a significant number of duplicate records. For example, let's compare the business listings shown in Table 2-1.

Table 2-1. The challenge of record linkage

Name	Address	City	State	Phone
Josh's Coffee Shop	1234 Sunset Boulevard	West Hollywood	CA	(213)-555-1212
Josh Coffee	1234 Sunset Blvd West	Hollywood	CA	555-1212
Coffee Chain #1234	1400 Sunset Blvd #2	Hollywood	CA	206-555-1212
Coffee Chain Regional Office	1400 Sunset Blvd Suite 2	Hollywood	California	206-555-1212

The first two entries in this table refer to the same small coffee shop, even though a data entry error makes it look as if they are in two different cities (West Hollywood and Hollywood). The second two entries, on the other hand, are actually referring to different business locations of the same chain of coffee shops that happen to share a common address: one of the entries refers to an actual coffee shop, and the other one refers to a local corporate office location. Both of the entries give the official phone number of corporate headquarters in Seattle.

This example illustrates everything that makes record linkage so difficult: even though both pairs of entries look similar to each other, the criteria that we use to make the duplicate/not-duplicate decision is different for each pair. This is the kind of distinction that is easy for a human to understand and identify at a glance, but is difficult for a computer to learn.

Getting Started: The Spark Shell and SparkContext

We're going to use a sample data set from the UC Irvine Machine Learning Repository, which is a fantastic source for interesting (and free) data sets for research and education. The data set we'll analyze was curated from a record linkage study performed at a German hospital in 2010, and it contains several million pairs of patient records that were matched according to several different criteria, such as the patient's name (first and last), address, and birthday. Each matching field was assigned a numerical score from 0.0 to 1.0 based on how similar the strings were, and the data was then hand-labeled to identify which pairs represented the same person and which did not. The underlying values of the fields that were used to create the data set were removed to protect the privacy of the patients. Numerical identifiers, the match scores for the fields, and the label for each pair (match versus nonmatch) were published for use in record linkage research.

From the shell, let's pull the data from the repository:

```
$ mkdir linkage
$ cd linkage/
$ curl -L -o donation.zip https://bit.ly/1Aoywaq
$ unzip donation.zip
$ unzip 'block_*.zip'
```

If you have a Hadoop cluster handy, you can create a directory for the block data in HDFS and copy the files from the data set there:

```
$ hadoop fs -mkdir linkage
$ hadoop fs -put block_*.csv linkage
```

The examples and code in this book assume you have Spark 2.1.0 available. Releases can be obtained from the Spark project site (*https://spark.apache.org/downloads.html*). Refer to the Spark documentation (*https://spark.apache.org/docs/latest/*) for instructions on setting up a Spark environment, whether on a cluster or simply on your local machine.

Now we're ready to launch the spark-shell, which is a REPL for the Scala language that also has some Spark-specific extensions. If you've never seen the term REPL before, you can think of it as something similar to the R environment: it's a console where you can define functions and manipulate data in the Scala programming language.

If you have a Hadoop cluster that runs a version of Hadoop that supports YARN, you can launch the Spark jobs on the cluster by using the value of yarn for the Spark master:

```
$ spark-shell --master yarn --deploy-mode client
```

However, if you're just running these examples on your personal computer, you can launch a local Spark cluster by specifying local[N], where N is the number of threads to run, or * to match the number of cores available on your machine. For example, to launch a local cluster that uses eight threads on an eight-core machine:

```
$ spark-shell --master local[*]
```

The examples will work the same way locally. You will simply pass paths to local files, rather than paths on HDFS beginning with hdfs://. Note that you will still need to cp block_*.csv into your chosen local directory rather than use the directory containing files you unzipped earlier, because it contains a number of other files in addition to the .csv data files.

The rest of the examples in this book will not show a --master argument to spark-shell, but you will typically need to specify this argument as appropriate for your environment.

You may need to specify additional arguments to make the Spark shell fully utilize your resources. For example, when running Spark with a local master, you can use --driver-memory 2g to let the single local process use 2 GB of memory. YARN memory configuration is more complex, and relevant options like --executor-memory are explained in the Spark on YARN documentation (*https://bit.ly/1BVpP9J*).

After running one of these commands, you will see a lot of log messages from Spark as it initializes itself, but you should also see a bit of ASCII art, followed by some additional log messages and a prompt:

```
Spark context Web UI available at http://10.0.1.39:4040
Spark context available as 'sc' (master = local[*], app id = ...).
Spark session available as 'spark'.
Welcome to
      ____              __
     / __/__  ___ _____/ /__
    _\ \/ _ \/ _ `/ __/  '_/
   /___/ .__/\_,_/_/ /_/\_\   version 2.1.0
      /_/

Using Scala version 2.11.8 (Java HotSpot(TM) 64-Bit Server VM, Java 1.8.0_60)
Type in expressions to have them evaluated.
```

```
Type :help for more information.
scala>
```

If this is your first time using the Spark shell (or any Scala REPL, for that matter), you should run the :help command to list available commands in the shell. :history and :h? can be helpful for finding the names of variables or functions that you wrote during a session but can't seem to find at the moment. :paste can help you correctly insert code from the clipboard—something you might want to do while following along with the book and its accompanying source code.

In addition to the note about :help, the Spark log messages indicated "Spark context available as sc." This is a reference to the SparkContext, which coordinates the execution of Spark jobs on the cluster. Go ahead and type sc at the command line:

```
sc
...
res: org.apache.spark.SparkContext =
    org.apache.spark.SparkContext@DEADBEEF
```

The REPL will print the string form of the object. For the SparkContext object, this is simply its name plus the hexadecimal address of the object in memory. (DEADBEEF is a placeholder; the exact value you see here will vary from run to run.)

It's good that the sc variable exists, but what exactly do we do with it? SparkContext is an object, so it has methods associated with it. We can see what those methods are in the Scala REPL by typing the name of a variable, followed by a period, followed by tab:

```
sc.[\t]
...
!=                          hashCode
##                          isInstanceOf
+                           isLocal
->                          isStopped
==                          jars
accumulable                 killExecutor
accumulableCollection       killExecutors
accumulator                 listFiles
addFile                     listJars
addJar                      longAccumulator
...  (lots of other methods)
getClass                    stop
getConf                     submitJob
getExecutorMemoryStatus     synchronized
getExecutorStorageStatus    textFile
getLocalProperty            toString
getPersistentRDDs           uiWebUrl
getPoolForName              union
getRDDStorageInfo           version
getSchedulingMode           wait
```

```
hadoopConfiguration          wholeTextFiles
hadoopFile                   →
```

The `SparkContext` has a long list of methods, but the ones that we're going to use most often allow us to create *Resilient Distributed Datasets*, or *RDDs*. An RDD is Spark's fundamental abstraction for representing a collection of objects that can be distributed across multiple machines in a cluster. There are two ways to create an RDD in Spark:

- Using the `SparkContext` to create an RDD from an external data source, like a file in HDFS, a database table via JDBC, or a local collection of objects that we create in the Spark shell
- Performing a transformation on one or more existing RDDs, like filtering records, aggregating records by a common key, or joining multiple RDDs together

RDDs are a convenient way to describe the computations that we want to perform on our data as a sequence of small, independent steps.

Resilient Distributed Datasets

An RDD is laid out across the cluster of machines as a collection of *partitions*, each including a subset of the data. Partitions define the unit of parallelism in Spark. The framework processes the objects within a partition in sequence, and processes multiple partitions in parallel. One of the simplest ways to create an RDD is to use the `parallelize` method on `SparkContext` with a local collection of objects:

```
val rdd = sc.parallelize(Array(1, 2, 2, 4), 4)
...
rdd: org.apache.spark.rdd.RDD[Int] = ...
```

The first argument is the collection of objects to parallelize. The second is the number of partitions. When the time comes to compute the objects within a partition, Spark fetches a subset of the collection from the driver process.

To create an RDD from a text file or directory of text files residing in a distributed filesystem like HDFS, we can pass the name of the file or directory to the `textFile` method:

```
val rdd2 = sc.textFile("hdfs:///some/path.txt")
...
rdd2: org.apache.spark.rdd.RDD[String] = ...
```

When you're running Spark in local mode, the `textFile` method can access paths that reside on the local filesystem. If Spark is given a directory instead of an individual file, it will consider all of the files in that directory as part of the given RDD. Finally, note that no actual data has been read by Spark or loaded into memory yet,

---

either on our client machine or the cluster. When the time comes to compute the objects within a partition, Spark reads a section (also known as a *split*) of the input file, and then applies any subsequent transformations (filtering, aggregation, etc.) that we defined via other RDDs.

Our record linkage data is stored in a text file, with one observation on each line. We will use the `textFile` method on `SparkContext` to get a reference to this data as an RDD:

```
val rawblocks = sc.textFile("linkage")
...
rawblocks: org.apache.spark.rdd.RDD[String] = ...
```

There are a few things happening on this line that are worth going over. First, we're declaring a new variable called `rawblocks`. As we can see from the shell, the `raw blocks` variable has a type of `RDD[String]`, even though we never specified that type information in our variable declaration. This is a feature of the Scala programming language called *type inference*, and it saves us a lot of typing when we're working with the language. Whenever possible, Scala figures out what type a variable has based on its context. In this case, Scala looks up the return type from the `textFile` function on the `SparkContext` object, sees that it returns an `RDD[String]`, and assigns that type to the `rawblocks` variable.

Whenever we create a new variable in Scala, we must preface the name of the variable with either `val` or `var`. Variables that are prefaced with `val` are immutable, and cannot be changed to refer to another value once they are assigned, whereas variables that are prefaced with `var` can be changed to refer to different objects of the same type. Watch what happens when we execute the following code:

```
rawblocks = sc.textFile("linkage")
...
<console>: error: reassignment to val

var varblocks = sc.textFile("linkage")
varblocks = sc.textFile("linkage")
```

Attempting to reassign the linkage data to the `rawblocks` val threw an error, but reassigning the `varblocks` var is fine. Within the Scala REPL, there is an exception to the reassignment of `val`s, because we are allowed to redeclare the same immutable variable, like the following:

```
val rawblocks = sc.textFile("linakge")
val rawblocks = sc.textFile("linkage")
```

In this case, no error is thrown on the second declaration of rawblocks. This isn't typically allowed in normal Scala code, but it's fine to do in the shell, and we will make extensive use of this feature throughout the examples in the book.

The REPL and Compilation

In addition to its interactive shell, Spark also supports compiled applications. We typically recommend using *Apache Maven* (*https://maven.apache.org*) for compiling and managing dependencies. The GitHub repository included with this book holds a self-contained Maven project in the *simplesparkproject/* directory (*http://bit.ly/2rnWGlI*) to help you get started.

With both the shell and compilation as options, which should you use when testing and building a data pipeline? It is often useful to start working entirely in the REPL. This enables quick prototyping, faster iteration, and less lag time between ideas and results. However, as the program builds in size, maintaining a monolithic file of code can become more onerous, and Scala's interpretation eats up more time. This can be exacerbated by the fact that, when you're dealing with massive data, it is not uncommon for an attempted operation to cause a Spark application to crash or otherwise render a SparkContext unusable. This means that any work and code typed in so far becomes lost. At this point, it is often useful to take a hybrid approach. Keep the frontier of development in the REPL and as pieces of code harden, move them over into a compiled library. You can make the compiled JAR available to spark-shell by passing it to the --jars command-line flag. When done right, the compiled JAR only needs to be rebuilt infrequently, and the REPL allows for fast iteration on code and approaches that still need ironing out.

What about referencing external Java and Scala libraries? To compile code that references external libraries, you need to specify the libraries inside the project's Maven configuration (*pom.xml*). To run code that accesses external libraries, you need to include the JARs for these libraries on the classpath of Spark's processes. A good way to make this happen is to use Maven to package a JAR that includes all of your application's dependencies. You can then reference this JAR when starting the shell by using the --jars property. The advantage of this approach is that the dependencies only need to be specified once: in the Maven *pom.xml*. Again, the *simplesparkproject/* directory in the GitHub repository shows you how to accomplish this.

If you know of a third-party JAR that is published to a Maven repository, you can tell the spark-shell to load the JAR by passing its Maven coordinates via the --packages command-line argument. For example, to load the Wisp Visualization Library for Scala 2.11, you would pass --packages "com.quantifind:wisp_2.11:0.0.4" to the spark-shell. If the JAR is stored in a repository besides Maven Central, you can tell Spark where to look for the JAR by passing the repository URL to the --repositories argument. Both the --packages and --repositories arguments can

---

take comma-separated arguments if you need to load from multiple packages or repositories.

Bringing Data from the Cluster to the Client

RDDs have a number of methods that allow us to read data from the cluster into the Scala REPL on our client machine. Perhaps the simplest of these is `first`, which returns the first element of the RDD into the client:

```
rawblocks.first
...
res: String = "id_1","id_2","cmp_fname_c1","cmp_fname_c2",...
```

The `first` method can be useful for sanity checking a data set, but we're generally interested in bringing back larger samples of an RDD into the client for analysis. When we know that an RDD only contains a small number of records, we can use the `collect` method to return all the contents of an RDD to the client as an array. Because we don't know how big the linkage data set is just yet, we'll hold off on doing this right now.

We can strike a balance between `first` and `collect` with the `take` method, which allows us to read a given number of records into an array on the client. Let's use `take` to get the first 10 lines from the linkage data set:

```
val head = rawblocks.take(10)
...
head: Array[String] = Array("id_1","id_2","cmp_fname_c1",...

head.length
...
res: Int = 10
```

Actions

The act of creating an RDD does not cause any distributed computation to take place on the cluster. Rather, RDDs define logical data sets that are intermediate steps in a computation. Distributed computation occurs upon invoking an *action* on an RDD. For example, the `count` action returns the number of objects in an RDD:

```
rdd.count()
14/09/10 17:36:09 INFO SparkContext: Starting job: count ...
14/09/10 17:36:09 INFO SparkContext: Job finished: count ...
res0: Long = 4
```

The `collect` action returns an `Array` with all the objects from the RDD. This `Array` resides in local memory, not on the cluster:

```
rdd.collect()
14/09/29 00:58:09 INFO SparkContext: Starting job: collect ...
14/09/29 00:58:09 INFO SparkContext: Job finished: collect ...
res2: Array[(Int, Int)] = Array((4,1), (1,1), (2,2))
```

Actions need not only return results to the local process. The saveAsTextFile action
saves the contents of an RDD to persistent storage, such as HDFS:

```
rdd.saveAsTextFile("hdfs:///user/ds/mynumbers")
14/09/29 00:38:47 INFO SparkContext: Starting job:
saveAsTextFile ...
14/09/29 00:38:49 INFO SparkContext: Job finished:
saveAsTextFile ...
```

The action creates a directory and writes out each partition as a file within it. From
the command line outside of the Spark shell:

```
hadoop fs -ls /user/ds/mynumbers

-rw-r--r--   3 ds supergroup          0 2014-09-29 00:38 myfile.txt/_SUCCESS
-rw-r--r--   3 ds supergroup          4 2014-09-29 00:38 myfile.txt/part-00000
-rw-r--r--   3 ds supergroup          4 2014-09-29 00:38 myfile.txt/part-00001
```

Remember that textFile can accept a directory of text files as input, meaning that a
future Spark job could refer to mynumbers as an input directory.

The raw form of data returned by the Scala REPL can be somewhat hard to read,
especially for arrays that contain more than a handful of elements. To make it easier
to read the contents of an array, we can use the foreach method in conjunction with
println to print out each value in the array on its own line:

```
head.foreach(println)
...
"id_1","id_2","cmp_fname_c1","cmp_fname_c2","cmp_lname_c1","cmp_lname_c2",
  "cmp_sex","cmp_bd","cmp_bm","cmp_by","cmp_plz","is_match"
37291,53113,0.833333333333333,?,1,?,1,1,1,1,0,TRUE
39086,47614,1,?,1,?,1,1,1,1,1,TRUE
70031,70237,1,?,1,?,1,1,1,1,1,TRUE
84795,97439,1,?,1,?,1,1,1,1,1,TRUE
36950,42116,1,?,1,1,1,1,1,1,1,TRUE
42413,48491,1,?,1,?,1,1,1,1,1,TRUE
25965,64753,1,?,1,?,1,1,1,1,1,TRUE
49451,90407,1,?,1,?,1,1,1,1,0,TRUE
39932,40902,1,?,1,?,1,1,1,1,1,TRUE
```

The foreach(println) pattern is one that we will frequently use in this book. It's an
example of a common functional programming pattern, where we pass one function
(println) as an argument to another function (foreach) in order to perform some
action. This kind of programming style will be familiar to data scientists who have
worked with R and are used to processing vectors and lists by avoiding for loops and

instead using higher-order functions like `apply` and `lapply`. Collections in Scala are similar to lists and vectors in R in that we generally want to avoid `for` loops and instead process the elements of the collection using higher-order functions.

Immediately, we see a couple of issues with the data that we need to address before we begin our analysis. First, the CSV files contain a header row that we'll want to filter out from our subsequent analysis. We can use the presence of the "id_1" string in the row as our filter condition, and write a small Scala function that tests for the presence of that string inside the line:

```
def isHeader(line: String) = line.contains("id_1")
isHeader: (line: String)Boolean
```

Like Python, we declare functions in Scala using the keyword `def`. Unlike Python, we have to specify the types of the arguments to our function; in this case, we have to indicate that the `line` argument is a `String`. The body of the function, which uses the `contains` method for the `String` class to test whether or not the characters "id_1" appear anywhere in the string, comes after the equals sign. Even though we had to specify a type for the `line` argument, note that we did not have to specify a return type for the function, because the Scala compiler was able to infer the type based on its knowledge of the `String` class and the fact that the `contains` method returns `true` or `false`.

Sometimes we will want to specify the return type of a function ourselves, especially for long, complex functions with multiple `return` statements, where the Scala compiler can't necessarily infer the return type itself. We might also want to specify a return type for our function in order to make it easier for someone else reading our code later to be able to understand what the function does without having to reread the entire method. We can declare the return type for the function right after the argument list, like this:

```
def isHeader(line: String): Boolean = {
  line.contains("id_1")
}
isHeader: (line: String)Boolean
```

We can test our new Scala function against the data in the `head` array by using the `filter` method on Scala's `Array` class and then printing the results:

```
head.filter(isHeader).foreach(println)
...
"id_1","id_2","cmp_fname_c1","cmp_fname_c2","cmp_lname_c1",...
```

It looks like our `isHeader` method works correctly; the only result that was returned from applying it to the `head` array via the `filter` method was the header line itself. But of course, what we really want to do is get all of the rows in the data *except* the header rows. There are a few ways that we can do this in Scala. Our first option is to take advantage of the `filterNot` method on the `Array` class:

```
head.filterNot(isHeader).length
...
res: Int = 9
```

We could also use Scala's support for anonymous functions to negate the `isHeader` function from inside `filter`:

```
head.filter(x => !isHeader(x)).length
...
res: Int = 9
```

Anonymous functions in Scala are somewhat like Python's lambda functions. In this case, we defined an anonymous function that takes a single argument called x, passes x to the `isHeader` function, and returns the negation of the result. Note that we did *not* have to specify any type information for the x variable in this instance; the Scala compiler was able to infer that x is a `String` from the fact that `head` is an `Array[String]`.

There is nothing that Scala programmers hate more than typing, so Scala has lots of little features designed to reduce the amount of typing necessary. For example, in our anonymous function definition, we had to type the characters x => to declare our anonymous function and give its argument a name. For simple anonymous functions like this one, we don't even have to do that—Scala allows us to use an underscore (_) to represent the argument to the function so that we can save four characters:

```
head.filter(!isHeader(_)).length
...
res: Int = 9
```

Sometimes, this abbreviated syntax makes the code easier to read because it avoids duplicating obvious identifiers. But other times, this shortcut just makes the code cryptic. The code listings throughout this book use one or the other according to our best judgment.

Shipping Code from the Client to the Cluster

We just saw a wide variety of ways to write and apply functions to data in Scala. All the code that we executed was done against the data inside the `head` array, which was contained on our client machine. Now we're going to take the code that we just wrote and apply it to the millions of linkage records contained in our cluster and represented by the `rawblocks` RDD in Spark.

Here's what the code for this looks like; it should feel eerily familiar to you:

```
val noheader = rawblocks.filter(x => !isHeader(x))
```

The syntax we used to express the filtering computation against the entire data set on the cluster is *exactly the same* as the syntax we used to express the filtering computation against the array in head on our local machine. We can use the first method on the noheader RDD to verify that the filtering rule worked correctly:

```
noheader.first
...
res: String = 37291,53113,0.833333333333333,?,1,?,1,1,1,0,TRUE
```

This is incredibly powerful. It means that we can interactively develop and debug our data-munging code against a small amount of data that we sample from the cluster, and then ship that code to the cluster to apply it to the entire data set when we're ready to transform the entire data set. Best of all, we never have to leave the shell. There really isn't another tool that gives you this kind of experience.

In the next several sections, we'll use this mix of local development and testing and cluster computation to perform more munging and analysis of the record linkage data, but if you need to take a moment to drink in the new world of awesome that you have just entered, we certainly understand.

From RDDs to Data Frames

In the first edition of this book, we spent the next several pages in this chapter using our newfound ability to mix local development and testing with cluster computations from inside the REPL to write code that parsed the CSV file of record linkage data, including splitting the line up by commas, converting each column to an appropriate data type (like Int or Double), and handling invalid values that we encountered. Having the option to work with data in this way is one of the most compelling aspects of working with Spark, especially when we're dealing with data sets that have an especially unusual or nonstandard structure that make them difficult to work with any other way.

At the same time, most data sets we encounter have a reasonable structure in place, either because they were born that way (like a database table) or because someone else has done the work of cleaning and structuring the data for us. For these data sets, it doesn't really make sense for us to have to write our own code to parse the data; we should simply use an existing library that can leverage the structure of the existing data set to parse the data into a form that we can use for immediate analysis. Spark 1.3 introduced just such a structure: the DataFrame.

In Spark, the DataFrame is an abstraction built on top of RDDs for data sets that have a regular structure in which each record is a row made up of a set of columns, and each column has a well-defined data type. You can think of a data frame as the Spark analogue of a table in a relational database. Even though the naming convention might make you think of a data.frame object in R or a pandas.DataFrame object in

Python, Spark's DataFrames are a different beast. This is because they represent distributed data sets on a cluster, not local data where every row in the data is stored on the same machine. Although there are similarities in how you use DataFrames and the role they play inside the Spark ecosystem, there are some things you may be used to doing when working with data frames in R and Python that do not apply to Spark, so it's best to think of them as their own distinct entity and try to approach them with an open mind.

To create a data frame for our record linkage data set, we're going to use the other object that was created for us when we started the Spark REPL, the SparkSession object named spark:

```
spark
...
res: org.apache.spark.sql.SparkSession = ...
```

SparkSession is a replacement for the now deprecated SQLContext object that was originally introduced in Spark 1.3. Like SQLContext, SparkSession is a wrapper around the SparkContext object, which you can access directly from the SparkSession:

```
spark.sparkContext
...
res: org.apache.spark.SparkContext = ...
```

You should see that the value of spark.sparkContext is identical to the value of the sc variable that we have been using to create RDDs thus far. To create a data frame from the SparkSession, we will use the csv method on its Reader API:

```
val prev = spark.read.csv("linkage")
...
prev: org.apache.spark.sql.DataFrame = [_c0: string, _c1: string, ...
```

By default, every column in a CSV file is treated as a string type, and the column names default to _c0, _c1, _c2, ... We can look at the head of a data frame in the shell by calling its show method:

```
prev.show()
```

We can see that the first row of the DataFrame is the name of the header columns, as we expected, and that the CSV file has been cleanly split up into its individual columns. We can also see the presence of the ? strings in some of the columns; we will need to handle these as missing values. In addition to naming each column correctly, it would be ideal if Spark could properly infer the data type of each of the columns for us.

Fortunately, Spark's CSV reader provides all of this functionality for us via options that we can set on the reader API. You can see the full list of options that the API takes at the spark-csv project's GitHub page (*http://bit.ly/2i8zW6y*), which was developed separately for Spark 1.x but is included in Spark 2.x. For now, we'll read and parse the linkage data like this:

```
val parsed = spark.read.
  option("header", "true").
  option("nullValue", "?").
  option("inferSchema", "true").
  csv("linkage")
```

When we call show on the parsed data, we see that the column names are set correctly and the ? strings have been replaced by null values. To see the inferred type for each column, we can print the schema of the parsed DataFrame like this:

```
parsed.printSchema()
...
root
 |-- id_1: integer (nullable = true)
 |-- id_2: integer (nullable = true)
 |-- cmp_fname_c1: double (nullable = true)
 |-- cmp_fname_c2: double (nullable = true)
...
```

Each StructField instance contains the name of the column, the most specific data type that could handle the type of data contained in each record, and a boolean field that indicates whether or not the column may contain null values, which is true by default. In order to perform the schema inference, Spark must do *two* passes over the data set: one pass to figure out the type of each column, and a second pass to do the actual parsing. If you know the schema that you want to use for a file ahead of time, you can create an instance of the org.apache.spark.sql.types.StructType class and pass it to the Reader API via the schema function, which can have a significant performance benefit when the data set is very large, since Spark will not need to perform an extra pass over the data to figure out the data type of each column.

Data Formats and Data Frames

Spark 2.0 ships with built-in support for reading and writing data frames in a variety of formats via the DataFrameReader and DataFrameWriter APIs. In addition to the CSV format discussed here, you can also read and write structured data from the following sources:

json
> Supports many of the same schema-inference functionality that the CSV format does

parquet *and* orc
> Competing columnar-oriented binary file formats

---

jdbc
: Connects to a relational database via the JDBC data connection standard

libsvm
: Popular text file format for representing labeled observations with sparse features

text
: Maps each line of a file to a data frame with a single column of type `string`

You access the methods of the DataFrameReader API by calling the `read` method on a SparkSession instance, and you can load data from a file using either the `format` and `load` methods, or one of the shortcut methods for built-in formats:

```
val d1 = spark.read.format("json").load("file.json")
val d2 = spark.read.json("file.json")
```

In this example, `d1` and `d2` reference the same underlying JSON data and will have the same contents. Each of the different file formats has its own set of options that can be set via the same `option` method that we used for CSV files.

To write data out again, you access the DataFrameWriter API via the `write` method on any DataFrame instance. The DataFrameWriter API supports the same built-in formats as the DataFrameReader API, so the following two methods are equivalent ways of writing the contents of the `d1` DataFrame as a Parquet file:

```
d1.write.format("parquet").save("file.parquet")
d1.write.parquet("file.parquet")
```

By default, Spark will throw an error if you try to save a data frame to a file that already exists. You can control Spark's behavior in this situation via the `SaveMode` enum on the DataFrameWriter API to either `Overwrite` the existing file, `Append` the data in the DataFrame to the file (if it exists), or `Ignore` the write operation if the file already exists and leave it in place:

```
d2.write.mode(SaveMode.Ignore).parquet("file.parquet")
```

You can also specify the `SaveMode` as a string literal (`"overwrite"`, `"append"`, `"ignore"`) in Scala, just as you can when working with the DataFrame API in R and Python.

Analyzing Data with the DataFrame API

Although the RDD API in Spark provides a small number of handy methods for analyzing data—like the `count` method to count the number of records an RDD contained, `countByValue` to get a histogram of the distinct values, or the `stats` method to get summary statistics like min, max, mean, and standard deviation for an `RDD[Double]`—the DataFrame API comes with a more powerful set of tools that will likely be familiar to data scientists who are used to R, Python, and SQL. In this section, we will begin to explore these tools and how to apply them to the record linkage data.

If we look at the schema of the `parsed` DataFrame and the first few rows of data, we see this:

- The first two fields are integer IDs that represent the patients that were matched in the record.
- The next nine values are (possibly missing) numeric values (either doubles or ints) that represent match scores on different fields of the patient records, such as their names, birthdays, and locations. The fields are stored as integers when the only possible values are match (1) or no-match (0), and doubles whenever partial matches are possible.
- The last field is a boolean value (`true` or `false`) indicating whether or not the pair of patient records represented by the line was a match.

Our goal is to come up with a simple classifier that allows us to predict whether a record will be a match based on the values of the match scores for the patient records. Let's start by getting an idea of the number of records we're dealing with via the `count` method, which works in exactly the same way for DataFrames and RDDs:

```
parsed.count()
...
res: Long = 5749132
```

This is a relatively small data set—certainly small enough to fit in memory on one of the nodes in a cluster or even on your local machine if you don't have a cluster available. Thus far, every time we've processed the data in the data set, Spark has reopened the file, reparsed the rows, and then performed the action requested, like showing the first few rows of the data or counting the number of records. When we ask another question, Spark will do these same operations, again and again, even if we have filtered the data down to a small number of records or are working with an aggregated version of the original data set.

This isn't an optimal use of our compute resources. After the data has been parsed once, we'd like to save the data in its parsed form on the cluster so that we don't have to reparse it every time we want to ask a new question of the data. Spark supports this use case by allowing us to signal that a given RDD or DataFrame should be cached in memory after it is generated by calling the `cache` method on the instance. Let's do that now for the `parsed` DataFrame:

```
parsed.cache()
```

Caching

Although the contents of DataFrames and RDDs are transient by default, Spark provides a mechanism for persisting the underlying data:

```
cached.cache()
cached.count()
cached.take(10)
```

The call to `cache` indicates that the contents of the DataFrame should be stored in memory the next time it's computed. In this example, the call to `count` computes the contents initially, and the `take` action returns the first 10 elements of the DataFrame as a local `Array[Row]`. When `take` is called, it accesses the cached elements of `cached` instead of recomputing them from their dependencies.

Spark defines a few different mechanisms, or `StorageLevel` values, for persisting data. `cache()` is shorthand for `persist(StorageLevel.MEMORY)`, which stores the rows as unserialized Java objects. When Spark estimates that a partition will not fit in memory, it simply will not store it, and it will be recomputed the next time it's needed. This level makes the most sense when the objects will be referenced frequently and/or require low-latency access, because it avoids any serialization overhead. Its drawback is that it takes up larger amounts of memory than its alternatives. Also, holding on to many small objects puts pressure on Java's garbage collection, which can result in stalls and general slowness.

Spark also exposes a `MEMORY_SER` storage level, which allocates large byte buffers in memory and serializes the records into them. When we use the right format (more on this in a bit), serialized data usually takes up two to five times less space than its raw equivalent.

Spark can use disk for caching data as well. The `MEMORY_AND_DISK` and `MEM ORY_AND_DISK_SER` are similar to the `MEMORY` and `MEMORY_SER` storage levels, respectively. For the latter two, if a partition will not fit in memory, it is simply not stored, meaning that it must be recomputed from its dependencies the next time an action uses it. For the former, Spark spills partitions that will not fit in memory to disk.

Although both DataFrames and RDDs can be cached, Spark can use the detailed knowledge of the data stored with a data frame available via the DataFrame's schema to persist the data far more efficiently than it can with Java objects stored inside of RDDs.

Deciding when to cache data can be an art. The decision typically involves trade-offs between space and speed, with the specter of garbage-collecting looming overhead to occasionally confound things further. In general, data should be cached when it is likely to be referenced by multiple actions, is relatively small compared to the amount of memory/disk available on the cluster, and is expensive to regenerate.

Once our data has been cached, the next thing we want to know is the relative fraction of records that were matches versus those that were nonmatches. With the RDD API, we would need to write an inlined Scala function to extract the value of the is_match column from each record and then call countByValue on the resulting RDD[Boolean] to sum up the frequency of each record and return it to the client as a Map[Boolean, Long]. In fact, we can still do this calculation against the RDD that underlies the parsed DataFrame:

```
parsed.rdd.
  map(_.getAs[Boolean]("is_match")).
  countByValue()
...
Map(true -> 20931, false -> 5728201)
```

The RDD that a data frame wraps is made up of instances of the org.apache.spark.sql.Row class, which has accessor methods for getting the values inside each record by index position (counting from zero) as well as the getAs[T] method, which allows us to look up fields of a given type by their name.

Although the RDD-based analysis gets us the result we want, it still leaves a lot to be desired as a general-purpose way of analyzing data in Spark. First, using the countBy Value function to do the counts is only the right thing to do when we know that there are just a few distinct values in the data set. If there are lots of distinct values, it's more efficient to use an RDD function that won't return the results to the client, like reduce ByKey. Second, if we require the results of the countByValue aggregation in a subsequent computation, we need to use the parallelize method of the SparkContext to ship the data back from the client to the cluster. In general, we prefer to have a single way of aggregating structured data that would work for any size data set, and this is exactly what the DataFrame API provides:

```
parsed.
  groupBy("is_match").
  count().
  orderBy($"count".desc)
  show()
...
+--------+-------+
|is_match|  count|
+--------+-------+
|   false|5728201|
|    true|  20931|
+--------+-------+
```

Instead of writing a function to extract the is_match column, we simply pass its name to the groupBy method on the DataFrame, call the count method to, well, count the number of records inside each grouping, sort the resulting data in descending order based on the count column, and then cleanly render the result of the computation in the REPL with show. Under the covers, the Spark engine determines the most efficient way to perform the aggregation and return the results, without us having to worry about the details of which RDD APIs to use. The result is a cleaner, faster, and more expressive way to do data analysis in Spark.

Note that there are two ways we can reference the names of the columns in the DataFrame: either as literal strings, like in groupBy("is_match"), or as Column objects by using the special $"<col>" syntax that we used on the count column. Either approach is valid in most cases, but we needed to use the $ syntax to call the desc method on the count column. If we had omitted the $ in front of the string, Scala would have thrown an error because the String class does not have a method named desc.

DataFrame Aggregation Functions

In addition to count, we can also compute more complex aggregations like sums, mins, maxes, means, and standard deviation using the agg method of the DataFrame API in conjunction with the aggregation functions defined in the org.apache.spark.sql.functions package. For example, to find the mean and standard deviation of the cmp_sex field in the overall parsed DataFrame, we could type:

```
parsed.agg(avg($"cmp_sex"), stddev($"cmp_sex")).show()
+------------------+--------------------+
|      avg(cmp_sex)|stddev_samp(cmp_sex)|
+------------------+--------------------+
|0.955001381078048|  0.2073011111689795|
+------------------+--------------------+
```

Note that by default, Spark computes the sample standard deviation; there is also a stddev_pop function for computing the population standard deviation.

You may have noticed that the functions on the DataFrame API are similar to the components of a SQL query. This isn't a coincidence, and in fact we have the option of treating any DataFrame we create as if it were a database table and expressing our questions using familiar and powerful SQL syntax. First, we need to tell the Spark SQL execution engine the name it should associate with the parsed DataFrame, since the name of the variable itself ("parsed") isn't available to Spark:

```
parsed.createOrReplaceTempView("linkage")
```

Because the parsed DataFrame is only available during the length of this Spark REPL session, it is a *temporary* table. Spark SQL may also be used to query persistent tables in HDFS if we configure Spark to connect to an Apache Hive metastore that tracks the schemas and locations of structured data sets.

Once our temporary table is registered with the Spark SQL engine, we can query it like this:

```
spark.sql("""
  SELECT is_match, COUNT(*) cnt
  FROM linkage
  GROUP BY is_match
  ORDER BY cnt DESC
""").show()
...
+--------+-------+
|is_match|    cnt|
+--------+-------+
|   false|5728201|
|    true|  20931|
+--------+-------+
```

Like Python, Scala allows us to write multiline strings via the convention of three double quotes in a row. In Spark 1.x, the Spark SQL compiler was primarily aimed at replicating the nonstandard syntax of HiveQL in order to support users who were migrating to Spark from Apache Hive. In Spark 2.0, you have the option of running Spark using either an ANSI 2003-compliant version of Spark SQL (the default) or in HiveQL mode by calling the `enableHiveSupport` method when you create a `Spark Session` instance via its Builder API.

Should you use Spark SQL or the DataFrame API to do your analysis in Spark? There are pros and cons to each: SQL has the benefit of being broadly familiar and expressive for simple queries. It is also the best way to quickly read and filter data stored in commonly used columnar file formats like ORC and Parquet. The downside of SQL is that it can be difficult to express complex, multistage analyses in a dynamic, readable, and testable way—all areas where the DataFrame API shines. Throughout the rest of the book, we use both Spark SQL and the DataFrame API, and leave it as an exercise for the reader to examine the choices we made and translate our computations from one interface to the other.

Connecting Spark SQL to Hive

Spark 1.x shipped with a `HiveContext` class that was a subclass of `SQLContext` and supported Hive's unique SQL dialect (HiveQL). This class could be used to talk to a Hive metastore by copying a *hive-site.xml* file into the *conf* directory of the Spark installation. In Spark 2.x, the `HiveContext` is deprecated, but you can still connect to a Hive metastore via a *hive-site.xml* file, and you can also use HiveQL in queries by calling the `enableHiveSupport` method on the SparkSession Builder API:

```
val sparkSession = SparkSession.builder.
  master("local[4]")
  .enableHiveSupport()
  .getOrCreate()
```

In Spark 2.x, you can treat any table in the Hive metastore as a data frame, execute Spark SQL queries against tables defined in the metastore, and persist the output of

---

those queries to the metastore so that they can be queried by other tools, including Hive itself, Apache Impala, or Presto.

Fast Summary Statistics for DataFrames

Although there are many kinds of analyses that may be expressed equally well in SQL or with the DataFrame API, there are certain common things that we want to be able to do with data frames that can be tedious to express in SQL. One such analysis that is especially helpful is computing the min, max, mean, and standard deviation of all the non-null values in the numerical columns of a data frame. In R, this function is named summary; and in Spark, this function has the same name that it does in Pandas, describe:

```
val summary = parsed.describe()
...
summary.show()
```

The summary DataFrame has one column for each variable in the parsed DataFrame, along with another column (also named summary) that indicates which metric— count, mean, stddev, min, or max—is present in the rest of the columns in the row. We can use the select method to choose a subset of the columns in order to make the summary statistics easier to read and compare:

```
summary.select("summary", "cmp_fname_c1", "cmp_fname_c2").show()
+-------+------------------+------------------+
|summary|      cmp_fname_c1|      cmp_fname_c2|
+-------+------------------+------------------+
|  count|           5748125|            103698|
|   mean|0.7129024704436274|0.9000176718903216|
| stddev|0.3887583596162788|0.2713176105782331|
|    min|               0.0|               0.0|
|    max|               1.0|               1.0|
+-------+------------------+------------------+
```

Note the difference in the value of the count variable between cmp_fname_c1 and cmp_fname_c2. While almost every record has a non-null value for cmp_fname_c1, less than 2% of the records have a non-null value for cmp_fname_c2. To create a useful classifier, we need to rely on variables that are almost always present in the data— unless their missingness indicates something meaningful about whether the record matches.

Once we have an overall feel for the distribution of the variables in our data, we want to understand how the values of those variables are correlated with the value of the is_match column. Therefore, our next step is to compute those same summary statistics for just the subsets of the parsed DataFrame that correspond to matches and nonmatches. We can filter DataFrames using either SQL-style where syntax or with

Column objects using the DataFrame API and then use `describe` on the resulting DataFrames:

```
val matches = parsed.where("is_match = true")
val matchSummary = matches.describe()

val misses = parsed.filter($"is_match" === false)
val missSummary = misses.describe()
```

The logic inside the string we pass to the `where` function can include statements that would be valid inside a `WHERE` clause in Spark SQL. The filtering condition that uses the DataFrame API is a bit more complex: we need to use the `===` operator on the `$"is_match"` column, and we need to wrap the boolean literal `false` with the `lit` function in order to turn it into another column object that `is_match` can be compared with. Note that the `where` function is an alias for the `filter` function; we could have reversed the `where` and `filter` calls in the above snippet and everything would have worked the same way.

We can now start to compare our `matchSummary` and `missSummary` DataFrames to see how the distribution of the variables changes depending on whether the record is a match or a miss. Although this is a relatively small data set, doing this comparison is still somewhat tedious—what we really want is to transpose the `matchSummary` and `missSummary` DataFrames so that the rows and columns are swapped, which would allow us to join the transposed DataFrames together by variable and analyze the summary statistics, a practice that most data scientists know as "pivoting" or "reshaping" a data set. In the next section, we'll show you how to perform these transforms in Spark.

Pivoting and Reshaping DataFrames

The first thing we need to do in order to transpose our summary statistics is to convert the `matchSummary` and `missSummary` from "wide" form, in which we have rows of metrics and columns of variables, into "long" form, where each row has one metric, one variable, and the value of that metric/variable pair. Once that is done, we will complete our transpose operation by transforming the long-form DataFrame into another wide-form DataFrame, only this time the variables will correspond to the rows and the metrics will be in the columns.

To convert from a wide form to a long form, we'll take advantage of the `DataFrame`'s `flatMap` function, which is a wrapper around `RDD.flatMap`. A `flatMap` is one of the most useful transforms in Spark: it takes a function argument that processes each input record and returns a sequence of zero or more output records. You can think of `flatMap` as a generalization of the `map` and `filter` transforms that we have used so far: a `map` is a specialization of `flatMap` for the case where each input record has exactly one output record, and a `filter` is a specialization of `flatMap` where the input and output types are the same and either zero or one records are returned based on a boolean condition function.

For our `flatMap` function to work for general data frames, we need to use the `schema` object of the `DataFrame` returned by a call to `describe` to get the names of the columns:

```
summary.printSchema()
...
root
 |-- summary: string (nullable = true)
 |-- id_1: string (nullable = true)
 |-- id_2: string (nullable = true)
 |-- cmp_fname_c1: string (nullable = true)
...
```

In the summary schema, every field is treated as a string. Since we want to analyze the summary statistics as numbers, we'll need to convert the values from strings to doubles as we process them. Our output should be a data frame that has three columns: the name of the metric (count, `mean`, etc.), the name of the column (id1, cmp_by, etc.), and the `Double` value of the summary statistic for that column:

```
val schema = summary.schema
val longForm = summary.flatMap(row => {
  val metric = row.getString(0)
  (1 until row.size).map(i => {
    (metric, schema(i).name, row.getString(i).toDouble)
  })
})
```

There is a lot going on in this snippet, so let's take each line one by one. For each `row` in the `summary` DataFrame, we are getting the name of the metric for that row positionally, by calling `row.getString(0)`. For the other columns in the row, from position 1 until the end, we are generating a sequence of tuples as the result of the `flatMap` operation, where the first entry in the tuple is the name of the metric, the second entry is the name of the column (which we access via the `schema(i).name` object), and the third entry is the value of the statistic, which we have coerced to a `Double` value from its original string by calling the `toDouble` method on `row.get String(i)`.

The `toDouble` method is an example of one of Scala's most powerful (and arguably dangerous) features: *implicit types*. In Scala, an instance of the `String` class is just a `java.lang.String`, and the `java.lang.String` class does not have a method named `toDouble`. Instead, the methods are defined in a Scala class called `StringOps`. Implicits work like this: if you call a method on a Scala object, and the Scala compiler does not see a definition for that method in the class definition for that object, the compiler will try to convert your object to an instance of a class that *does* have that method defined. In this case, the compiler will see that Java's `String` class does not have a toDouble method defined but that the StringOps class does, and that the StringOps class has a method that can convert an instance of the String class into an instance of the StringOps class. The compiler silently performs the conversion of our String object into a StringOps object, and then calls the toDouble method on the new object.

Developers who write libraries in Scala (including the core Spark developers) really like implicit type conversion; it allows them to enhance the functionality of core classes like String that are otherwise closed to modification. For a user of these tools, implicit type conversions are more of a mixed bag, because they can make it difficult to figure out exactly where a particular class method is defined. Nonetheless, we're going to encounter implicit conversions throughout our examples, so it's best that we get used to them now.

The last thing to note about this snippet is the type of the longForm variable:

```
longForm: org.apache.spark.sql.Dataset[(String, String, Double)]
```

This is our first direct encounter with the Dataset[T] interface, although we have been using it all along—a data frame is simply an alias for the Dataset[Row] type! Dataset[T] is a new addition to the Spark 2.0 APIs and generalizes the DataFrame type that was introduced in Spark 1.3 to be able to handle a richer set of data types than just instances of the Row class. We'll look at the Dataset interface a bit more closely later in the chapter, but for now, all you need to know is that we can always convert a Dataset back to a data frame thanks to some implicit conversion magic in the Spark API:

```
val longDF = longForm.toDF("metric", "field", "value")
longDF.show()
+------+-----------+-------------------+
|metric|      field|              value|
+------+-----------+-------------------+
| count|       id_1|          5749132.0|
| count|       id_2|          5749132.0|
| count|cmp_fname_c1|         5748125.0|
...
| count|     cmp_by|          5748337.0|
| count|    cmp_plz|          5736289.0|
|  mean|       id_1|   33324.48559643438|
|  mean|       id_2|   66587.43558331935|
|  mean|cmp_fname_c1|  0.7129024704436274|
...
|  mean|     cmp_bd|0.22446526708507172|
|  mean|     cmp_bm|0.48885529849763504|
+------+-----------+-------------------+
```

Given a data frame in long form, we can transform it to a wide form by using the groupBy operator on the column that we want to use as the pivot table's row followed by the `pivot` operator on the column that we want to use as the pivot table's column. The `pivot` operator needs to know the distinct set of values of the pivot column that we want to use for the columns, and we can specify the value in each cell of the wide table by using an `agg(first)` operation on the `values` column, which works correctly because there is only a single value for each combination of `field` and `metric`:

```scala
val wideDF = longDF.
  groupBy("field").
  pivot("metric", Seq("count", "mean", "stddev", "min", "max")).
  agg(first("value"))
wideDF.select("field", "count", "mean").show()
...
+------------+---------+--------------------+
|       field|    count|                mean|
+------------+---------+--------------------+
|     cmp_plz|5736289.0|0.00552866147434343|
|cmp_lname_c1|5749132.0|  0.3156278193084133|
|cmp_lname_c2|   2464.0|0.31841283153174377|
|     cmp_sex|5749132.0|   0.955001381078048|
|      cmp_bm|5748337.0|0.48885529849763504|
...
|      cmp_bd|5748337.0|0.22446526708507172|
|      cmp_by|5748337.0|  0.2227485966810923|
+------------+---------+--------------------+
```

Now that we have figured out how to transpose a summary DataFrame, let's implement our logic into a function that we can reuse on the `matchSummary` and `missSummary` DataFrames. Using a text editor in another shell window, copy and paste the following code and save it in a file called `Pivot.scala`:

```scala
import org.apache.spark.sql.DataFrame
import org.apache.spark.sql.functions.first

def pivotSummary(desc: DataFrame): DataFrame = {
  val schema = desc.schema
  import desc.sparkSession.implicits._

  val lf = desc.flatMap(row => {
    val metric = row.getString(0)
    (1 until row.size).map(i => {
      (metric, schema(i).name, row.getString(i).toDouble)
    })
  }).toDF("metric", "field", "value")

  lf.groupBy("field").
    pivot("metric", Seq("count", "mean", "stddev", "min", "max")).
    agg(first("value"))
}
```

Now in your Spark shell, type :load Pivot.scala, and the Scala REPL will compile your code on the fly and make the pivotSummary function available for use on the matchSummary and missSummary DataFrames:

```scala
val matchSummaryT = pivotSummary(matchSummary)
val missSummaryT = pivotSummary(missSummary)
```

Joining DataFrames and Selecting Features

So far, we have only used Spark SQL and the DataFrame API to filter and aggregate the records from a data set, but we can also use these tools in order to perform joins (inner, left outer, right outer, or full outer) on DataFrames as well. Although the Data-Frame API includes a join function, it's often easier to express these joins using Spark SQL, especially when the tables we are joining have a large number of column names in common and we want to be able to clearly indicate which column we are referring to in our select expressions. Let's create temporary views for the matchSummaryT and missSummaryT DataFrames, join them on the field column, and compute some simple summary statistics on the resulting rows:

```scala
matchSummaryT.createOrReplaceTempView("match_desc")
missSummaryT.createOrReplaceTempView("miss_desc")
spark.sql("""
  SELECT a.field, a.count + b.count total, a.mean - b.mean delta
  FROM match_desc a INNER JOIN miss_desc b ON a.field = b.field
  WHERE a.field NOT IN ("id_1", "id_2")
  ORDER BY delta DESC, total DESC
""").show()
...
```

field	total	delta
cmp_plz	5736289.0	0.9563812499852176
cmp_lname_c2	2464.0	0.8064147192926264
cmp_by	5748337.0	0.7762059675300512
cmp_bd	5748337.0	0.775442311783404
cmp_lname_c1	5749132.0	0.6838772482590526
cmp_bm	5748337.0	0.5109496938298685
cmp_fname_c1	5748125.0	0.2854529057460786
cmp_fname_c2	103698.0	0.09104268062280008
cmp_sex	5749132.0	0.032408185250332844

A good feature has two properties: it tends to have significantly different values for matches and nonmatches (so the difference between the means will be large) and it occurs often enough in the data that we can rely on it to be regularly available for any pair of records. By this measure, cmp_fname_c2 isn't very useful because it's missing a lot of the time and the difference in the mean value for matches and nonmatches is relatively small—0.09, for a score that ranges from 0 to 1. The cmp_sex feature also isn't particularly helpful because even though it's available for any pair of records, the difference in means is just 0.03.

Features cmp_plz and cmp_by, on the other hand, are excellent. They almost always occur for any pair of records, and there is a very large difference in the mean values (more than 0.77 for both features.) Features cmp_bd, cmp_lname_c1, and cmp_bm also seem beneficial: they are generally available in the data set and the difference, in mean values for matches and nonmatches are substantial.

Features cmp_fname_c1 and cmp_lname_c2 are more of a mixed bag: cmp_fname_c1 doesn't discriminate all that well (the difference in the means is only 0.28) even though it's usually available for a pair of records, whereas cmp_lname_c2 has a large difference in the means but it's almost always missing. It's not quite obvious under what circumstances we should include these features in our model based on this data.

For now, we're going to use a simple scoring model that ranks the similarity of pairs of records based on the sums of the values of the obviously good features: cmp_plz, cmp_by, cmp_bd, cmp_lname_c1, and cmp_bm. For the few records where the values of these features are missing, we'll use 0 in place of the null value in our sum. We can get a rough feel for the performance of our simple model by creating a data frame of the computed scores and the value of the is_match column and evaluating how well the score discriminates between matches and nonmatches at various thresholds.

Preparing Models for Production Environments

Although we could write this scoring function as a Spark SQL query, there are many situations in which we want to be able to deploy a scoring rule or machine learning model into a production environment, and where we may not have enough time to run a Spark SQL to generate an answer to our question. For these situations, we want to be able to write and test functions that are able to work with Spark but that do not require any production code to depend on the Spark JARs or require that a SparkSession be run in order to excecute the code.

To abstract away the Spark-specific components of our model, we would like to have a way of creating a simple record type that allows us to work with the fields in the DataFrame as statically typed variables instead of as fields that we look up dynamically inside a Row. Fortunately, Scala provides a convenient syntax for creating these records, called *case classes*. A case class is a simple type of immutable class that comes with implementations of all of the basic Java class methods, like toString, equals, and hashCode, which makes them very easy to use. Let's declare a case class for our record linkage data, where the names and types of the fields map exactly to the names and types of the columns in the parsed DataFrame:

```
case class MatchData(
  id_1: Int,
  id_2: Int,
  cmp_fname_c1: Option[Double],
  cmp_fname_c2: Option[Double],
  cmp_lname_c1: Option[Double],
  cmp_lname_c2: Option[Double],
  cmp_sex: Option[Int],
  cmp_bd: Option[Int],
  cmp_bm: Option[Int],
  cmp_by: Option[Int],
  cmp_plz: Option[Int],
  is_match: Boolean
)
```

Note that we are using Scala's built-in Option[T] type to represent fields whose values may be null in our input data. The Option class requires that client code check to see whether a particular field is absent (represented by the None object) before it is used, which significantly reduces the occurrence of NullPointerExceptions in Scala code. For fields that can never be null, like id_1, id_2, and is_match, we can omit the Option wrapper.

Once our class is defined, we can use the as[T] method to convert the parsed Data-Frame into a Dataset[MatchData]:

```
val matchData = parsed.as[MatchData]
matchData.show()
```

As you can see, all of the columns and values of the matchData data set are the same as the data in the parsed DataFrame, and we can still use all of the SQL-style Data-Frame API methods and Spark SQL code against the matchData data set. The major difference between the two is that when we call functions like map, flatMap, or fil ter against matchData, we are processing instances of the MatchData case class instead of the Row class.

For our scoring function, we are going to sum up the value of one field of type Option[Double] (cmp_lname_c1) and four fields of type Option[Int] (cmp_plz, cmp_by, cmp_bd, and cmp_bm). Let's write a small helper case class to cut down on some of the boilerplate code associated with checking for the presence of the Option values:

```
case class Score(value: Double) {
  def +(oi: Option[Int]) = {
    Score(value + oi.getOrElse(0))
  }
}
```

The Score case class starts with a value of type Double (the running sum) and defines a \+ method that allows us to merge an Option[Int] value into the running sum by getting the value of the Option or returning 0 if it is missing. Here, we're taking advantage of the fact that Scala lets you define functions using a much broader set of names than Java to make our scoring function a bit eaiser to read:

```
def scoreMatchData(md: MatchData): Double = {
  (Score(md.cmp_lname_c1.getOrElse(0.0)) + md.cmp_plz +
      md.cmp_by + md.cmp_bd + md.cmp_bm).value
}
```

With our scoring function in hand, we can now compute our scores and the value of the is_match field for each MatchData object in the matchData data set and store the results in a data frame:

```
val scored = matchData.map { md =>
(scoreMatchData(md), md.is_match)
}.toDF("score", "is_match")
```

Model Evaluation

The final step in creating our scoring function is to decide on what threshold the score must exceed in order for us to predict that the two records represent a match. If we set the threshold too high, then we will incorrectly mark a matching record as a miss (called the *false-negative* rate), whereas if we set the threshold too low, we will incorrectly label misses as matches (the *false-positive* rate.) For any nontrivial problem, we always have to trade some false positives for some false negatives, and the question of what the threshold value should be usually comes down to the relative cost of the two kinds of errors in the situation to which the model is being applied.

To help us choose a threshold, it's helpful to create a 2×2 *contingency table* (which is sometimes called a *cross tabulation*, or *crosstab*) that counts the number of records whose scores fall above/below the threshold value crossed with the number of records in each of those categories that were/were not matches. Since we don't know what threshold value we're going to use yet, let's write a function that takes the scored DataFrame and the choice of threshold as parameters and computes the crosstabs using the DataFrame API:

```
def crossTabs(scored: DataFrame, t: Double): DataFrame = {
  scored.
    selectExpr(s"score >= $t as above", "is_match").
    groupBy("above").
    pivot("is_match", Seq("true", "false")).
    count()
}
```

Note that we are including the selectExpr method of the DataFrame API to dynamically determine the value of the field named above based on the value of the t argument using Scala's string interpolation syntax, which allows us to substitute variables by name if we preface the string literal with the letter s (yet another handy bit of Scala implicit magic). Once the `above` field is defined, we create the crosstab with a standard combination of the `groupBy`, `pivot`, and `count` methods that we used before.

Applying a high threshold value of 4.0, meaning that the average of the five features is 0.8, we can filter out almost all of the nonmatches while keeping over 90% of the matches:

```
crossTabs(scored, 4.0).show()
...
+-----+-----+-------+
|above| true| false|
+-----+-----+-------+
| true|20871|    637|
|false|   60|5727564|
+-----+-----+-------+
```

Applying the lower threshold of 2.0, we can ensure that we capture *all* of the known matching records, but at a substantial cost in terms of false positive (top-right cell):

```
crossTabs(scored, 2.0).show()
...
+-----+-----+-------+
|above| true| false|
+-----+-----+-------+
| true|20931| 596414|
|false| null|5131787|
+-----+-----+-------+
```

Even though the number of false positives is higher than we want, this more generous filter still removes 90% of the nonmatching records from our consideration while including every positive match. Even though this is pretty good, it's possible to do even better; see if you can find a way to use some of the other values from `MatchData` (both missing and not) to come up with a scoring function that successfully identifies every `true` match at the cost of less than 100 false positives.

Where to Go from Here

If this chapter was your first time carrying out data preparation and analysis with Scala and Spark, or if you're familiar with the Spark 1.0 APIs and are getting up to speed with the new techniques in Spark 2.0, we hope that you got a feel for what a powerful foundation these tools provide. If you have been using Scala and Spark for a while, we hope that you will pass this chapter along to your friends and colleagues as a way of introducing them to that power as well.

Our goal for this chapter was to provide you with enough Scala knowledge to be able to understand and complete the rest of the examples in this book. If you are the kind of person who learns best through practical examples, your next step is to continue on to the next set of chapters, where we will introduce you to MLlib, the machine learning library designed for Spark.

As you become a seasoned user of Spark and Scala for data analysis, it's likely that you will reach a point where you begin to build tools and libraries designed to help other analysts and data scientists apply Spark to solve their own problems. At that point in your development, it would be helpful to pick up additional books on Scala, like *Programming Scala* by Dean Wampler and Alex Payne, and *The Scala Cookbook* by Alvin Alexander (both from O'Reilly).

## CHAPTER 3

Recommending Music and the Audioscrobbler Data Set

Sean Owen

De gustibus non est disputandum.
(There's no accounting for taste.)

—Anonymous

When somebody asks what it is I do for a living, the direct answer of "data science" or "machine learning" sounds impressive but usually draws a blank stare. Fair enough; even actual data scientists seem to struggle to define what these mean—storing lots of data, computing, predicting something? Inevitably, I jump straight to a relatable example: *"OK, you know how Amazon will tell you about books like the ones you bought? Yes? Yes! It's like that."*

Empirically, the recommender engine seems to be an example of large-scale machine learning that everyone understands, and most people have seen Amazon's. It is a common denominator because recommender engines are everywhere, from social networks to video sites to online retailers. We can also directly observe them in action. We're aware that a computer is picking tracks to play on Spotify, in much the same way we don't necessarily notice that Gmail is deciding whether inbound email is spam.

The output of a recommender is more intuitively understandable than other machine learning algorithms. It's exciting, even. For as much as we think that musical taste is personal and inexplicable, recommenders do a surprisingly good job of identifying tracks we didn't know we would like.

Finally, for domains like music or movies where recommenders are usually deployed, it's comparatively easy to reason about why a recommended piece of music fits with someone's listening history. Not all clustering or classification algorithms match that description. For example, a support vector machine classifier is a set of coefficients, and it's hard even for practitioners to articulate what the numbers mean when they make predictions.

So, it seems fitting to kick off the next three chapters, which will explore key machine learning algorithms on Spark, with a chapter built around recommender engines, and recommending music in particular. It's an accessible way to introduce real-world use of Spark and MLlib, and some basic machine learning ideas that will be developed in subsequent chapters.

Data Set

This example will use a data set published by Audioscrobbler. Audioscrobbler was the first music recommendation system for last.fm, one of the first internet streaming radio sites, founded in 2002. Audioscrobbler provided an open API for "scrobbling," or recording listeners' song plays. last.fm used this information to build a powerful music recommender engine. The system reached millions of users because third-party apps and sites could provide listening data back to the recommender engine.

At that time, research on recommender engines was mostly confined to learning from rating-like data. That is, recommenders were usually viewed as tools that operated on input like "Bob rates Prince 3.5 stars."

The Audioscrobbler data set is interesting because it merely records plays: "Bob played a Prince track." A play carries less information than a rating. Just because Bob played the track doesn't mean he actually liked it. You or I may occasionally play a song by an artist we don't care for, or even play an album and walk out of the room.

However, listeners rate music far less frequently than they play music. A data set like this is therefore much larger, covers more users and artists, and contains more total information than a rating data set, even if each individual data point carries less information. This type of data is often called *implicit feedback* data because the user-artist connections are implied as a side effect of other actions, and not given as explicit ratings or thumbs-up.

A snapshot of a data set distributed by last.fm in 2005 can be found online as a compressed archive (*https://bit.ly/1KiJdOR*). Download the archive, and find within it several files. The main data set is in the *user_artist_data.txt* file. It contains about 141,000 unique users, and 1.6 million unique artists. About 24.2 million users' plays of artists are recorded, along with their counts.

The data set also gives the names of each artist by ID in the *artist_data.txt* file. Note that when plays are scrobbled, the client application submits the name of the artist being played. This name could be misspelled or nonstandard, and this may only be detected later. For example, "The Smiths," "Smiths, The," and "the smiths" may appear as distinct artist IDs in the data set even though they are plainly the same. So, the data set also includes *artist_alias.txt*, which maps artist IDs that are known misspellings or variants to the canonical ID of that artist.

The Alternating Least Squares Recommender Algorithm

We need to choose a recommender algorithm that is suitable for this implicit feedback data. The data set consists entirely of interactions between users and artists' songs. It contains no information about the users, or about the artists other than their names. We need an algorithm that learns without access to user or artist attributes. These are typically called collaborative filtering (*https://en.wikipedia.org/wiki/Collaborative_filtering*) algorithms. For example, deciding that two users might share similar tastes because they are the same age *is not* an example of collaborative filtering. Deciding that two users might both like the same song because they play many other same songs *is* an example.

This data set looks large because it contains tens of millions of play counts. But in a different sense, it is small and skimpy, because it is sparse. On average, each user has played songs from about 171 artists—out of 1.6 million. Some users have listened to only one artist. We need an algorithm that can provide decent recommendations to even these users. After all, every single listener must have started with just one play at some point!

Finally, we need an algorithm that scales, both in its ability to build large models and to create recommendations quickly. Recommendations are typically required in near real time—within a second, not tomorrow.

This example will employ a member of a broad class of algorithms called latent-factor (*https://en.wikipedia.org/wiki/Factor_analysis*) models. They try to explain *observed interactions* between large numbers of users and items through a relatively small number of *unobserved, underlying reasons*. It is analogous to explaining why millions of people buy a particular few of thousands of possible albums by describing users and albums in terms of tastes for perhaps tens of genres—tastes that are not directly observable or given as data.

For example, consider a customer who has bought albums by metal bands Megadeth and Pantera, but also classical composer Mozart. It may be difficult to explain why exactly these albums were bought and nothing else. However, it's probably a small window on a much larger set of tastes. Maybe the customer likes a coherent spectrum of music from metal to progressive rock to classical. That explanation is simpler, and as a bonus, suggests many other albums that would be of interest. In this example, "liking metal, progressive rock, and classical" are three latent factors that could explain tens of thousands of individual album preferences.

More specifically, this example will use a type of matrix factorization (*https://en.wiki pedia.org/wiki/Non-negative_matrix_factorization*) model. Mathematically, these algorithms treat the user and product data as if it were a large matrix A, where the entry at row i and column j exists if user i has played artist j. A is sparse: most entries of A are 0, because only a few of all possible user-artist combinations actually appear in the data. They factor A as the matrix product of two smaller matrices, X and Y. They are very skinny—both have many rows because A has many rows and columns, but both have just a few columns (k). The k columns correspond to the latent factors that are being used to explain the interaction data.

The factorization can only be approximate because k is small, as shown in Figure 3-1.

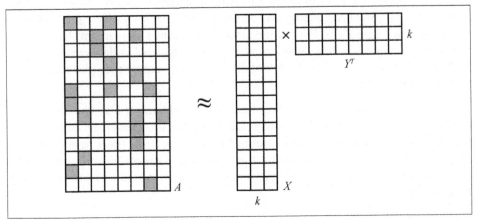

Figure 3-1. Matrix factorization

These algorithms are sometimes called matrix completion algorithms, because the original matrix A may be quite sparse, but the product XY^T is dense. Very few, if any, entries are 0, and therefore the model is only an approximation to A. It is a model in the sense that it produces ("completes") a value for even the many entries that are missing (that is, 0) in the original A.

This is a case where, happily, the linear algebra maps directly and elegantly to intuition. These two matrices contain a row for each user and each artist, respectively. The rows have few values—k. Each value corresponds to a latent feature in the model. So the rows express how much users and artists associate with these k latent features, which might correspond to tastes or genres. And it is simply the product of a user-feature and feature-artist matrix that yields a complete estimation of the entire, dense user-artist interaction matrix. This product might be thought of as mapping items to their attributes, and then weighting those by user attributes.

The bad news is that $A = XY^T$ generally has no exact solution at all, because X and Y aren't large enough (technically speaking, too low rank (*https://bit.ly/1ALoQFK*)) to perfectly represent A. This is actually a good thing. A is just a tiny sample of all interactions that *could* happen. In a way, we believe A is a terribly spotty and therefore hard-to-explain view of a simpler underlying reality that is well explained by just some small number of factors, k, of them. Think of a jigsaw puzzle depicting a cat. The final puzzle is simple to describe: a cat. When you're holding just a few pieces, however, the picture you see is quite difficult to describe.

XY^T should still be as close to A as possible. After all, it's all we've got to go on. It will not and should not reproduce it exactly. The bad news again is that this can't be solved directly for both the best X and best Y at the same time. The good news is that it's trivial to solve for the best X if Y is known, and vice versa. But neither is known beforehand!

Fortunately, there are algorithms that can escape this catch-22 and find a decent solution. More specifically still, the example in this chapter will use the Alternating Least Squares (*https://bit.ly/16ilZZV*) (ALS) algorithm to compute X and Y. This type of approach was popularized around the time of the Netflix Prize (*https://en.wikipe dia.org/wiki/Netflix_Prize*) by papers like "Collaborative Filtering for Implicit Feedback Datasets" (*http://yifanhu.net/PUB/cf.pdf*) and "Large-Scale Parallel Collaborative Filtering for the Netflix Prize" (*http://bit.ly/2rtogOx*). In fact, Spark MLlib's ALS implementation draws on ideas from both of these papers.

Y isn't known, but it can be initialized to a matrix full of randomly chosen row vectors. Then simple linear algebra gives the best solution for X, given A and Y. In fact, it's trivial to compute each row i of X separately as a function of Y and of one row of A. Because it can be done separately, it can be done in parallel, and that is an excellent property for large-scale computation:

$$A_i Y (Y^T Y)^{-1} = X_i$$

Equality can't be achieved exactly, so in fact the goal is to minimize $|A_i Y (Y^T Y)^{-1} - X_i|$, or the sum of squared differences between the two matrices' entries. This is where the "least squares" in the name comes from. In practice, this is never solved by actually computing inverses but faster and more directly via methods like the QR decomposition (*https://en.wikipedia.org/wiki/QR_decomposition*). This equation simply elaborates on the theory of how the row vector is computed.

The same thing can be done to compute each Y_j from X. And again, to compute X from Y, and so on. This is where the "alternating" part comes from. There's just one small problem: Y was made up, and random! X was computed optimally, yes, but given a bogus solution for Y. Fortunately, if this process is repeated, X and Y do eventually converge to decent solutions.

When used to factor a matrix representing implicit data, there is a little more complexity to the ALS factorization. It is not factoring the input matrix A directly, but a matrix P of 0s and 1s, containing 1 where A contains a positive value and 0 elsewhere.

The values in *A* are incorporated later as weights. This detail is beyond the scope of this book, but is not necessary to understand how to use the algorithm.

Finally, the ALS algorithm can take advantage of the sparsity of the input data as well. This, and its reliance on simple, optimized linear algebra and its data-parallel nature, make it very fast at large scale. This is much of the reason it is the topic of this chapter —that, and the fact that ALS is the only recommender algorithm currently implemented in Spark MLlib!

Preparing the Data

First, the data set's files need to be made available. Copy all three data files into HDFS. This chapter will assume that the files are available at */user/ds/*. Start `spark-shell`. Note that this computation will take up more memory than simple applications. If you are running locally rather than on a cluster, for example, you will likely need to specify something like `--driver-memory 4g` to have enough memory to complete these computations.

The first step in building a model is to understand the data that is available, and parse or transform it into forms that are useful for analysis in Spark.

Spark MLlib's ALS implementation does not strictly require numeric IDs for users and items, but is more efficient when the IDs are in fact representable as 32-bit integers. It's advantageous to use `Int` to represent IDs, but this would mean that the IDs can't exceed `Int.MaxValue`, or 2147483647. Does this data set conform to this requirement already? Access the file as a data set of `Strings` in Spark with `SparkSes sion`'s `textFile` method:

```
val rawUserArtistData =
  spark.read.textFile("hdfs:///user/ds/user_artist_data.txt")

rawUserArtistData.take(5).foreach(println)


...
1000002 1 55
1000002 1000006 33
1000002 1000007 8
1000002 1000009 144
1000002 1000010 314
```

By default, the data set will contain one partition for each HDFS block. Because this file consumes about 400 MB on HDFS, it will split into about three to six partitions given typical HDFS block sizes. This is normally fine, but machine learning tasks like ALS are likely to be more compute-intensive than simple text processing. It may be better to break the data into smaller pieces—more partitions—for processing. This can let Spark put more processor cores to work on the problem at once, because each can run a task that processes one partition independently. You can chain a call to `.repartition(n)` after reading the text file to specify a different and larger number of partitions. You might set this higher to match the number of cores in your cluster, for example.

Each line of the file contains a user ID, an artist ID, and a play count, separated by spaces. To compute statistics on the user ID, we split the line by a space character, and parse the first two values as integers. The result is conceptually two "columns": a user ID and artist ID as `Ints`. It makes sense to transform this to a data frame with columns named "user" and "artist," because it then becomes simple to compute simple statistics like the maximum and minimum of both columns:

```
val userArtistDF = rawUserArtistData.map { line =>
  val Array(user, artist, _*) = line.split(' ') ❶
  (user.toInt, artist.toInt)
}.toDF("user", "artist")

userArtistDF.agg(
  min("user"), max("user"), min("artist"), max("artist")).show()

...

+---------+---------+-----------+-----------+
|min(user)|max(user)|min(artist)|max(artist)|
+---------+---------+-----------+-----------+
|       90|  2443548|          1|   10794401|
+---------+---------+-----------+-----------+
```

❶ Match and discard remaining tokens.

The maximum user and artist IDs are 2443548 and 10794401, respectively (and their minimums are 90 and 1; no negative values). These are comfortably smaller than 2147483647. No additional transformation will be necessary to use these IDs.

It will be useful later in this example to know the artist names corresponding to the opaque numeric IDs. This information is contained in *artist_data.txt*. This time, it contains the artist ID and name separated by a tab. However, a straightforward parsing of the file into (`Int,String`) tuples will fail:

```
val rawArtistData = spark.read.textFile("hdfs:///user/ds/artist_data.txt")

rawArtistData.map { line =>
  val (id, name) = line.span(_ != '\t') ❶
  (id.toInt, name.trim)
}.count() ❷

...
java.lang.NumberFormatException: For input string: "Aya Hisakawa"
```

❶ Split line at first tab.

❷ Trigger parsing with .count; this will fail!

Here, span() splits the line by its first tab by consuming characters that aren't tabs. It then parses the first portion as the numeric artist ID, and retains the rest as the artist name (with whitespace—the tab—removed). A small number of the lines appear to be corrupted. They don't contain a tab or they inadvertently include a newline character. These lines cause a NumberFormatException, and ideally, they would not map to anything at all.

However, the map() function must return exactly one value for every input, so it can't be used. It's possible to remove the lines that don't parse with filter(), but this would duplicate the parsing logic. The flatMap() function is appropriate when each element maps to zero, one, or more results because it simply "flattens" these collections of zero or more results from each input into one big data set. It works with Scala Collections, but also with Scala's Option class. Option represents a value that might only optionally exist. It is like a simple collection of 1 or 0 values, corresponding to its Some and None subclasses. So, while the function in flatMap in the following code could just as easily return an empty List or a List of one element, this is a reasonable place to instead use the simpler and clearer Some and None:

```
val artistByID = rawArtistData.flatMap { line =>
  val (id, name) = line.span(_ != '\t')
  if (name.isEmpty) {
    None
  } else {
    try {
      Some((id.toInt, name.trim))
    } catch {
      case _: NumberFormatException => None
    }
  }
}.toDF("id", "name")
```

This gives a data frame with the artist ID and name as columns "id" and "name".

The *artist_alias.txt* file maps artist IDs that may be misspelled or nonstandard to the ID of the artist's canonical name. It contains two IDs per line, separated by a tab. This file is relatively small, containing about 200,000 entries. It will be useful to collect it as a Map, mapping "bad" artist IDs to "good" ones, instead of just using it as a data set of pairs of artist IDs. Again, some lines are missing the first artist ID for some reason, and are skipped:

```
val rawArtistAlias = spark.read.textFile("hdfs:///user/ds/artist_alias.txt")
val artistAlias = rawArtistAlias.flatMap { line =>
  val Array(artist, alias) = line.split('\t')
  if (artist.isEmpty) {
    None
  } else {
```

```
      Some((artist.toInt, alias.toInt))
  }
}.collect().toMap

artistAlias.head
...
(1208690,1003926)
```

The first entry, for instance, maps ID 1208690 to 1003926. We can look these up from the DataFrame containing artist names:

```
artistByID.filter($"id" isin (1208690, 1003926)).show()
```

```
...
+-------+----------------+
|     id|            name|
+-------+----------------+
|1208690|Collective Souls|
|1003926| Collective Soul|
+-------+----------------+
```

This entry evidently maps "Collective Souls" to "Collective Soul," which is in fact the correct name for the band.

Building a First Model

Although the data set is in nearly the right form for use with Spark MLlib's ALS implementation, it requires a small extra transformation. The aliases data set should be applied to convert all artist IDs to a canonical ID, if a different canonical ID exists. Aside from that, all that's required is to parse the lines of input into suitable columns. A helper function is defined to do this, for later reuse.

```
import org.apache.spark.sql._
import org.apache.spark.broadcast._

def buildCounts(
    rawUserArtistData: Dataset[String],
    bArtistAlias: Broadcast[Map[Int,Int]]): DataFrame = {
  rawUserArtistData.map { line =>
    val Array(userID, artistID, count) = line.split(' ').map(_.toInt)
    val finalArtistID =
      bArtistAlias.value.getOrElse(artistID, artistID) ❶
    (userID, finalArtistID, count)
  }.toDF("user", "artist", "count")
}

val bArtistAlias = spark.sparkContext.broadcast(artistAlias)

val trainData = buildCounts(rawUserArtistData, bArtistAlias)
trainData.cache()
```

❶ Get artist's alias if it exists, otherwise get original artist.

The `artistAlias` mapping created earlier could be referenced directly in a `map()` function even though it is a local `Map` on the driver. This works, because it would be copied automatically with every task. However, it is not tiny, consuming about 15 megabytes in memory and at least several megabytes in serialized form. Because many tasks execute in one JVM, it is wasteful to send and store so many copies of the data.

Instead, we create a broadcast variable (*https://bit.ly/1ALqojd*) called `bArtistAlias` for `artistAlias`. This makes Spark send and hold in memory just one copy for *each executor* in the cluster. When there are thousands of tasks and many execute in parallel on each executor, this can save significant network traffic and memory.

Broadcast Variables

When Spark runs a stage, it creates a binary representation of all the information needed to run tasks in that stage; this is called the *closure* of the function that needs to be executed. This closure includes all the data structures on the driver referenced in the function. Spark distributes it with every task that is sent to an executor on the cluster.

Broadcast variables are useful when many tasks need access to the same (immutable) data structure. They extend normal handling of task closures to enable:

- Caching data as raw Java objects on each executor, so they need not be deserialized for each task
- Caching data across multiple jobs, stages, and tasks

For example, consider a natural language processing application that requires a large dictionary of English words, and has a `score` function that accepts a line of input and dictionary of words. Broadcasting the dictionary means it is transferred to each executor only once:

```
val dict: Seq[String] = ...
val bDict = spark.sparkContext.broadcast(dict)

def query(path: String) = {
  spark.read.textFile(path).map(score(_, bDict.value))
  ...
}
```

Although it's beyond the scope of this book, `DataFrame` operations can at times also automatically take advantage of broadcasts when performing joins between a large and small table. Just broadcasting the small table is advantageous sometimes. This is called a *broadcast hash join*.

The call to `cache()` suggests to Spark that this DataFrame should be temporarily stored after being computed, and furthermore, kept in memory in the cluster. This is helpful because the ALS algorithm is iterative, and will typically need to access this data 10 times or more. Without this, the DataFrame could be repeatedly recomputed from the original data each time it is accessed! The Storage tab in the Spark UI will show how much of the DataFrame is cached and how much memory it uses, as shown in Figure 3-2. This one consumes about 120 MB across the cluster.

Storage Level	Cached Partitions	Fraction Cached	Size in Memory	Size on Disk
Memory Deserialized 1x Replicated	8	100%	120.3 MB	0.0 B

Figure 3-2. Storage tab in the Spark UI, showing cached DataFrame memory usage

Note that the label "Deserialized" in the UI above is actually only relevant for RDDs, where "Serialized" means data are stored in memory not as objects, but as serialized bytes. However, `Dataset` and `DataFrame` instances like this one perform their own "encoding" of common data types in memory separately.

Actually, 120 MB is surprisingly small. Given that there are about 24 million plays stored here, a quick back-of-the-envelope calculation suggests that this would mean that each user-artist-count entry consumes only 5 bytes on average. However, the three 32-bit integers alone ought to consume 12 bytes. This is one of the advantages of a DataFrame. Because the types of data stored are primitive 32-bit integers, their representation can be optimized in memory internally. In the original RDD-based API for ALS, which would have required storing a collection of 24 million `Rating` objects in memory, the RDD would have consumed over 900 MB.

Finally, we can build a model:

```
import org.apache.spark.ml.recommendation._
import scala.util.Random

val model = new ALS().
    setSeed(Random.nextLong()). ❶
    setImplicitPrefs(true).
    setRank(10).
    setRegParam(0.01).
    setAlpha(1.0).
    setMaxIter(5).
    setUserCol("user").
    setItemCol("artist").
    setRatingCol("count").
    setPredictionCol("prediction").
    fit(trainData)
```

❶ Use random seed

This constructs model as an ALSModel with some default configuration. The operation will likely take minutes or more depending on your cluster. Compared to some machine learning models, whose final form may consist of just a few parameters or coefficients, this type of model is huge. It contains a feature vector of 10 values for each user and product in the model, and in this case there are more than 1.7 million of them. The model contains these large user-feature and product-feature matrices as DataFrames of their own.

The values in your results may be somewhat different. The final model depends on a randomly chosen initial set of feature vectors. The default behavior of this and other components in MLlib, however, is to use the same set of random choices every time by defaulting to a fixed seed. This is unlike other libraries, where behavior of random elements is typically not fixed by default. So, here and elsewhere, a random seed is set with setSeed(Random.nextLong()).

To see some feature vectors, try the following, which displays just one row and does not truncate the wide display of the feature vector:

```
model.userFactors.show(1, truncate = false)
```

```
...
+---+-------------------------------------------------- ...
|id |features                                           ...
+---+-------------------------------------------------- ...
|90 |[-0.2738046, 0.03154172, 1.046261, -0.52314466, ...
+---+-------------------------------------------------- ...
```

The other methods invoked on ALS, like setAlpha, set *hyperparameters* whose value can affect the quality of the recommendations that the model makes. These will be explained later. The more important first question is, is the model any good? Does it produce good recommendations?

Spot Checking Recommendations

We should first see if the artist recommendations make any intuitive sense, by examining a user, plays, and recommendations for that user. Take, for example, user 2093760. First, let's look at his or her plays to get a sense of the person's tastes. Extract the IDs of artists that this user has listened to and print their names. This means searching the input for artist IDs played by this user, and then filtering the set of artists by these IDs in order to print the names in order:

```
val userID = 2093760

val existingArtistIDs = trainData.
  filter($"user" === userID). ❶
```

```
    select("artist").as[Int].collect() ❷

artistByID.filter($"id" isin (existingArtistIDs:_*)).show() ❸

...
+-------+---------------+
|     id|           name|
+-------+---------------+
|   1180|     David Gray|
|    378|   Blackalicious|
|    813|      Jurassic 5|
|1255340|The Saw Doctors|
|    942|         Xzibit|
+-------+---------------+
```

❶ Find lines whose user is 2093760.

❷ Collect data set of `Int` artist ID.

❸ Filter in those artists; note `:_*` varargs syntax.

The artists look like a mix of mainstream pop and hip-hop. A Jurassic 5 fan? Remember, it's 2005. In case you're wondering, the Saw Doctors are a very Irish rock band popular in Ireland.

The bad news is that, surprisingly, `ALSModel` does not have a method that directly computes top recommendations for a user. Its purpose is to estimate a user's preference for any given artist. Spark 2.2 will add a `recommendAll` method to address this, but this has not been released at the time fo this writing. This can be used to score all artists for a user and then return the few with the highest predicted score:

```
def makeRecommendations(
    model: ALSModel,
    userID: Int,
    howMany: Int): DataFrame = {

  val toRecommend = model.itemFactors.
    select($"id".as("artist")).
    withColumn("user", lit(userID)) ❶

  model.transform(toRecommend).
    select("artist", "prediction").
    orderBy($"prediction".desc).
    limit(howMany) ❷
}
```

❶ Select all artist IDs and pair with target user ID.

❷ Score all artists, return top by score.

Note that this method does not bother to filter out the IDs of artists the user has already listened to. Although this is common, it's not always desirable, and won't matter for our purposes anyway.

Now, it's simple to make recommendations, though computing them this way will take a few moments. It's suitable for batch scoring but not real-time use cases:

```
val topRecommendations = makeRecommendations(model, userID, 5)
topRecommendations.show()
```

```
...
+-------+-----------+
| artist| prediction|
+-------+-----------+
|   2814|0.030201003|
|1300642|0.029290354|
|1001819|0.029130368|
|1007614|0.028773561|
|1037970|0.028646756|
+-------+-----------+
```

The results contain an artist ID of course, and also a "prediction." For this type of ALS algorithm, the prediction is an opaque value normally between 0 and 1, where higher values mean a better recommendation. It is not a probability, but can be thought of as an estimate of a 0/1 value indicating whether the user won't or will interact with the artist, respectively.

After extracting the artist IDs for the recommendations, we can look up artist names in a similar way:

```
val recommendedArtistIDs =
  topRecommendations.select("artist").as[Int].collect()

artistByID.filter($"id" isin (recommendedArtistIDs:_*)).show()
```

```
...
+-------+-----------+
|    id|       name|
+-------+-----------+
|   2814|    50 Cent|
|1007614|      Jay-Z|
|1037970|Kanye West|
|1001819|       2Pac|
|1300642|  The Game|
+-------+-----------+
```

The result is all hip-hop. This doesn't look like a great set of recommendations, at first glance. While these are generally popular artists, they don't appear to be personalized to this user's listening habits.

Evaluating Recommendation Quality

Of course, that's just one subjective judgment about one user's results. It's hard for anyone but that user to quantify how good the recommendations are. Moreover, it's infeasible to have any human manually score even a small sample of the output to evaluate the results.

It's reasonable to assume that users tend to play songs from artists who are appealing, and not play songs from artists who aren't appealing. So, the plays for a user give a partial picture of "good" and "bad" artist recommendations. This is a problematic assumption but about the best that can be done without any other data. For example, presumably user 2093760 likes many more artists than the 5 listed previously, and among the 1.7 million other artists not played, a few are of interest and not all are "bad" recommendations.

What if a recommender were evaluated on its ability to rank good artists high in a list of recommendations? This is one of several generic metrics that can be applied to a system that ranks things, like a recommender. The problem is that "good" is defined as "artists the user has listened to," and the recommender system has already received all of this information as input. It could trivially return the user's previously listened-to artists as top recommendations and score perfectly. But this is not useful, especially because the recommender's role is to recommend artists that the user has never listened to.

To make this meaningful, some of the artist play data can be set aside and hidden from the ALS model-building process. Then, this held-out data can be interpreted as a collection of good recommendations for each user but one that the recommender has not already been given. The recommender is asked to rank all items in the model, and the ranks of the held-out artists are examined. Ideally, the recommender places all of them at or near the top of the list.

We can then compute the recommender's score by comparing all held-out artists' ranks to the rest. (In practice, we compute this by examining only a sample of all such pairs, because a potentially huge number of such pairs may exist.) The fraction of pairs where the held-out artist is ranked higher is its score. A score of 1.0 is perfect, 0.0 is the worst possible score, and 0.5 is the expected value achieved from randomly ranking artists.

This metric is directly related to an information retrieval concept called the receiver operating characteristic (*https://bit.ly/18sUUQK*) (ROC) curve. The metric in the preceding paragraph equals the area under this ROC curve, and is indeed known as AUC, or Area Under the Curve. AUC may be viewed as the probability that a randomly chosen good recommendation ranks above a randomly chosen bad recommendation.

The AUC metric is also used in the evaluation of classifiers. It is implemented, along with related methods, in the MLlib class BinaryClassificationMetrics. For recommenders, we will compute AUC *per user* and average the result. The resulting metric is slightly different, and might be called "mean AUC." We will implement this, because it is not (quite) implemented in Spark.

Other evaluation metrics that are relevant to systems that rank things are implemented in RankingMetrics. These include metrics like precision, recall, and mean average precision (*https://bit.ly/1ALr1cG*) (MAP). MAP is also frequently used and focuses more narrowly on the quality of the top recommendations. However, AUC will be used here as a common and broad measure of the quality of the entire model output.

In fact, the process of holding out some data to select a model and evaluate its accuracy is common practice in all of machine learning. Typically, data is divided into three subsets: training, cross-validation (CV), and test sets. For simplicity in this initial example, only two sets will be used: training and CV. This will be sufficient to choose a model. In Chapter 4, this idea will be extended to include the test set.

Computing AUC

An implementation of mean AUC is provided in the source code accompanying this book. It is complex and not reproduced here, but is explained in some detail in comments in the source code. It accepts the CV set as the "positive" or "good" artists for each user, and a prediction function. This function translates a data frame containing each user-artist pair into a data frame that also contains its estimated strength of interaction as a "prediction," a number wherein higher values mean higher rank in the recommendations.

In order to use it, we must split the input data into a training and CV set. The ALS model will be trained on the training data set only, and the CV set will be used to evaluate the model. Here, 90% of the data is used for training and the remaining 10% for cross-validation:

```
def areaUnderCurve(
    positiveData: DataFrame,
    bAllArtistIDs: Broadcast[Array[Int]],
    predictFunction: (DataFrame => DataFrame)): Double = {
  ...
}

val allData = buildCounts(rawUserArtistData, bArtistAlias) ❶
val Array(trainData, cvData) = allData.randomSplit(Array(0.9, 0.1))
trainData.cache()
cvData.cache()

val allArtistIDs = allData.select("artist").as[Int].distinct().collect() ❷
```

```
val bAllArtistIDs = spark.sparkContext.broadcast(allArtistIDs)

val model = new ALS().
    setSeed(Random.nextLong()).
    setImplicitPrefs(true).
    setRank(10).setRegParam(0.01).setAlpha(1.0).setMaxIter(5).
    setUserCol("user").setItemCol("artist").
    setRatingCol("count").setPredictionCol("prediction").
    fit(trainData)
areaUnderCurve(cvData, bAllArtistIDs, model.transform)
```

❶ Note that this function is defined above.

❷ Remove duplicates, and collect to driver.

Note that `areaUnderCurve()` accepts a *function* as its third argument. Here, the `trans form` method from `ALSModel` is passed in, but it will shortly be swapped out for an alternative.

The result is about 0.879. Is this good? It is certainly higher than the 0.5 that is expected from making recommendations randomly, and it's close to 1.0, which is the maximum possible score. Generally, an AUC over 0.9 would be considered high.

But is it an accurate evaluation? This evaluation could be repeated with a different 90% as the training set. The resulting AUC values' average might be a better estimate of the algorithm's performance on the data set. In fact, one common practice is to divide the data into *k* subsets of similar size, use *k* – 1 subsets together for training, and evaluate on the remaining subset. We can repeat this *k* times, using a different set of subsets each time. This is called *k-fold cross-validation* (*https://bit.ly/1BVTEa9*). This won't be implemented in examples here, for simplicity, but some support for this technique exists in MLlib in its `CrossValidator` API. The validation API will be revisited in Chapter 4.

It's helpful to benchmark this against a simpler approach. For example, consider recommending the globally most-played artists to every user. This is not personalized, but it is simple and may be effective. Define this simple prediction function and evaluate its AUC score:

```
def predictMostListened(train: DataFrame)(allData: DataFrame) = {

  val listenCounts = train.
    groupBy("artist").
    agg(sum("count").as("prediction")).
    select("artist", "prediction")

  allData.
    join(listenCounts, Seq("artist"), "left_outer").
    select("user", "artist", "prediction")
}
```

```
areaUnderCurve(cvData, bAllArtistIDs, predictMostListened(trainData))
```

This is another interesting demonstration of Scala syntax, where the function appears to be defined to take two lists of arguments. Calling the function and supplying the first argument creates a *partially applied function*, which itself takes an argument (all Data) in order to return predictions. The result of predictMostListened(train Data) is a *function*.

The result is also about 0.880. This suggests that nonpersonalized recommendations are already fairly effective according to this metric. However, we'd expect the "personalized" recommendations to score better in comparison. Clearly, the model needs some tuning. Can it be made better?

Hyperparameter Selection

So far, the hyperparameter values used to build the ALSModel were simply given without comment. They are not learned by the algorithm and must be chosen by the caller. The configured hyperparameters were:

setRank(10)
> The number of latent factors in the model, or equivalently, the number of columns k in the user-feature and product-feature matrices. In nontrivial cases, this is also their rank.

setMaxIter(5)
> The number of iterations that the factorization runs. More iterations take more time but may produce a better factorization.

setRegParam(0.01)
> A standard overfitting parameter, also usually called *lambda*. Higher values resist overfitting, but values that are too high hurt the factorization's accuracy.

setAlpha(1.0)
> Controls the relative weight of observed versus unobserved user-product interactions in the factorization.

rank, regParam, and alpha can be considered *hyperparameters* to the model. (max Iter is more of a constraint on resources used in the factorization.) These are not values that end up in the matrices inside the ALSModel—those are simply its *parameters* and are chosen by the algorithm. These hyperparameters are instead parameters to the process of building itself.

The values used in the preceding list are not necessarily optimal. Choosing good hyperparameter values is a common problem in machine learning. The most basic way to choose values is to simply try combinations of values and evaluate a metric for each of them, and choose the combination that produces the best value of the metric.

In the following example, eight possible combinations are tried: rank = 5 or 30, regParam = 4.0 or 0.0001, and alpha = 1.0 or 40.0. These values are still something of a guess, but are chosen to cover a broad range of parameter values. The results are printed in order by top AUC score:

```
val evaluations =
  for (rank     <- Seq(5,  30);
       regParam <- Seq(4.0, 0.0001);
       alpha    <- Seq(1.0, 40.0)) ❶
    yield {
      val model = new ALS().
        setSeed(Random.nextLong()).
        setImplicitPrefs(true).
        setRank(rank).setRegParam(regParam).
        setAlpha(alpha).setMaxIter(20).
        setUserCol("user").setItemCol("artist").
        setRatingCol("count").setPredictionCol("prediction").
        fit(trainData)

      val auc = areaUnderCurve(cvData, bAllArtistIDs, model.transform)

      model.userFactors.unpersist() ❷
      model.itemFactors.unpersist()

      (auc, (rank, regParam, alpha))
    }

evaluations.sorted.reverse.foreach(println) ❸

...
(0.8928367485129145,(30,4.0,40.0))
(0.891835487024326,(30,1.0E-4,40.0))
(0.8912376926662007,(30,4.0,1.0))
(0.889240668173946,(5,4.0,40.0))
(0.8886268430389741,(5,4.0,1.0))
(0.8883278461068959,(5,1.0E-4,40.0))
(0.8825350012228627,(5,1.0E-4,1.0))
(0.8770527940660278,(30,1.0E-4,1.0))
```

❶ Read as a triply nested for loop.

❷ Free up model resources immediately.

❸ Sort by first value (AUC), descending, and print.

The for syntax here is a way to write nested loops in Scala. It is like a loop over alpha, inside a loop over regParam, inside a loop over rank.

The differences are small in absolute terms, but are still somewhat significant for AUC values. Interestingly, the parameter alpha seems consistently better at 40 than 1. (For the curious, 40 was a value proposed as a default in one of the original ALS papers mentioned earlier.) This can be interpreted as indicating that the model is better off focusing far more on what the user did listen to than what he or she did not listen to.

A higher regParam looks better too. This suggests the model is somewhat susceptible to overfitting, and so needs a higher regParam to resist trying to fit the sparse input given from each user too exactly. Overfitting will be revisited in more detail in Chapter 4.

As expected, 5 features is pretty low for a model of this size, and underperforms the model that uses 30 features to explain tastes. It's possible that the best number of features is actually higher than 30, and that these values are alike in being too small.

Of course, this process can be repeated for different ranges of values or more values. It is a brute-force means of choosing hyperparameters. However, in a world where clusters with terabytes of memory and hundreds of cores are not uncommon, and with frameworks like Spark that can exploit parallelism and memory for speed, it becomes quite feasible.

It is not strictly required to understand what the hyperparameters mean, although it is helpful to know what normal ranges of values are like in order to start the search over a parameter space that is neither too large nor too tiny.

This was a fairly manual way to loop over hyperparameters, build models, and evaluate them. In Chapter 4, after learning more about the Spark ML API, we'll find that there is a more automated way to compute this using Pipelines and TrainValidationSplit.

Making Recommendations

Proceeding for the moment with the best set of hyperparameters, what does the new model recommend for user 2093760?

```
+-----------+
|       name|
+-----------+
|  [unknown]|
|The Beatles|
```

```
|      Eminem|
|          U2|
|   Green Day|
+-----------+
```

Anecdotally, this makes a bit more sense for this user, being dominated by pop rock instead of all hip-hop. [unknown] is plainly not an artist. Querying the original data set reveals that it occurs 429,447 times, putting it nearly in the top 100! This is some default value for plays without an artist, maybe supplied by a certain scrobbling client. It is not useful information and we should discard it from the input before starting again. It is an example of how the practice of data science is often iterative, with discoveries about the data occurring at every stage.

This model can be used to make recommendations for all users. This could be useful in a batch process that recomputes a model and recommendations for users every hour or even less, depending on the size of the data and speed of the cluster.

At the moment, however, Spark MLlib's ALS implementation does not support a method to recommend to all users. It is possible to recommend to one user at a time, as shown above, although each will launch a short-lived distributed job that takes a few seconds. This may be suitable for rapidly recomputing recommendations for small groups of users. Here, recommendations are made to 100 users taken from the data and printed:

```scala
val someUsers = allData.select("user").as[Int].distinct().take(100) ❶
val someRecommendations =
  someUsers.map(userID => (userID, makeRecommendations(model, userID, 5))) ❷
someRecommendations.foreach { case (userID, recsDF) =>
  val recommendedArtists = recsDF.select("artist").as[Int].collect()
  println(s"$userID -> ${recommendedArtists.mkString(", ")}") ❸
}

...
1000190 -> 6694932, 435, 1005820, 58, 1244362
1001043 -> 1854, 4267, 1006016, 4468, 1274
1001129 -> 234, 1411, 1307, 189, 121
...
```

❶ Copy 100 (distinct) users to the driver.

❷ map() is a local Scala operation here.

❸ mkString joins a collection to a string with a delimiter.

Here, the recommendations are just printed. They could just as easily be written to an external store like HBase (*https://hbase.apache.org*), which provides fast lookup at runtime.

Interestingly, this entire process could also be used to recommend *users* to *artists*. This could be used to answer questions like "Which 100 users are most likely to be interested in the new album by artist X?" Doing so would only require swapping the user and artist field when parsing the input:

```
rawArtistData.map { line =>
  val (id, name) = line.span(_ != '\t')
  (name.trim, id.int)
}
```

Where to Go from Here

Naturally, it's possible to spend more time tuning the model parameters, and finding and fixing anomalies in the input, like the [unknown] artist. For example, a quick analysis of play counts reveals that user 2064012 played artist 4468 an astonishing 439,771 times! Artist 4468 is the implausibly successful alterna-metal band System of a Down (*https://en.wikipedia.org/wiki/System_of_a_Down*), who turned up earlier in recommendations. Assuming an average song length of 4 minutes, this is over 33 years of playing hits like "Chop Suey!" and "B.Y.O.B." Because the band started making records in 1998, this would require playing four or five tracks at once for seven years. It must be spam or a data error, and another example of the types of real-world data problems that a production system would have to address.

ALS is not the only possible recommender algorithm, but at this time, it is the only one supported by Spark MLlib. However, MLlib also supports a variant of ALS for non-implicit data. Its use is identical, except that ALS is configured with setImplicit Prefs(false). This is appropriate when data is rating-like, rather than count-like. For example, it is appropriate when the data set is user ratings of artists on a 1–5 scale. The resulting prediction column returned from ALSModel.transform recommendation methods then really is an estimated rating. In this case, the simple RMSE (root mean squared error) metric is appropriate for evaluating the recommender.

Later, other recommender algorithms may be available in Spark MLlib or other libraries.

In production, recommender engines often need to make recommendations in real time, because they are used in contexts like ecommerce sites where recommendations are requested frequently as customers browse product pages. Precomputing and storing recommendations in a NoSQL store, as mentioned previously, is a reasonable way to make recommendations available at scale. One disadvantage of this approach is that it requires precomputing recommendations for all users who might need recommendations soon, which is potentially any of them. For example, if only 10,000 of 1 million users visit a site in a day, precomputing all million users' recommendations each day is 99% wasted effort.

It would be nicer to compute recommendations on the fly, as needed. While we can compute recommendations for one user using the ALSModel, this is necessarily a distributed operation that takes several seconds, because ALSModel is uniquely large and therefore actually a distributed data set. This is not true of other models, which afford much faster scoring. Projects like Oryx 2 (*https://github.com/OryxProject/oryx*) attempt to implement real-time on-demand recommendations with libraries like MLlib by efficiently accessing the model data in memory.

## CHAPTER 4

Predicting Forest Cover with Decision Trees

Sean Owen

Prediction is very difficult, especially if it's about the future.
—Niels Bohr

In the late nineteenth century, the English scientist Sir Francis Galton was busy measuring things like peas and people. He found that large peas (and people) had larger-than-average offspring. This isn't surprising. However, the offspring were, on average, smaller than their parents. In terms of people: the child of a seven-foot-tall basketball player is likely to be taller than the global average but still more likely than not to be less than seven feet tall.

As almost a side effect of his study, Galton plotted child versus parent size and noticed there was a roughly linear relationship between the two. Large parent peas had large children, but slightly smaller than themselves; small parents had small children, but generally a bit larger than themselves. The line's slope was therefore positive but less than 1, and Galton described this phenomenon as we do today, as *regression to the mean*.

Although maybe not perceived this way at the time, this line was, to me, an early example of a predictive model. The line links the two values, and implies that the value of one suggests a lot about the value of the other. Given the size of a new pea, this relationship could lead to a more accurate estimate of its offspring's size than simply assuming the offspring would be like the parent or like every other pea.

Fast Forward to Regression

More than a century of statistics later, and since the advent of modern machine learning and data science, we still talk about the idea of predicting a value from other values as regression (*https://en.wikipedia.org/wiki/Regression_analysis*), even though it has nothing to do with slipping back toward a mean value, or indeed moving backward at all. Regression techniques also relate to classification (*https://en.wikipedia.org/wiki/Statistical_classification*) techniques. Generally, *regression* refers to predicting a numeric quantity like size or income or temperature, whereas *classification* refers to predicting a label or category, like "spam" or "picture of a cat."

The common thread linking regression and classification is that both involve predicting one (or more) values given one (or more) other values. To do so, both require a body of inputs and outputs to learn from. They need to be fed both questions and known answers. For this reason, they are known as types of *supervised learning* (*https://en.wikipedia.org/wiki/Supervised_learning*).

Classification and regression are the oldest and most well-studied types of predictive analytics. Most algorithms you will likely encounter in analytics packages and libraries are classification or regression techniques, like support vector machines, logistic regression, naïve Bayes, neural networks, and deep learning. Recommenders, the topic of Chapter 3, were comparatively more intuitive to introduce, but are also just a relatively recent and separate subtopic within machine learning.

This chapter will focus on a popular and flexible type of algorithm for both classification and regression: decision trees (*https://en.wikipedia.org/wiki/Decision_tree*), and the algorithm's extension, random decision forests (*https://en.wikipedia.org/wiki/Random_forest*). The exciting thing about these algorithms is that, with all due respect to Mr. Bohr, they can help predict the future—or at least, predict the things we don't yet know for sure, like the likelihood you will buy a car based on your online behavior, whether an email is spam given its words, or which acres of land are likely to grow the most crops given their location and soil chemistry.

Vectors and Features

To explain the choice of the data set and algorithm featured in this chapter, and to begin to explain how regression and classification operate, it is necessary to briefly define the terms that describe their input and output.

Consider predicting tomorrow's high temperature given today's weather. There is nothing wrong with this idea, but "today's weather" is a casual concept that requires structuring before it can be fed into a learning algorithm.

Really, it is certain *features* of today's weather that may predict tomorrow's temperature, such as:

- Today's high temperature
- Today's low temperature
- Today's average humidity

- Whether it's cloudy, rainy, or clear today
- The number of weather forecasters predicting a cold snap tomorrow

These features are also sometimes called *dimensions*, *predictors*, or just *variables*. Each of these features can be quantified. For example, high and low temperatures are measured in degrees Celsius, humidity can be measured as a fraction between 0 and 1, and weather type can be labeled `cloudy`, `rainy`, or `clear`. The number of forecasters is, of course, an integer count. Today's weather might therefore be reduced to a list of values like `13.1,19.0,0.73,cloudy,1`.

These five features together, in order, are known as a *feature vector*, and can describe any day's weather. This usage bears some resemblance to use of the term *vector* in linear algebra, except that a vector in this sense can conceptually contain nonnumeric values, and even lack some values.

These features are not all of the same type. The first two features are measured in degrees Celsius, but the third is unitless, a fraction. The fourth is not a number at all, and the fifth is a number that is always a nonnegative integer.

For purposes of discussion, this book will talk about features in two broad groups only: *categorical* features and *numeric* features. In this context, numeric features are those that can be quantified by a number and have a meaningful ordering. For example, it's meaningful to say that today's high was 23°C, and that this is higher than yesterday's high of 22°C. All of the features mentioned previously are numeric, except the weather type. Terms like `clear` are not numbers, and have no ordering. It is meaningless to say that `cloudy` is larger than `clear`. This is a categorical feature, which instead takes on one of several discrete values.

Training Examples

A learning algorithm needs to train on data in order to make predictions. It requires a large number of inputs, and known correct outputs, from historical data. For example, in this problem, the learning algorithm would be given that, one day, the weather was between 12° and 16°C, with 10% humidity, clear, with no forecast of a cold snap; and the following day, the high temperature was 17.2°C. With enough of these *examples*, a learning algorithm might learn to predict the following day's high temperature with some accuracy.

Feature vectors provide an organized way to describe input to a learning algorithm (here: `12.5,15.5,0.10,clear,0`). The output, or *target*, of the prediction can also be thought of as a feature. Here, it is a numeric feature: `17.2`. It's not uncommon to simply include the target as another feature in the feature vector. The entire training example might be thought of as `12.5,15.5,0.10,clear,0,17.2`. The collection of all of these examples is known as the *training set*.

Note that regression problems are just those where the target is a numeric feature, and classification problems are those where the target is categorical. Not every regression or classification algorithm can handle categorical features or categorical targets; some are limited to numeric features.

Decision Trees and Forests

It turns out that the family of algorithms known as *decision trees* can naturally handle both categorical and numeric features. Building a single tree can be done in parallel, and many trees can be built in parallel at once. They are robust to outliers in the data, meaning that a few extreme and possibly erroneous data points might not affect predictions at all. They can consume data of different types and on different scales without the need for preprocessing or normalization, which is an issue that will reappear in Chapter 5.

Decision trees generalize into a more powerful algorithm, called *random decision forests*. Their flexibility makes these algorithms worthwhile to examine in this chapter, where Spark MLlib's `DecisionTree` and `RandomForest` implementation will be applied to a data set.

Decision tree–based algorithms have the further advantage of being comparatively intuitive to understand and reason about. In fact, we all probably use the same reasoning embodied in decision trees, implicitly, in everyday life. For example, I sit down to have morning coffee with milk. Before I commit to that milk and add it to my brew, I want to predict: is the milk spoiled? I don't know for sure. I might check if the use-by date has passed. If not, I predict no, it's not spoiled. If the date has passed, but that was three or fewer days ago, I take my chances and predict no, it's not spoiled. Otherwise, I sniff the milk. If it smells funny, I predict yes, and otherwise no.

This series of yes/no decisions that lead to a prediction are what decision trees embody. Each decision leads to one of two results, which is either a prediction or another decision, as shown in Figure 4-1. In this sense, it is natural to think of the process as a tree of decisions, where each internal node in the tree is a decision, and each leaf node is a final answer.

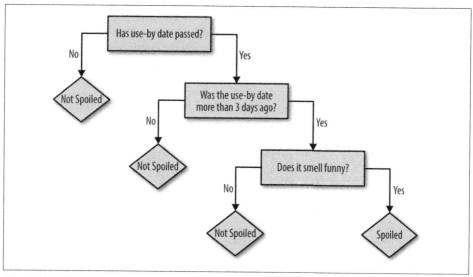

Figure 4-1. Decision tree: is it spoiled?

The preceding rules were ones I learned to apply intuitively over years of bachelor life —they seemed like rules that were both simple and also usefully differentiated cases of spoiled and nonspoiled milk. These are also properties of a good decision tree.

That is a simplistic decision tree, and was not built with any rigor. To elaborate, consider another example. A robot has taken a job in an exotic pet store. It wants to learn, before the shop opens, which animals in the shop would make a good pet for a child. The owner lists nine pets that would and wouldn't be suitable before hurrying off. The robot compiles the information found in Table 4-1 from examining the animals.

Table 4-1. Exotic pet store "feature vectors"

Name	Weight (kg)	# Legs	Color	Good pet?
Fido	20.5	4	Brown	Yes
Mr. Slither	3.1	0	Green	No
Nemo	0.2	0	Tan	Yes
Dumbo	1390.8	4	Gray	No
Kitty	12.1	4	Gray	Yes
Jim	150.9	2	Tan	No
Millie	0.1	100	Brown	No
McPigeon	1.0	2	Gray	No
Spot	10.0	4	Brown	Yes

Although a name is given, it will not be included as a feature. There is little reason to believe the name alone is predictive; "Felix" could name a cat or a poisonous tarantula, for all the robot knows. So, there are two numeric features (weight, number of legs) and one categorical feature (color) predicting a categorical target (is/is not a good pet for a child).

The robot might try to fit a simple decision tree to this training data to start, consisting of a single decision based on weight, as shown in Figure 4-2.

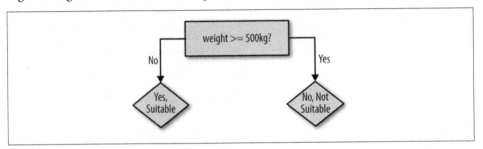

Figure 4-2. Robot's first decision tree

The logic of the decision tree is easy to read and make some sense of: 500kg animals certainly sound unsuitable as pets. This rule predicts the correct value in five of nine cases. A quick glance suggests that we could improve the rule by lowering the weight threshold to 100kg. This gets six of nine examples correct. The heavy animals are now predicted correctly; the lighter animals are only partly correct.

So, a second decision can be constructed to further refine the prediction for examples with weights less than 100kg. It would be good to pick a feature that changes some of the incorrect Yes predictions to No. For example, there is one small green animal, sounding suspiciously like a snake, that the robot could predict correctly by deciding on color, as shown in Figure 4-3.

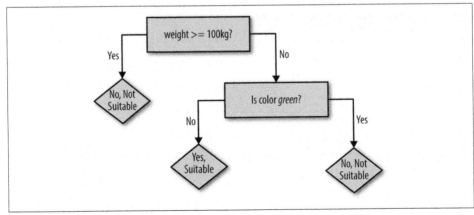

Figure 4-3. Robot's next decision tree

Now, seven of nine examples are correct. Of course, decision rules could be added until all nine were correctly predicted. The logic embodied in the resulting decision tree would probably sound implausible when translated into common speech: "If the animal's weight is less than 100kg, and its color is brown instead of green, and it has fewer than 10 legs, then yes it is a suitable pet." While perfectly fitting the given examples, a decision tree like this would fail to predict that a small, brown, four-legged wolverine is not a suitable pet. Some balance is needed to avoid this phenomenon, known as *overfitting*.

This is enough of an introduction to decision trees for us to begin using them with Spark. The remainder of the chapter will explore how to pick decision rules, how to know when to stop, and how to gain accuracy by creating a forest of trees.

Covtype Data Set

The data set used in this chapter is the well-known Covtype data set, available online (*https://bit.ly/1KiJRfg*) as a compressed CSV-format data file, *covtype.data.gz*, and accompanying info file, *covtype.info*.

The data set records the types of forest-covering parcels of land in Colorado, USA. It's only a coincidence that the data set concerns real-world forests! Each example contains several features describing each parcel of land—like its elevation, slope, distance to water, shade, and soil type—along with the known forest type covering the land. The forest cover type is to be predicted from the rest of the features, of which there are 54 in total.

This data set has been used in research and even a Kaggle competition (*https://www.kaggle.com/c/forest-cover-type-prediction*). It is an interesting data set to explore in this chapter because it contains both categorical and numeric features. There are 581,012 examples in the data set, which does not exactly qualify as big data but is large enough to be manageable as an example and still highlight some issues of scale.

Preparing the Data

Thankfully, the data is already in a simple CSV format and does not require much cleansing or other preparation to be used with Spark MLlib. Later, it will be of interest to explore some transformations of the data, but it can be used as is to start.

The *covtype.data* file should be extracted and copied into HDFS. This chapter will assume that the file is available at */user/ds/*. Start `spark-shell`. You may again find it helpful to give the shell a healthy amount of memory to work with, as building decision forests can be resource-intensive. If you have the memory, specify `--driver-memory 8g` or similar.

CSV files contain fundamentally tabular data, organized into rows of columns. Sometimes these columns are given names in a header line, although that's not the case here. The column names are given in the companion file, *covtype.info*. Conceptually, each column of a CSV file has a type as well—a number, a string—but a CSV file doesn't specify this.

It's natural to parse this data as a data frame because this is Spark's abstraction for tabular data, with a defined column schema, including column names and types. Spark has built-in support for reading CSV data, in fact:

```
val dataWithoutHeader = spark.read.
  option("inferSchema", true).
  option("header", false).
  csv("hdfs:///user/ds/covtype.data")

...
org.apache.spark.sql.DataFrame = [_c0: int, _c1: int ... 53 more fields]
```

This code reads the input as CSV and does not attempt to parse the first line as a header of column names. It also requests that the type of each column be inferred by examining the data. It correctly infers that all of the columns are numbers, and more specifically, integers. Unfortunately it can only name the columns "_c0" and so on.

Looking at the column names, it's clear that some features are indeed numeric. "Elevation" is an elevation in meters; "Slope" is measured in degrees. However, "Wilderness_Area" is something different, because it is said to span four columns, each of which is a 0 or 1. In reality, "Wilderness_Area" is a categorical value, not a numeric one.

These four columns are actually a one-hot (*https://en.wikipedia.org/wiki/One-hot*) or 1-of-n encoding, in which one categorical feature that takes on N distinct values becomes N numeric features, each taking on the value 0 or 1. Exactly one of the N values has value 1, and the others are 0. For example, a categorical feature for weather that can be cloudy, rainy, or clear would become three numeric features, where cloudy is represented by 1,0,0; rainy by 0,1,0; and so on. These three numeric features might be thought of as is_cloudy, is_rainy, and is_clear features. Likewise, 40 of the columns are really one Soil_Type categorical feature.

This isn't the only possible way to encode a categorical feature as a number. Another possible encoding simply assigns a distinct numeric value to each possible value of the categorical feature. For example, cloudy may become 1.0, rainy 2.0, and so on. The target itself, "Cover_Type", is a categorical value encoded as a value 1 to 7.

Be careful when encoding a categorical feature as a single numeric feature. The original categorical values have no ordering, but when encoded as a number, they appear to. Treating the encoded feature as numeric leads to meaningless results because the algorithm is effectively pretending that rainy is somehow greater than, and two times larger than, cloudy. It's OK as long as the encoding's numeric value is not used as a number.

So we see both types of encodings of categorical features. It would have, perhaps, been simpler and more straightforward to not encode such features (and in two ways, no less), and instead simply include their values directly like "Rawah Wilderness Area." This may be an artifact of history; the data set was released in 1998. For performance reasons or to match the format expected by libraries of the day, which were built more for regression problems, data sets often contain data encoded in these ways.

In any event, before proceeding, it is useful to add column names to this DataFrame in order to make it easier to work with:

```
val colNames = Seq(
    "Elevation", "Aspect", "Slope",
    "Horizontal_Distance_To_Hydrology", "Vertical_Distance_To_Hydrology",
    "Horizontal_Distance_To_Roadways",
    "Hillshade_9am", "Hillshade_Noon", "Hillshade_3pm",
    "Horizontal_Distance_To_Fire_Points"
) ++ ( ❶
    (0 until 4).map(i => s"Wilderness_Area_$i")
) ++ (
    (0 until 40).map(i => s"Soil_Type_$i")
) ++ Seq("Cover_Type")

val data = dataWithoutHeader.toDF(colNames:_*).
    withColumn("Cover_Type", $"Cover_Type".cast("double"))

data.head
...
org.apache.spark.sql.Row = [2596,51,3,258,0,510,221,232,148,6279,1,0,0,0,...
```

❶ ++ concatenates collections

The wilderness- and soil-related columns are named "Wilderness_Area_0", "Soil_Type_0", and a bit of Scala can generate these 44 names without having to type them all out. Finally, the target "Cover_Type" column is cast to a double value upfront, because it will actually be necessary to consume it as a double rather than int in all Spark MLlib APIs. This will become apparent later.

You can call data.show() to see some rows of the data set, but the display is so wide that it will be difficult to read at all. data.head displays it as a raw Row object, which will be more readable in this case.

A First Decision Tree

In Chapter 3, we built a recommender model right away on all of the available data. This created a recommender that could be sense-checked by anyone with some knowledge of music: looking at a user's listening habits and recommendations, we got some sense that it was producing good results. Here, that is not possible. We would have no idea how to make up a new 54-feature description of a new parcel of land in Colorado or what kind of forest cover to expect from such a parcel.

Instead, we must jump straight to holding out some data for purposes of evaluating the resulting model. Before, the AUC metric was used to assess the agreement between held-out listening data and predictions from recommendations. The principle is the same here, although the evaluation metric will be different: *accuracy*. The majority—90%—of the data will again be used for training, and later, we'll see that a subset of this training set will be held out for cross-validation (the CV set). The other 10% held out here is actually a third subset, a proper test set.

```
val Array(trainData, testData) = data.randomSplit(Array(0.9, 0.1))
trainData.cache()
testData.cache()
```

The data needs a little more preparation to be used with a classifier in Spark MLlib. The input DataFrame contains many columns, each holding one feature that could be used to predict the target column. Spark MLlib requires all of the inputs to be collected into *one* column, whose value is a vector. This class is an abstraction for vectors in the linear algebra sense, and contains only numbers. For most intents and purposes, they work like a simple array of double values (floating-point numbers). Of course, some of the input features are conceptually categorical, even if they're all represented with numbers in the input. For now, we'll overlook this point and return to it later.

Fortunately, the VectorAssembler class can do this work:

```
import org.apache.spark.ml.feature.VectorAssembler

val inputCols = trainData.columns.filter(_ != "Cover_Type")
val assembler = new VectorAssembler().
  setInputCols(inputCols).
  setOutputCol("featureVector")

val assembledTrainData = assembler.transform(trainData)
assembledTrainData.select("featureVector").show(truncate = false)


...
+-------------------------------------------------------------- ...
|featureVector                                                  ...
+-------------------------------------------------------------- ...
|(54,[0,1,2,3,4,5,6,7,8,9,13,15],[1863.0,37.0,17.0,120.0,18.0,90.0,2 ...
|(54,[0,1,2,5,6,7,8,9,13,18],[1874.0,18.0,14.0,90.0,208.0,209.0,135. ...
```

```
|(54,[0,1,2,3,4,5,6,7,8,9,13,18],[1879.0,28.0,19.0,30.0,12.0,95.0,20 ...
  ...
```

Its key parameters are the columns to combine into the feature vector, and the name of the new column containing the feature vector. Here, all columns—*except*—the target, of course—are included as input features. The resulting DataFrame has a new "featureVector" column, as shown.

The output doesn't look exactly like a sequence of numbers, but that's because this shows a raw representation of the vector, represented as a `SparseVector` instance to save storage. Because most of the 54 values are 0, it only stores nonzero values and their indices. This detail won't matter in classification.

`VectorAssembler` is an example of `Transformer` within the current Spark MLlib "Pipelines" API. It transforms another DataFrame into a DataFrame, and is composable with other transformations into a pipeline. Later in this chapter, these transformations will be connected into an actual `Pipeline`. Here, the transformation is just invoked directly, which is sufficient to build a first decision tree classifier model.

```
import org.apache.spark.ml.classification.DecisionTreeClassifier
import scala.util.Random

val classifier = new DecisionTreeClassifier().
  setSeed(Random.nextLong()). ❶
  setLabelCol("Cover_Type").
  setFeaturesCol("featureVector").
  setPredictionCol("prediction")

val model = classifier.fit(assembledTrainData)
println(model.toDebugString)

...
DecisionTreeClassificationModel (uid=dtc_29cfe1281b30) of depth 5 with 63 nodes
  If (feature 0 <= 3039.0)
   If (feature 0 <= 2555.0)
    If (feature 10 <= 0.0)
     If (feature 0 <= 2453.0)
      If (feature 3 <= 0.0)
       Predict: 4.0
      Else (feature 3 > 0.0)
       Predict: 3.0
       ...
```

❶ Use random seed

Again, the essential configuration for the classifier consists of column names: the column containing the input feature vectors and the column containing the target value to predict. Because the model will later be used to predict new values of the target, it is given the name of a column to store predictions.

Printing a representation of the model shows some of its tree structure. It consists of a series of nested decisions about features, comparing feature values to thresholds. (Here, for historical reasons, the features are only referred to by number, not name, unfortunately.)

Decision trees are able to assess the importance of input features as part of their building process. That is, they can estimate how much each input feature contributes to making correct predictions. This information is simple to access from the model.

```
model.featureImportances.toArray.zip(inputCols).
  sorted.reverse.foreach(println)

...
(0.7931809106979147,Elevation)
(0.050122380231328235,Horizontal_Distance_To_Hydrology)
(0.030609364695664505,Wilderness_Area_0)
(0.03052094489457567,Soil_Type_3)
(0.026170212644908816,Hillshade_Noon)
(0.024374024564392027,Soil_Type_1)
(0.01670006142176787,Soil_Type_31)
(0.012596990926899494,Horizontal_Distance_To_Roadways)
(0.011205482194428473,Wilderness_Area_2)
(0.0024194271152490235,Hillshade_3pm)
(0.0018551637821715788,Horizontal_Distance_To_Fire_Points)
(2.450368306995527E-4,Soil_Type_8)
(0.0,Wilderness_Area_3)
...
```

This pairs importance values (higher is better) with column names and prints them in order from most to least important. Elevation seems to dominate as the most important feature; most features are estimated to have virtually no importance when predicting the cover type!

The resulting DecisionTreeClassificationModel is itself a transformer because it can transform a data frame containing feature vectors into a data frame also containing predictions.

For example, it might be interesting to see what the model predicts on the *training* data, and compare its prediction with the known correct cover type.

```
val predictions = model.transform(assembledTrainData)
predictions.select("Cover_Type", "prediction", "probability").
  show(truncate = false)

...
+----------+----------+----------------------------------------------------- ...
|Cover_Type|prediction|probability                                           ...
+----------+----------+----------------------------------------------------- ...
|6.0       |3.0       |[0.0,0.0,0.03421818804589827,0.6318547696523378, ...
|6.0       |4.0       |[0.0,0.0,0.043440860215053764,0.283870967741935, ...
|6.0       |3.0       |[0.0,0.0,0.03421818804589827,0.6318547696523378, ...
```

```
|6.0        |3.0        |[0.0,0.0,0.03421818804589827,0.6318547696523378, ...
...
```

Interestingly, the output also contains a "probability" column that gives the model's estimate of how likely it is that each possible outcome is correct. This shows that in these instances, it's fairly sure the answer is 3 in several cases and quite sure the answer isn't 1.

Eagle-eyed readers might note that the probability vectors actually have eight values even though there are only seven possible outcomes. The vector's values at indices 1 to 7 do contain the probability of outcomes 1 to 7. However, there is also a value at index 0, which always shows as probability 0.0. This can be ignored, as 0 isn't even a valid outcome, as this says. It's a quirk of representing this information as a vector that's worth being aware of.

Based on this snippet, it looks like the model could use some work. Its predictions look like they are often wrong. As with the ALS implementation, the DecisionTree Classifier implementation has several hyperparameters for which a value must be chosen, and they've all been left to defaults here. Here, the test set can be used to produce an unbiased evaluation of the expected accuracy of a model built with these default hyperparameters.

MulticlassClassificationEvaluator can compute accuracy and other metrics that evaluate the quality of the model's predictions. It's an example of an evaluator in Spark MLlib, which is responsible for assessing the quality of an output DataFrame in some way.

```
import org.apache.spark.ml.evaluation.MulticlassClassificationEvaluator

val evaluator = new MulticlassClassificationEvaluator().
  setLabelCol("Cover_Type").
  setPredictionCol("prediction")

evaluator.setMetricName("accuracy").evaluate(predictions)
evaluator.setMetricName("f1").evaluate(predictions)


...
0.6976371385502989
0.6815943874214012
```

After being given the column containing the "label" (target, or known correct output value) and the name of the column containing the prediction, it finds that the two match about 70% of the time. This is the accuracy of this classifier. It can compute other related measures, like the F1 score (*https://en.wikipedia.org/wiki/F1_score*). For purposes here, accuracy will be used to evaluate classifiers.

This single number gives a good summary of the quality of the classifier's output. Sometimes, however, it can be useful to look at the *confusion matrix*. This is a table with a row and a column for every possible value of the target. Because there are seven target category values, this is a 7×7 matrix, where each row corresponds to an actual correct value, and each column to a predicted value, in order. The entry at row *i* and column *j* counts the number of times an example with true category *i* was predicted as category *j*. So, the correct predictions are the counts along the diagonal and the predictions are everything else.

Fortunately, Spark provides support code to compute the confusion matrix. Unfortunately, that implementation exists as part of the older MLlib APIs that operate on RDDs. However, that's no big deal, because data frames and data sets can freely be turned into RDDs and used with these older APIs. Here, `MulticlassMetrics` is appropriate for a data frame containing predictions.

```
import org.apache.spark.mllib.evaluation.MulticlassMetrics

val predictionRDD = predictions.
  select("prediction", "Cover_Type").
  as[(Double,Double)]. ❶
  rdd ❷
val multiclassMetrics = new MulticlassMetrics(predictionRDD)
multiclassMetrics.confusionMatrix

...
143125.0  41769.0    164.0    0.0    0.0   0.0  5396.0
65865.0   184360.0  3930.0  102.0   39.0   0.0   677.0
0.0         5680.0  25772.0  674.0    0.0   0.0     0.0
0.0           21.0   1481.0  973.0    0.0   0.0     0.0
87.0        7761.0    648.0    0.0   69.0   0.0     0.0
0.0         6175.0   8902.0  559.0    0.0   0.0     0.0
8058.0        24.0     50.0    0.0    0.0   0.0 10395.0
```

❶ Convert to data set.

❷ Convert to RDD.

 Your values will be a little different. The process of building a decision tree includes some random choices that can lead to slightly different classifications.

Counts are high along the diagonal, which is good. However, there are certainly a number of misclassifications, and, for example, category 5 is never predicted at all.

Of course, it's also possible to calculate something like a confusion matrix directly with the DataFrame API, using its more general operators. It is not necessary to rely on a specialized method anymore.

```
val confusionMatrix = predictions.
  groupBy("Cover_Type").
  pivot("prediction", (1 to 7)).
  count().
  na.fill(0.0).  ❶
  orderBy("Cover_Type")

confusionMatrix.show()

...
+----------+------+------+-----+---+---+---+-----+
|Cover_Type|     1|     2|    3|  4|  5|  6|    7|
+----------+------+------+-----+---+---+---+-----+
|       1.0|143125| 41769|  164|  0|  0|  0| 5396|
|       2.0| 65865|184360| 3930|102| 39|  0|  677|
|       3.0|     0|  5680|25772|674|  0|  0|    0|
|       4.0|     0|    21| 1481|973|  0|  0|    0|
|       5.0|    87|  7761|  648|  0| 69|  0|    0|
|       6.0|     0|  6175| 8902|559|  0|  0|    0|
|       7.0|  8058|    24|   50|  0|  0|  0|10395|
+----------+------+------+-----+---+---+---+-----+
```

❶ Replace null with 0

Microsoft Excel users may have recognized the problem as just like that of computing a pivot table (*https://en.wikipedia.org/wiki/Pivot_table*). A pivot table groups values by two dimensions whose values become rows and columns of the output, and compute some aggregation within those groupings, like a count here. This is also available as a PIVOT function in several databases, and is supported by Spark SQL. It's arguably more elegant and powerful to compute it this way.

Although 70% accuracy sounds decent, it's not immediately clear whether it is outstanding or poor. How well would a simplistic approach do to establish a baseline? Just as a broken clock is correct twice a day, randomly guessing a classification for each example would also occasionally produce the correct answer.

We could construct such a random "classifier" by picking a class at random in proportion to its prevalence in the training set. For example, if 30% of the training set were cover type 1, then the random classifier would guess "1" 33% of the time. Each classification would be correct in proportion to its prevalence in the test set. If 40% of the test set were cover type 1, then guessing "1" would be correct 40% of the time. Cover type 1 would then be guessed correctly 30% x 40% = 12% of the time and contribute 12% to overall accuracy. Therefore, we can evaluate the accuracy by summing these products of probabilities:

```
import org.apache.spark.sql.DataFrame

def classProbabilities(data: DataFrame): Array[Double] = {
  val total = data.count()
```

```
    data.groupBy("Cover_Type").count().  ❶
      orderBy("Cover_Type").  ❷
      select("count").as[Double].  ❸
      map(_ / total).
      collect()
  }

  val trainPriorProbabilities = classProbabilities(trainData)
  val testPriorProbabilities = classProbabilities(testData)
  trainPriorProbabilities.zip(testPriorProbabilities).map {  ❹
    case (trainProb, cvProb) => trainProb * cvProb
  }.sum


  ...
  0.3771270477245849
```

❶ Count by category

❷ Order counts by category

❸ To data set

❹ Sum products of pairs in training, test sets

Random guessing achieves 37% accuracy then, which makes 70% seem like a good result after all. But this result was achieved with default hyperparameters. We can do even better by exploring what these actually mean for the tree-building process.

Decision Tree Hyperparameters

In Chapter 3, the ALS algorithm exposed several hyperparameters whose values we had to choose by building models with various combinations of values and then assessing the quality of each result using some metric. The process is the same here, although the metric is now multiclass accuracy instead of AUC. The hyperparameters controlling how the tree's decisions are chosen will be quite different as well: maximum depth, maximum bins, impurity measure, and minimum information gain.

Maximum depth simply limits the number of levels in the decision tree. It is the maximum number of chained decisions that the classifier will make to classify an example. It is useful to limit this to avoid overfitting the training data, as illustrated previously in the pet store example.

The decision tree algorithm is responsible for coming up with potential decision rules to try at each level, like the weight >= 100 or weight >= 500 decisions in the pet store example. Decisions are always of the same form: for numeric features, decisions are of the form feature >= value; and for categorical features, they are of the form feature in (value1, value2, …). So, the set of decision rules to try is really a set of values to plug in to the decision rule. These are referred to as "bins" in the Spark MLlib implementation. A larger number of bins requires more processing time but might lead to finding a more optimal decision rule.

What makes a decision rule good? Intuitively, a good rule would meaningfully distinguish examples by target category value. For example, a rule that divides the Covtype data set into examples with only categories 1–3 on the one hand and 4–7 on the other would be excellent because it clearly separates some categories from others. A rule that resulted in about the same mix of all categories as are found in the whole data set doesn't seem helpful. Following either branch of such a decision leads to about the same distribution of possible target values, and so doesn't really make progress toward a confident classification.

Put another way, good rules divide the training data's target values into relatively homogeneous, or "pure," subsets. Picking a best rule means minimizing the impurity of the two subsets it induces. There are two commonly used measures of impurity: Gini impurity (*https://en.wikipedia.org/wiki/Decision_tree_learning#Gini_impurity*) and entropy (*https://en.wikipedia.org/wiki/Entropy_(information_theory)*).

Gini impurity is directly related to the accuracy of the random-guess classifier. Within a subset, it is the probability that a randomly chosen classification of a randomly chosen example (both according to the distribution of classes in the subset) is *incorrect*. This is the sum of products of proportions of classes, but with themselves and subtracted from 1. If a subset has N classes and p_i is the proportion of examples of class i, then its Gini impurity is given in the Gini impurity equation:

$$I_G(p) = 1 - \sum_{i=1}^{N} p_i^2$$

If the subset contains only one class, this value is 0 because it is completely "pure." When there are N classes in the subset, this value is larger than 0 and is largest when the classes occur the same number of times—maximally impure.

Entropy is another measure of impurity, borrowed from information theory. Its nature is more difficult to explain, but it captures how much uncertainty the collection of target values in the subset implies about predictions for data that falls in that subset. A subset containing one class suggests that the outcome for the subset is completely certain and has 0 entropy—no uncertainty. A subset containing one of each possible class, on the other hand, suggests a lot of uncertainty about predictions for that subset because data have been observed with all kinds of target values. This has high entropy. Hence, low entropy, like low Gini impurity, is a good thing. Entropy is defined by the entropy equation:

$$I_E(p) = \sum_{i=1}^{N} p_i \log \left(\frac{1}{p}\right) = -\sum_{i=1}^{N} p_i \log (p_i)$$

 Interestingly, uncertainty has units. Because the logarithm is the natural log (base e), the units are *nats*, the base-e counterpart to more familiar *bits* (which we can obtain by using log base 2 instead). It really is measuring information, so it's also common to talk about the *information gain* of a decision rule when using entropy with decision trees.

One or the other measure may be a better metric for picking decision rules in a given data set. They are, in a way, similar. Both involve a weighted average: a sum over values weighted by p_i. The default in Spark's implementation is Gini impurity.

Finally, minimum information gain is a hyperparameter that imposes a minimum information gain, or decrease in impurity, for candidate decision rules. Rules that do not improve the subsets impurity enough are rejected. Like a lower maximum depth, this can help the model resist overfitting because decisions that barely help divide the training input may in fact not helpfully divide future data at all.

Tuning Decision Trees

It's not obvious from looking at the data which impurity measure leads to better accuracy, or what maximum depth or number of bins is enough without being excessive. Fortunately, as in Chapter 3, it's simple to let Spark try a number of combinations of these values and report the results.

First, it's necessary to set up a pipeline encapsulating the same two steps above. Creating the VectorAssembler and DecisionTreeClassifier and chaining these two Transformers together results in a single Pipeline object that represents these two operations together as one operation:

```
import org.apache.spark.ml.Pipeline

val inputCols = trainData.columns.filter(_ != "Cover_Type")
val assembler = new VectorAssembler().
  setInputCols(inputCols).
  setOutputCol("featureVector")

val classifier = new DecisionTreeClassifier().
  setSeed(Random.nextLong()).
  setLabelCol("Cover_Type").
  setFeaturesCol("featureVector").
  setPredictionCol("prediction")

val pipeline = new Pipeline().setStages(Array(assembler, classifier))
```

Naturally, pipelines can be much longer and more complex. This is about as simple as it gets. Now we can also define the combinations of hyperparameters that should be tested using the Spark ML API's built-in support, `ParamGridBuilder`. It's also time to define the evaluation metric that will be used to pick the "best" hyperparameters, and that is again `MulticlassClassificationEvaluator` here.

```
import org.apache.spark.ml.tuning.ParamGridBuilder

val paramGrid = new ParamGridBuilder().
  addGrid(classifier.impurity, Seq("gini", "entropy")).
  addGrid(classifier.maxDepth, Seq(1, 20)).
  addGrid(classifier.maxBins, Seq(40, 300)).
  addGrid(classifier.minInfoGain, Seq(0.0, 0.05)).
  build()

val multiclassEval = new MulticlassClassificationEvaluator().
  setLabelCol("Cover_Type").
  setPredictionCol("prediction").
  setMetricName("accuracy")
```

This means that a model will be built and evaluated for two values of four hyperparameters. That's 16 models. They'll be evaluated by multiclass accuracy. Finally, `TrainValidationSplit` brings these components together—the pipeline that makes models, model evaluation metrics, and hyperparameters to try—and can run the evaluation on the training data. It's worth noting that `CrossValidator` could be used here as well to perform full k-fold cross-validation, but it is k times more expensive and doesn't add as much value in the presence of big data. So, `TrainValidationSplit` is used here.

```
import org.apache.spark.ml.tuning.TrainValidationSplit

val validator = new TrainValidationSplit().
  setSeed(Random.nextLong()).
  setEstimator(pipeline).
  setEvaluator(multiclassEval).
  setEstimatorParamMaps(paramGrid).
  setTrainRatio(0.9)

val validatorModel = validator.fit(trainData)
```

This will take minutes or more, depending on your hardware, because it's building and evaluating many models. Note the train ratio parameter is set to 0.9. This means that the training data is actually further subdivided by `TrainValidationSplit` into 90%/10% subsets. The former is used for training each model. The remaining 10% of the input is held out as a cross-validation set to evaluate the model. If it's already holding out some data for evaluation, then why did we hold out 10% of the original data as a test set?

If the purpose of the CV set was to evaluate *parameters* that fit to the *training* set, then the purpose of the test set is to evaluate *hyperparameters* that were "fit" to the CV set. That is, the test set ensures an unbiased estimate of the accuracy of the final, chosen model and its hyperparameters.

Say that the best model chosen by this process exhibits 90% accuracy on the CV set. It seems reasonable to expect it will exhibit 90% accuracy on future data. However, there's an element of randomness in how these models are built. By chance, this model and evaluation could have turned out unusually well. The top model and evaluation result could have benefited from a bit of luck, so its accuracy estimate is likely to be slightly optimistic. Put another way, hyperparameters can overfit too.

To really assess how well this best model is likely to perform on future examples, we need to evaluate it on examples that were not used to train it. But we also need to avoid examples in the CV set that were used to evaluate it. That is why a third subset, the test set, was held out.

The result of the validator contains the best model it found. This itself is a representation of the best overall *pipeline* it found, because we provided an instance of a pipeline to run. In order to query the parameters chosen by `DecisionTreeClassifier`, it's necessary to manually extract `DecisionTreeClassificationModel` from the resulting `PipelineModel`, which is the final stage in the pipeline.

```
import org.apache.spark.ml.PipelineModel

val bestModel = validatorModel.bestModel
bestModel.asInstanceOf[PipelineModel].stages.last.extractParamMap
```

```
...
{
        dtc_9136220619b4-cacheNodeIds: false,
        dtc_9136220619b4-checkpointInterval: 10,
        dtc_9136220619b4-featuresCol: featureVector,
        dtc_9136220619b4-impurity: entropy,
        dtc_9136220619b4-labelCol: Cover_Type,
        dtc_9136220619b4-maxBins: 40,
        dtc_9136220619b4-maxDepth: 20,
        dtc_9136220619b4-maxMemoryInMB: 256,
        dtc_9136220619b4-minInfoGain: 0.0,
        dtc_9136220619b4-minInstancesPerNode: 1,
        dtc_9136220619b4-predictionCol: prediction,
        dtc_9136220619b4-probabilityCol: probability,
        dtc_9136220619b4-rawPredictionCol: rawPrediction,
        dtc_9136220619b4-seed: 159147643
}
```

This contains a lot of information about the fitted model, but it also tells us that "entropy" apparently worked best as the impurity measure and that a max depth of 20 was not surprisingly better than 1. It might be surprising that the best model was fit with just 40 bins, but this is probably a sign that 40 was "plenty" rather than "better" than 300. Lastly, no minimum information gain was better than a small minimum, which could imply that the model is more prone to underfit than overfit.

You may wonder if it is possible to see the accuracy that each of the models achieved for each combination of hyperparameters. The hyperparameters as well as the evaluations are exposed by `getEstimatorParamMaps` and `validationMetrics`, respectively. They can be combined to display all of the parameter combinations sorted by metric value:

```
val validatorModel = validator.fit(trainData)

val paramsAndMetrics = validatorModel.validationMetrics.
  zip(validatorModel.getEstimatorParamMaps).sortBy(-_._1)

paramsAndMetrics.foreach { case (metric, params) =>
    println(metric)
    println(params)
    println()
}

...
0.9138483377774368
{
        dtc_3e3b8bb692d1-impurity: entropy,
        dtc_3e3b8bb692d1-maxBins: 40,
        dtc_3e3b8bb692d1-maxDepth: 20,
        dtc_3e3b8bb692d1-minInfoGain: 0.0
}

0.9122369506416774
{
        dtc_3e3b8bb692d1-impurity: entropy,
        dtc_3e3b8bb692d1-maxBins: 300,
        dtc_3e3b8bb692d1-maxDepth: 20,
        dtc_3e3b8bb692d1-minInfoGain: 0.0
}
...
```

What was the accuracy that this model achieved on the CV set? And finally, what accuracy does the model achieve on the test set?

```
validatorModel.validationMetrics.max
multiclassEval.evaluate(bestModel.transform(testData)) ❶

...
0.9138483377774368
0.9139978718291971
```

❶   bestModel is a complete pipeline.

The results are both about 91%. It happens that the estimate from the CV set was pretty fine to begin with. In fact, it is not usual for the test set to show a very different result.

This is an interesting point at which to revisit the issue of overfitting. As discussed previously, it's possible to build a decision tree so deep and elaborate that it fits the given training examples very well or perfectly but fails to generalize to other examples because it has fit the idiosyncrasies and noise of the training data too closely. This is a problem common to most machine learning algorithms, not just decision trees.

When a decision tree has overfit, it will exhibit high accuracy when run on the same training data that it fit the model to, but low accuracy on other examples. Here, the final model's accuracy was about 91% on other, new examples. Accuracy can just as easily be evaluated over the same data that the model was trained on, `trainData`. This gives an accuracy of about 95%.

The difference is not large but suggests that the decision tree has overfit the training data to some extent. A lower maximum depth might be a better choice.

Categorical Features Revisited

So far, the code examples have implicitly treated all input features as if they're numeric (though "Cover_Type", despite being encoded as numeric, has actually been correctly treated as a categorical value.) This isn't exactly wrong, because the categorical features here are one-hot encoded as several binary 0/1 values. Treating these individual features as numeric turns out to be fine, because any decision rule on the "numeric" features will choose thresholds between 0 and 1, and all are equivalent since all values are 0 or 1.

Of course, this encoding forces the decision tree algorithm to consider the values of the underlying categorical features individually. Because features like soil type are broken down into many features, and because decision trees treat features individually, it is harder to relate information about related soil types.

For example, nine different soil types are actually part of the Leighcan family, and they may be related in ways that the decision tree can exploit. If soil type were encoded as a single categorical feature with 40 soil values, then the tree could express rules like "if the soil type is one of the nine Leighton family types" directly. However, when encoded as 40 features, the tree would have to learn a sequence of nine decisions on soil type to do the same, this expressiveness may lead to better decisions and more efficient trees.

However, having 40 numeric features represent one 40-valued categorical feature increases memory usage and slows things down.

What about undoing the one-hot encoding? This would replace, for example, the four columns encoding wilderness type with one column that encodes the wilderness type as a number between 0 and 3, like "Cover_Type".

```
import org.apache.spark.sql.functions._

def unencodeOneHot(data: DataFrame): DataFrame = {
  val wildernessCols = (0 until 4).map(i => s"Wilderness_Area_$i").toArray

  val wildernessAssembler = new VectorAssembler().
    setInputCols(wildernessCols).
    setOutputCol("wilderness")

  val unhotUDF = udf((vec: Vector) => vec.toArray.indexOf(1.0).toDouble) ❶

  val withWilderness = wildernessAssembler.transform(data).
    drop(wildernessCols:_*). ❷
    withColumn("wilderness", unhotUDF($"wilderness")) ❸

  val soilCols = (0 until 40).map(i => s"Soil_Type_$i").toArray

  val soilAssembler = new VectorAssembler().
    setInputCols(soilCols).
    setOutputCol("soil")

  soilAssembler.transform(withWilderness).
    drop(soilCols:_*).
    withColumn("soil", unhotUDF($"soil"))
}
```

❶ Note UDF definition

❷ Drop one-hot columns; no longer needed

❸ Overwrite column with numeric one of same name

Here `VectorAssembler` is deployed to combine the 4 and 40 wilderness and soil type columns into two `Vector` columns. The values in these `Vector`s are all 0, except for one location that has a 1. There's no simple DataFrame function for this, so we have to define our own UDF that can be used to operate on columns. This turns these two new columns into numbers of just the type we need.

From here, nearly the same process as above can be used to tune the hyperparameters of a decision tree model built on this data and to choose and evaluate a best model. There's one important difference, however. The two new numeric columns have nothing about them that indicates they're actually an encoding of categorical values. To treat them as numbers would be wrong, as their ordering is meaningless. However, it would silently succeed; the information in these features would be all but lost though.

Internally Spark MLlib can store additional metadata about each column. The details of this data are generally hidden from the caller, but includes information such as whether the column encodes a categorical value and how many distinct values it takes on. In order to add this metadata, it's necessary to put the data through VectorIn dexer. Its job is to turn input into properly labeled categorical feature columns. Although we did much of the work already to turn the categorical features into 0-indexed values, VectorIndexer will take care of the metadata.

We need to add this stage to the Pipeline:

```
import org.apache.spark.ml.feature.VectorIndexer

val inputCols = unencTrainData.columns.filter(_ != "Cover_Type")
val assembler = new VectorAssembler().
  setInputCols(inputCols).
  setOutputCol("featureVector")

val indexer = new VectorIndexer().
  setMaxCategories(40). ❶
  setInputCol("featureVector").
  setOutputCol("indexedVector")

val classifier = new DecisionTreeClassifier().
  setSeed(Random.nextLong()).
  setLabelCol("Cover_Type").
  setFeaturesCol("indexedVector").
  setPredictionCol("prediction")

val pipeline = new Pipeline().setStages(Array(assembler, indexer, classifier))
```

❶ >= 40 because soil has 40 values

The approach assumes that the training set contains all possible values of each of the categorical features at least once. That is, it works correctly only if all 4 soil values and all 40 wilderness values appear in the training set so that all possible values get a mapping. Here, that happens to be true, but may not be for small training sets of data in which some labels appear very infrequently. In those cases, it could be necessary to manually create and add a VectorIndexerModel with the complete value mapping supplied manually.

Aside from that, the process is the same as before. You should find that it chose a similar best model but that accuracy on the test set is about 93%. By treating categorical features as actual categorical features, the classifier improved its accuracy by almost 2%.

Random Decision Forests

If you have been following along with the code examples, you may have noticed that your results differ slightly from those presented in the code listings in the book. That is because there is an element of randomness in building decision trees, and the randomness comes into play when you're deciding what data to use and what decision rules to explore.

The algorithm does not consider every possible decision rule at every level. To do so would take an incredible amount of time. For a categorical feature over N values, there are 2^N-2 possible decision rules (every subset except the empty set and entire set). For even moderately large N, this would create billions of candidate decision rules.

Instead, decision trees use several heuristics to determine which few rules to actually consider. The process of picking rules also involves some randomness; only a few features picked at random are looked at each time, and only values from a random subset of the training data. This trades a bit of accuracy for a lot of speed, but it also means that the decision tree algorithm won't build the same tree every time. This is a good thing.

It's good for the same reason that the "wisdom of the crowds" usually beats individual predictions. To illustrate, take this quick quiz: How many black taxis operate in London?

Don't peek at the answer; guess first.

I guessed 10,000, which is well off the correct answer of about 19,000. Because I guessed low, you're a bit more likely to have guessed higher than I did, and so the average of our answers will tend to be more accurate. There's that regression to the mean again. The average guess from an informal poll of 13 people in the office was indeed closer: 11,170.

A key to this effect is that the guesses were independent and didn't influence one another. (You didn't peek, did you?) The exercise would be useless if we had all agreed on and used the same methodology to make a guess, because the guesses would have been the same answer—the same potentially quite wrong answer. It would even have been different and worse if I'd merely influenced you by stating my guess upfront.

It would be great to have not one tree, but many trees, each producing reasonable but different and independent estimations of the right target value. Their collective average prediction should fall close to the true answer, more than any individual tree's does. It's the *randomness* in the process of building that helps create this independence. This is the key to *random decision forests*.

Randomness is injected by building many trees, each of which sees a different random subset of data—and even of features. This makes the forest as a whole less prone to overfitting. If a particular feature contains noisy data or is deceptively predictive only in the *training* set, then most trees will not consider this problem feature most of the time. Most trees will not fit the noise and will tend to "outvote" the trees that have fit the noise in the forest.

The prediction of a random decision forest is simply a weighted average of the trees' predictions. For a categorical target, this can be a majority vote or the most probable value based on the average of probabilities produced by the trees. Random decision forests, like decision trees, also support regression, and the forest's prediction in this case is the average of the number predicted by each tree.

While random decision forests are a more powerful and complex classification technique, the good news is that it's virtually no different to use it in the pipeline that has been developed in this chapter. Simply drop in a `RandomForestClassifier` in place of `DecisionTreeClassifier` and proceed as before. There's really no more code or API to understand in order to use it.

```
import org.apache.spark.ml.classification.RandomForestClassifier

val classifier = new RandomForestClassifier().
  setSeed(Random.nextLong()).
  setLabelCol("Cover_Type").
  setFeaturesCol("indexedVector").
  setPredictionCol("prediction")
```

Note that this classifier has another hyperparameter: the number of trees to build. Like the max bins hyperparameter, higher values should give better results up to a point. The cost, however, is that building many trees of course takes many times longer than building one.

The accuracy of the best random decision forest model produced from a similar tuning process is 95% off the bat—about 2% better already, although viewed another way, that's a 28% reduction in the error rate over the best decision tree built previously, from 7% down to 5%. You may do better with further tuning.

Incidentally, at this point we have a more reliable picture of feature importance:

```
import org.apache.spark.ml.classification.RandomForestClassificationModel

val forestModel = bestModel.asInstanceOf[PipelineModel].
  stages.last.asInstanceOf[RandomForestClassificationModel]

forestModel.featureImportances.toArray.zip(inputCols).
  sorted.reverse.foreach(println)

...
(0.28877055118903183,Elevation)
```

```
(0.17288279582959612,soil)
(0.12105056811661499,Horizontal_Distance_To_Roadways)
(0.1121550648692802,Horizontal_Distance_To_Fire_Points)
(0.08805270405239551,wilderness)
(0.04467393191338021,Vertical_Distance_To_Hydrology)
(0.04293099150373547,Horizontal_Distance_To_Hydrology)
(0.03149644050848614,Hillshade_Noon)
(0.028408483578137605,Hillshade_9am)
(0.027185325937200706,Aspect)
(0.027075578474331806,Hillshade_3pm)
(0.015317564027809389,Slope)
```

Random decision forests are appealing in the context of big data because trees are supposed to be built independently, and big data technologies like Spark and Map-Reduce inherently need *data-parallel* problems, where parts of the overall solution can be computed independently on parts of the data. The fact that trees can, and should, train on only a subset of features or input data makes it trivial to parallelize building the trees.

Making Predictions

Building a classifier, while an interesting and nuanced process, is not the end goal. The goal is to make predictions. This is the payoff, and it is comparatively quite easy.

The resulting "best model" is actually a whole pipeline of operations, which encapsulate how input is transformed for use with the model and includes the model itself, which can make predictions. It can operate on a data frame of new input. The only difference from the data DataFrame we started with is that it lacks the "Cover_Type" column. When we're making predictions—especially about the future, says Mr. Bohr —the output is of course not known.

To prove it, try dropping the "Cover_Type" from the test data input and obtaining a prediction:

```
bestModel.transform(unencTestData.drop("Cover_Type")).select("prediction").show()

...
+----------+
|prediction|
+----------+
|       6.0|
+----------+
```

The result should be 6.0, which corresponds to class 7 (the original feature was 1-indexed) in the original Covtype data set. The predicted cover type for the land described in this example is Krummholz. Obviously.

Where to Go from Here

This chapter introduced two related and important types of machine learning, classification and regression, along with some foundational concepts in building and tuning models: features, vectors, training, and cross-validation. It demonstrated how to predict a type of forest cover from things like location and soil type using the Covtype data set, with decision trees and forests implemented in Spark MLlib.

As with recommenders in Chapter 3, it could be useful to continue exploring the effect of hyperparameters on accuracy. Most decision tree hyperparameters trade time for accuracy: more bins and trees generally produce better accuracy but hit a point of diminishing returns.

The classifier here turned out to be very accurate. It's unusual to achieve more than 95% accuracy. In general, you will achieve further improvements in accuracy by including more features or transforming existing features into a more predictive form. This is a common, repeated step in iteratively improving a classifier model. For example, for this data set, the two features encoding horizontal and vertical distance-to-surface-water features could produce a third feature: straight-line distance-to-surface-water features. This might turn out to be more useful than either original feature. Or, if it were possible to collect more data, we might try adding new information like soil moisture in order to improve classification.

Of course, not all prediction problems in the real world are exactly like the Covtype data set. For example, some problems require predicting a continuous numeric value, not a categorical value. Much of the same analysis and code applies to this type of *regression* problem; the `RandomForestRegressor` class will be of use in this case.

Furthermore, decision trees and forests are not the only classification or regression algorithms, and not the only ones implemented in Spark MLlib. For classification, it includes implementations of:

- Naïve Bayes (*https://en.wikipedia.org/wiki/Naive_Bayes_classifier*)
- Gradient boosting (*https://en.wikipedia.org/wiki/Gradient_boosting*)
- Logistic regression (*https://en.wikipedia.org/wiki/Logistic_regression*)
- Multilayer perceptron (*https://en.wikipedia.org/wiki/Multilayer_perceptron*)

Yes, logistic regression is a classification technique. Underneath the hood, it classifies by predicting a continuous function of a class probability. This detail is not necessary to understand.

Each of these algorithms operates quite differently from decision trees and forests. However, many elements are the same: they plug into a `Pipeline` and operate on columns in a data frame, and have hyperparameters that you must select using training, cross-validation, and test subsets of the input data. The same general principles, with these other algorithms, can also be deployed to model classification and regression problems.

These have been examples of supervised learning. What happens when some, or all, of the target values are unknown? The following chapter will explore what can be done in this situation.

## CHAPTER 5

Anomaly Detection in Network Traffic with K-means Clustering

Sean Owen

There are known knowns; there are things that we know that we know. We also know there are known unknowns; that is to say, we know there are some things we do not know. But there are also unknown unknowns, the ones we don't know we don't know.

—Donald Rumsfeld

Classification and regression are powerful, well-studied techniques in machine learning. Chapter 4 demonstrated using a classifier as a predictor of unknown values. But there was a catch: in order to predict unknown values for new data, we had to know the target values for many previously seen examples. Classifiers can only help if we, the data scientists, know what we are looking for and can provide plenty of examples where input produced a known output. These were collectively known as *supervised learning* (*https://en.wikipedia.org/wiki/Supervised_learning*) techniques, because their learning process receives the correct output value for each example in the input.

However, sometimes the correct output is unknown for some or all examples. Consider the problem of dividing up an ecommerce site's customers by their shopping habits and tastes. The input features are their purchases, clicks, demographic information, and more. The output should be groupings of customers: perhaps one group will represent fashion-conscious buyers, another will turn out to correspond to price-sensitive bargain hunters, and so on.

If you were asked to determine this target label for each new customer, you would quickly run into a problem in applying a supervised learning technique like a classifier: you don't know *a priori* who should be considered fashion-conscious, for example. In fact, you're not even sure if "fashion-conscious" is a meaningful grouping of the site's customers to begin with!

Fortunately, *unsupervised learning* (*https://en.wikipedia.org/wiki/Unsupervised_learn ing*) techniques can help. These techniques do not learn to predict a target value, because none is available. They can, however, learn structure in data and find groupings of similar inputs, or learn what types of input are likely to occur and what types are not. This chapter will introduce unsupervised learning using clustering implementations in MLlib.

Anomaly Detection

The inherent problem of anomaly detection is, as its name implies, that of finding unusual things. If we already knew what "anomalous" meant for a data set, we could easily detect anomalies in the data with supervised learning. An algorithm would receive inputs labeled "normal" and "anomaly", and learn to distinguish the two. However, the nature of anomalies is that they are unknown unknowns. Put another way, an anomaly that has been observed and understood is no longer an anomaly.

Anomaly detection is often used to find fraud, detect network attacks, or discover problems in servers or other sensor-equipped machinery. In these cases, it's important to be able to find new types of anomalies that have never been seen before—new forms of fraud, intrusions, and failure modes for servers.

Unsupervised learning techniques are useful in these cases because they can learn what input data normally looks like, and therefore detect when new data is unlike past data. Such new data is not necessarily attacks or fraud; it is simply unusual, and therefore, worth further investigation.

K-means Clustering

Clustering is the best-known type of unsupervised learning. Clustering algorithms try to find natural groupings in data. Data points that are like one another but unlike others are likely to represent a meaningful grouping, so clustering algorithms try to put such data into the same cluster.

K-means (*https://en.wikipedia.org/wiki/K-means_clustering*) clustering may be the most widely used clustering algorithm. It attempts to detect k clusters in a data set, where k is given by the data scientist. k is a hyperparameter of the model, and the right value will depend on the data set. In fact, choosing a good value for k will be a central plot point in this chapter.

What does "like" mean when the data set contains information like customer activity? Or transactions? K-means requires a notion of distance between data points. It is common to use simple Euclidean distance to measure distance between data points with K-means, and as it happens, this is the only distance function supported by Spark MLlib as of this writing. The Euclidean distance is defined for data points whose features are all numeric. "Like" points are those whose intervening distance is small.

To K-means, a cluster is simply a point: the center of all the points that make up the cluster. These are, in fact, just feature vectors containing all numeric features, and can be called vectors. However, it may be more intuitive to think of them as points here, because they are treated as points in a Euclidean space.

This center is called the cluster *centroid*, and is the arithmetic mean of the points—hence the name K-*means*. To start, the algorithm picks some data points as the initial cluster centroids. Then each data point is assigned to the nearest centroid. Then for each cluster, a new cluster centroid is computed as the mean of the data points just assigned to that cluster. This process is repeated.

Enough about K-means for now. Some more interesting details will emerge in the use case to follow.

Network Intrusion

So-called cyberattacks are increasingly visible in the news. Some attacks attempt to flood a computer with network traffic to crowd out legitimate traffic. But in other cases, attacks attempt to exploit flaws in networking software to gain unauthorized access to a computer. While it's quite obvious when a computer is being bombarded with traffic, detecting an exploit can be like searching for a needle in an incredibly large haystack of network requests.

Some exploit behaviors follow known patterns. For example, accessing every port on a machine in rapid succession is not something any normal software program should ever need to do. However, it is a typical first step for an attacker looking for services running on the computer that may be exploitable.

If you were to count the number of distinct ports accessed by a remote host in a short time, you would have a feature that probably predicts a port-scanning attack quite well. A handful is probably normal; hundreds indicates an attack. The same goes for detecting other types of attacks from other features of network connections—number of bytes sent and received, TCP errors, and so forth.

But what about those unknown unknowns? The biggest threat may be the one that has never yet been detected and classified. Part of detecting potential network intrusions is detecting anomalies. These are connections that aren't known to be attacks but do not resemble connections that have been observed in the past.

Here, unsupervised learning techniques like K-means can be used to detect anomalous network connections. K-means can cluster connections based on statistics about each of them. The resulting clusters themselves aren't interesting per se, but they collectively define types of connections that are like past connections. Anything not close to a cluster could be anomalous. Clusters are interesting insofar as they define regions of normal connections; everything else outside is unusual and potentially anomalous.

KDD Cup 1999 Data Set

The KDD Cup (*http://www.kdd.org/kdd-cup*) was an annual data mining competition organized by a special interest group of the Assocation for Computing Machinery (ACM). Each year, a machine learning problem was posed, along with a data set, and researchers were invited to submit a paper detailing their best solution to the problem. It was like Kaggle (*https://www.kaggle.com*) before there was Kaggle. In 1999, the topic was network intrusion, and the data set is still available (*https://bit.ly/1ALCuZN*). The remainder of this chapter will walk through building a system to detect anomalous network traffic using Spark, by learning from this data.

 Don't use this data set to build a real network intrusion system! The data did not necessarily reflect real network traffic at the time—even if it did, it reflects traffic patterns from 17 years ago.

Fortunately, the organizers had already processed raw network packet data into summary information about individual network connections. The data set is about 708 MB in size and contains about 4.9 million connections. This is large, if not massive, and is certainly sufficient for our purposes here. For each connection, the data set contains information like the number of bytes sent, login attempts, TCP errors, and so on. Each connection is one line of CSV-formatted data set, containing 38 features, like this:

```
0,tcp,http,SF,215,45076,
0,0,0,0,0,1,0,0,0,0,0,0,0,0,0,0,1,1,
0.00,0.00,0.00,0.00,1.00,0.00,0.00,0,0,0.00,
0.00,0.00,0.00,0.00,0.00,0.00,0.00,normal.
```

This connection, for example, was a TCP connection to an HTTP service—215 bytes were sent and 45,706 bytes were received. The user was logged in, and so on. Many features are counts, like num_file_creations in the 17th column.

Many features take on the value 0 or 1, indicating the presence or absence of a behavior, like su_attempted in the 15th column. They look like the one-hot encoded categorical features from Chapter 4, but are not grouped and related in the same way. Each is like a yes/no feature, and is therefore arguably a categorical feature. It is not always valid to translate categorical features as numbers and treat them as if they had an ordering. However, in the special case of a binary categorical feature, in most machine learning algorithms, mapping these to a numeric feature taking on v̇ and 1 will work well.

The rest are ratios like `dst_host_srv_rerror_rate` in the next-to-last colum take on values from 0.0 to 1.0, inclusive.

Interestingly, a label is given in the last field. Most connections are labeled `normal.`, but some have been identified as examples of various types of network attacks. These would be useful in learning to distinguish a known attack from a normal connection, but the problem here is anomaly detection and finding potentially new and unknown attacks. This label will be mostly set aside for our purposes.

A First Take on Clustering

Unzip the *kddcup.data.gz* data file and copy it into HDFS. This example, like others, will assume the file is available at */user/ds/kddcup.data*. Open the `spark-shell`, and load the CSV data as a data frame. It's a CSV file again, but without header information. It's necessary to supply column names as given in the accompanying *kddcup.names* file.

```
val dataWithoutHeader = spark.read.
  option("inferSchema", true).
  option("header", false).
  csv("hdfs:///user/ds/kddcup.data")

val data = dataWithoutHeader.toDF(
  "duration", "protocol_type", "service", "flag",
  "src_bytes", "dst_bytes", "land", "wrong_fragment", "urgent",
  "hot", "num_failed_logins", "logged_in", "num_compromised",
  "root_shell", "su_attempted", "num_root", "num_file_creations",
  "num_shells", "num_access_files", "num_outbound_cmds",
  "is_host_login", "is_guest_login", "count", "srv_count",
  "serror_rate", "srv_serror_rate", "rerror_rate", "srv_rerror_rate",
  "same_srv_rate", "diff_srv_rate", "srv_diff_host_rate",
  "dst_host_count", "dst_host_srv_count",
  "dst_host_same_srv_rate", "dst_host_diff_srv_rate",
  "dst_host_same_src_port_rate", "dst_host_srv_diff_host_rate",
  "dst_host_serror_rate", "dst_host_srv_serror_rate",
  "dst_host_rerror_rate", "dst_host_srv_rerror_rate",
  "label")
```

Begin by exploring the data set. What labels are present in the data, and how many are there of each? The following code simply counts by label and prints the results in descending order by count.

```
data.select("label").groupBy("label").count().orderBy($"count".desc).show(25)

...
+----------------+-------+
|           label|  count|
```

```
+----------------+-------+
|         smurf.|2807886|
|       neptune.|1072017|
|        normal.| 972781|
|         satan.|  15892|
...
|           phf.|      4|
|          perl.|      3|
|           spy.|      2|
+----------------+-------+
```

There are 23 distinct labels, and the most frequent are smurf. and neptune. attacks.

Note that the data contains nonnumeric features. For example, the second column may be tcp, udp, or icmp, but K-means clustering requires numeric features. The final label column is also nonnumeric. To begin, these will simply be ignored.

Aside from this, creating a K-means clustering of the data follows the same pattern as was seen in Chapter 4. A VectorAssembler creates a feature vector, a KMeans implementation creates a model from the feature vectors, and a Pipeline stitches it all together. From the resulting model, it's possible to extract and examine the cluster centers.

```
import org.apache.spark.ml.Pipeline
import org.apache.spark.ml.clustering.{KMeans, KMeansModel}
import org.apache.spark.ml.feature.VectorAssembler

val numericOnly = data.drop("protocol_type", "service", "flag").cache()

val assembler = new VectorAssembler().
  setInputCols(numericOnly.columns.filter(_ != "label")).
  setOutputCol("featureVector")

val kmeans = new KMeans().
  setPredictionCol("cluster").
  setFeaturesCol("featureVector")

val pipeline = new Pipeline().setStages(Array(assembler, kmeans))
val pipelineModel = pipeline.fit(numericOnly)
val kmeansModel = pipelineModel.stages.last.asInstanceOf[KMeansModel]

kmeansModel.clusterCenters.foreach(println)


...
[48.34019491959669,1834.6215497618625,826.2031900016945,793027561892E-4,...
[10999.0,0.0,1.309937401E9,0.0,0.0,0.0,0.0,0.0,0.0,0.0,0.0,0.0,0.0,0.0,0.0,...
```

It's not easy to interpret the numbers intuitively, but each of these represents the center (also known as centroid) of one of the clusters that the model produced. The values are the coordinates of the centroid in terms of each of the numeric input features.

Two vectors are printed, meaning K-means was fitting $k=2$ clusters to the data. For a complex data set that is known to exhibit at least 23 distinct types of connections, this is almost certainly not enough to accurately model the distinct groupings within the data.

This is a good opportunity to use the given labels to get an intuitive sense of what went into these two clusters by counting the labels within each cluster.

```
val withCluster = pipelineModel.transform(numericOnly)

withCluster.select("cluster", "label").
  groupBy("cluster", "label").count().
  orderBy($"cluster", $"count".desc).
  show(25)
```

```
...
+-------+-----------------+-------+
|cluster|            label|  count|
+-------+-----------------+-------+
|      0|           smurf.|2807886|
|      0|         neptune.|1072017|
|      0|          normal.| 972781|
|      0|           satan.|  15892|
|      0|         ipsweep.|  12481|
...
|      0|             phf.|      4|
|      0|            perl.|      3|
|      0|             spy.|      2|
|      1|       portsweep.|      1|
+-------+-----------------+-------+
```

The result shows that the clustering was not at all helpful. Only one data point ended up in cluster 1!

Choosing k

Two clusters are plainly insufficient. How many clusters are appropriate for this data set? It's clear that there are 23 distinct patterns in the data, so it seems that k could be at least 23, or likely even more. Typically, many values of k are tried to find the best one. But what is "best"?

A clustering could be considered good if each data point were near its closest centroid, where "near" is defined by the Euclidean distance. This is a simple, common way to evaluate the quality of a clustering, by the mean of these distances over all points, or sometimes, the mean of the distances squared. In fact, KMeansModel offers a computeCost method that computes the sum of squared distances and can easily be used to compute the mean squared distance.

Unfortunately, there is no simple `Evaluator` implementation to compute this measure, not like those available to compute multiclass classification metrics. It's simple enough to manually evaluate the clustering cost for several values of *k*. Note that this code could take 10 minutes or more to run.

```
import org.apache.spark.sql.DataFrame

def clusteringScore0(data: DataFrame, k: Int): Double = {
  val assembler = new VectorAssembler().
    setInputCols(data.columns.filter(_ != "label")).
    setOutputCol("featureVector")
  val kmeans = new KMeans().
    setSeed(Random.nextLong()).
    setK(k).
    setPredictionCol("cluster").
    setFeaturesCol("featureVector")
  val pipeline = new Pipeline().setStages(Array(assembler, kmeans))
  val kmeansModel = pipeline.fit(data).stages.last.asInstanceOf[KMeansModel]
  kmeansModel.computeCost(assembler.transform(data)) / data.count() ❶
}

(20 to 100 by 20).map(k => (k, clusteringScore0(numericOnly, k))).
  foreach(println)

...
(20,6.649218115128446E7)
(40,2.5031424366033625E7)
(60,1.027261913057096E7)
(80,1.2514131711109027E7)
(100,7235531.565096531)
```

❶ Compute mean from total squared distance ("cost")

The `(x to y by z)` syntax is a Scala idiom for creating a collection of numbers between a start and end (inclusive), with a given difference between successive elements. This is a compact way to create the values "20, 40, ..., 100" for *k*, and then do something with each.

The printed result shows that the score decreases as *k* increases. Note that scores are shown in scientific notation; the first value is over 10^7, not just a bit over 6.

 Again, your values will be somewhat different. The clustering depends on a randomly chosen initial set of centroids.

However, this much is obvious. As more clusters are added, it should always be possible to put data points closer to the nearest centroid. In fact, if *k* is chosen to equal the number of data points, the average distance will be 0 because every point will be its own cluster of one!

Worse, in the preceding results, the distance for *k=80* is higher than for *k=60*. This shouldn't happen because higher *k* always permits at least as good a clustering as a lower *k*. The problem is that K-means is not necessarily able to find the optimal clustering for a given *k*. Its iterative process can converge from a random starting point to a local minimum, which may be good but is not optimal.

This is still true even when more intelligent methods are used to choose initial centroids. K-means++ and K-means|| (*https://stanford.io/1ALCOaN*) are variants of selection algorithms that are more likely to choose diverse, separated centroids and lead more reliably to a good clustering. Spark MLlib, in fact, implements K-means||. However, all still have an element of randomness in selection and can't guarantee an optimal clustering.

The random starting set of clusters chosen for *k=80* perhaps led to a particularly suboptimal clustering, or it may have stopped early before it reached its local optimum.

We can improve it by running the iteration longer. The algorithm has a threshold via setTol() that controls the minimum amount of cluster centroid movement considered significant; lower values mean the K-means algorithm will let the centroids continue to move longer. Increasing the maximum number of iterations with setMaxIter() also prevents it from potentially stopping too early at the cost of possibly more computation.

```
def clusteringScore1(data: DataFrame, k: Int): Double = {
  ...
    setMaxIter(40). ❶
    setTol(1.0e-5) ❷
  ...
}

(20 to 100 by 20).map(k => (k, clusteringScore1(numericOnly, k))).
  foreach(println)
```

❶ Increase from default 20

❷ Decrease from default 1.0e-4

This time, at least the scores decrease consistently:

```
(20,1.8041795813813403E8)
(40,6.33056876207124E7)
(60,9474961.544965891)
(80,9388117.93747141)
(100,8783628.926311461)
```

We want to find a point past which increasing k stops reducing the score much—or an "elbow" in a graph of k versus score, which is generally decreasing but eventually flattens out. Here, it seems to be decreasing notably past 100. The right value of k may be past 100.

Visualization with SparkR

At this point, it could be useful to step back and understand more about the data before clustering again. In particular, looking at a plot of the data points could be helpful.

Spark itself has no tools for visualization, but the popular open source statistical environment R (*https://www.r-project.org*) has libraries for both data exploration and data visualization. Furthermore, Spark also provides some basic integration with R via SparkR (*https://spark.apache.org/docs/latest/sparkr.html*). This brief section will demonstrate using R and SparkR to cluster the data and explore the clustering.

SparkR is a variant of the `spark-shell` used throughout this book, and is invoked with the command sparkR. It runs a local R interpreter, like `spark-shell` runs a variant of the Scala shell as a local process. The machine that runs sparkR needs a local installation of R, which is not included with Spark. This can be installed, for example, with `sudo apt-get install r-base` on Linux distributions like Ubuntu, or `brew install R` with Homebrew (*http://brew.sh/*) on macOS.

sparkR is a command-line shell environment, like R. To view visualizations, it's necessary to run these commands within an IDE-like environment that can display images. RStudio (*https://www.rstudio.com*) is an IDE for R (and works with SparkR); it runs on a desktop operating system so it will only be usable here if you are experimenting with Spark locally rather than on a cluster.

If you are running Spark locally, download (*http://bit.ly/2qdhxHy*) the free version of RStudio and install it. If not, then most of the rest of this example can still be run with sparkR on a command line; for example, on a cluster. It won't be possible to display visualizations this way though.

If running via RStudio, launch the IDE and configure SPARK_HOME and JAVA_HOME, if your local environment does not already set them, to point to the Spark and JDK installation directories, respectively.

```
Sys.setenv(SPARK_HOME = "/path/to/spark") ❶
Sys.setenv(JAVA_HOME = "/path/to/java")
library(SparkR, lib.loc = c(file.path(Sys.getenv("SPARK_HOME"), "R", "lib")))
sparkR.session(master = "local[*]",
    sparkConfig = list(spark.driver.memory = "4g"))
```

❶ Replace with actual paths, of course.

Note that these steps aren't needed if you are running sparkR on the command line. Instead, it accepts command-line configuration parameters like --driver-memory, just like spark-shell.

SparkR is an R-language wrapper around the same DataFrame and MLlib APIs that have been demonstrated in this chapter. It's therefore possible to recreate a K-means simple clustering of the data:

```
clusters_data <- read.df("/path/to/kddcup.data", "csv", ❶
                         inferSchema = "true", header = "false")
colnames(clusters_data) <- c( ❷
  "duration", "protocol_type", "service", "flag",
  "src_bytes", "dst_bytes", "land", "wrong_fragment", "urgent",
  "hot", "num_failed_logins", "logged_in", "num_compromised",
  "root_shell", "su_attempted", "num_root", "num_file_creations",
  "num_shells", "num_access_files", "num_outbound_cmds",
  "is_host_login", "is_guest_login", "count", "srv_count",
  "serror_rate", "srv_serror_rate", "rerror_rate", "srv_rerror_rate",
  "same_srv_rate", "diff_srv_rate", "srv_diff_host_rate",
  "dst_host_count", "dst_host_srv_count",
  "dst_host_same_srv_rate", "dst_host_diff_srv_rate",
  "dst_host_same_src_port_rate", "dst_host_srv_diff_host_rate",
  "dst_host_serror_rate", "dst_host_srv_serror_rate",
  "dst_host_rerror_rate", "dst_host_srv_rerror_rate",
  "label")

numeric_only <- cache(drop(clusters_data, ❸
                      c("protocol_type", "service", "flag", "label")))

kmeans_model <- spark.kmeans(numeric_only, ~ ., ❹
                      k = 100, maxIter = 40, initMode = "k-means||")
```

❶ Replace with path to *kddcup.data*.

❷ Name columns.

❸ Drop nonnumeric columns again.

❹ ~ . means all columns.

From here, it's straightforward to assign a cluster to each data point. The operations above show usage of the SparkR APIs, which naturally correspond to core Spark APIs but are expressed as R libraries in R-like syntax. The actual clustering is executed using the same JVM-based, Scala-language implementation in MLlib. These operations are effectively a *handle* or remote control to distributed operations that are not executing in R.

R has its own rich set of libraries for analysis, and its own similar concept of a data frame. It is sometimes useful, therefore, to pull some data down into the R interpreter in order to be able to use these native R libraries, which are unrelated to Spark.

Of course, R and its libraries are not distributed, and so it's not feasible to pull the whole data set of 4,898,431 data points into R. However, it's easy to pull only a sample:

```
clustering <- predict(kmeans_model, numeric_only)
clustering_sample <- collect(sample(clustering, FALSE, 0.01))  ❶

str(clustering_sample)

...
'data.frame': 48984 obs. of  39 variables:
 $ duration      : int  0 0 0 0 0 0 0 0 0 ...
 $ src_bytes     : int  181 185 162 254 282 310 212 214 181 ...
 $ dst_bytes     : int  5450 9020 4528 849 424 1981 2917 3404 ...
 $ land          : int  0 0 0 0 0 0 0 0 0 ...
...
 $ prediction    : int  33 33 33 0 0 0 0 0 33 33 ...
```

❶ 1% sample without replacement

`clustering_sample` is actually a local R data frame, not a Spark DataFrame, so it can be manipulated like any other data in R. Above, `str()` shows the structure of the data frame.

For example, it's possible to extract the cluster assignment and then show statistics about the distribution of assignments:

```
clusters <- clustering_sample["prediction"]  ❶
data <- data.matrix(within(clustering_sample, rm("prediction")))  ❷

table(clusters)

...
clusters
    0    11    14    18    23    25    28    30    31    33    36   ...
47294     3     1     2     2   308   105     1    27  1219    15   ...
```

❶ Only the clustering assignment column

❷ Everything but the clustering assignment

For example, this shows that most points fell into cluster 0. Although much more could be done with this data in R, further coverage of this is beyond the scope of this book.

To visualize the data, a library called `rgl` is required. It will only be functional if running this example in RStudio. First, install (once) and load the library:

```
install.packages("rgl")
library(rgl)
```

Note that R may prompt you to download other packages or compiler tools to complete installation, because installing the package means compiling its source code.

This data set is 38-dimensional. It will have to be projected down into at most three dimensions in order to visualize it with a *random projection*:

```
random_projection <- matrix(data = rnorm(3*ncol(data)), ncol = 3) ❶
random_projection_norm <-
  random_projection / sqrt(rowSums(random_projection*random_projection))

projected_data <- data.frame(data %*% random_projection_norm) ❷
```

❶ Make a random 3D projection and normalize

❷ Project and make a new data frame

This creates a 3D data set out of a 38D data set by choosing three random unit vectors and projecting the data onto them. This is a simplistic, rough-and-ready form of dimension reduction. Of course, there are more sophisticated dimension reduction algorithms, like principal component analysis (PCA) (*https://en.wikipedia.org/wiki/Principal_component_analysis*) or the singular value decomposition (SVD) (*https://en.wikipedia.org/wiki/Singular_value_decomposition*). These are available in R but take much longer to run. For purposes of visualization in this example, a random projection achieves much the same result, faster.

Finally, the clustered points can be plotted in an interactive 3D visualization:

```
num_clusters <- max(clusters)
palette <- rainbow(num_clusters)
colors = sapply(clusters, function(c) palette[c])
plot3d(projected_data, col = colors, size = 10)
```

Note that this will require running RStudio in an environment that supports the `rgl` library and graphics. For example, on macOS, it requires that X11 from Apple's Developer Tools be installed.

The resulting visualization in Figure 5-1 shows data points in 3D space. Many points fall on top of one another, and the result is sparse and hard to interpret. However, the dominant feature of the visualization is its L shape. The points seem to vary along two distinct dimensions, and little in other dimensions.

This makes sense because the data set has two features that are on a much larger scale than the others. Whereas most features have values between 0 and 1, the bytes-sent and bytes-received features vary from 0 to tens of thousands. The Euclidean distance between points is therefore almost completely determined by these two features. It's almost as if the other features don't exist! So it's important to normalize away these differences in scale to put features on near-equal footing.

Feature Normalization

We can normalize each feature by converting it to a standard score (*https://en.wikipe dia.org/wiki/Standard_score*). This means subtracting the mean of the feature's values from each value, and dividing by the standard deviation, as shown in the standard score equation:

$$normalized_i = \frac{feature_i - \mu_i}{\sigma_i}$$

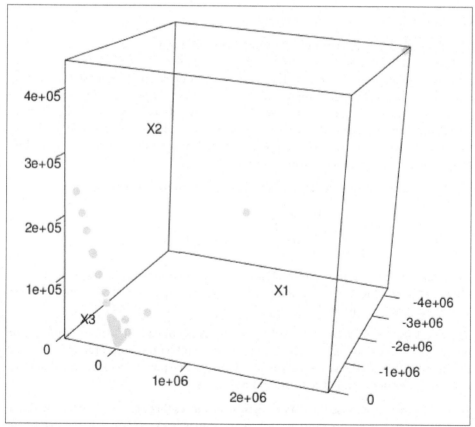

Figure 5-1. Random 3D projection

In fact, subtracting means has no effect on the clustering because the subtraction effectively shifts all the data points by the same amount in the same directions. This does not affect interpoint Euclidean distances.

MLlib provides `StandardScaler`, a component that can perform this kind of standardization and be easily added to the clustering pipeline.

We can run the same test with normalized data on a higher range of k:

```
import org.apache.spark.ml.feature.StandardScaler

def clusteringScore2(data: DataFrame, k: Int): Double = {
  val assembler = new VectorAssembler().
    setInputCols(data.columns.filter(_ != "label")).
    setOutputCol("featureVector")
  val scaler = new StandardScaler()
    .setInputCol("featureVector")
    .setOutputCol("scaledFeatureVector")
    .setWithStd(true)
    .setWithMean(false)
  val kmeans = new KMeans().
    setSeed(Random.nextLong()).
    setK(k).
    setPredictionCol("cluster").
    setFeaturesCol("scaledFeatureVector").
    setMaxIter(40).
    setTol(1.0e-5)
  val pipeline = new Pipeline().setStages(Array(assembler, scaler, kmeans))
  val pipelineModel = pipeline.fit(data)
  val kmeansModel = pipelineModel.stages.last.asInstanceOf[KMeansModel]
  kmeansModel.computeCost(pipelineModel.transform(data)) / data.count()
}

(60 to 270 by 30).map(k => (k, clusteringScore2(numericOnly, k))).
  foreach(println)
```

This has helped put dimensions on more equal footing, and the absolute distances between points (and thus the cost) is much smaller in absolute terms. However, there isn't yet an obvious value of k beyond which increasing it does little to improve the cost:

```
(60,1.2454250178069293)
(90,0.7767730051608682)
(120,0.5070473497003614)
(150,0.4077081720067704)
(180,0.3344486714980788)
(210,0.276237617334138)
(240,0.24571877339169032)
(270,0.21818167354866858)
```

Another 3D visualization of the normalized data points reveals a richer structure, as expected. Some points are spaced in regular, discrete intervals in a direction; these are likely projections of discrete dimensions in the data, like counts. With 100 clusters, it's hard to make out which points come from which clusters. One large cluster seems to dominate, and many clusters correspond to small compact subregions (some of which are omitted from this zoomed detail of the entire 3D visualization). The result, shown in Figure 5-2, does not necessarily advance the analysis but is an interesting sanity check.

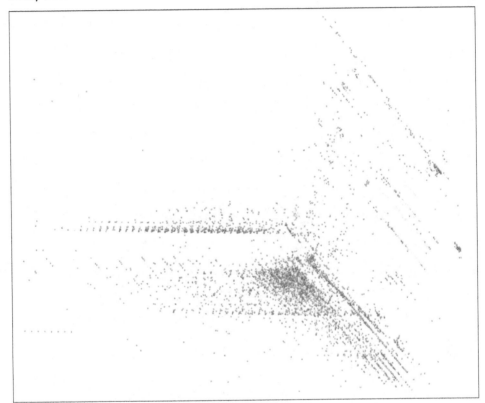

Figure 5-2. Random 3D projection, normalized

Categorical Variables

Normalization was a valuable step forward, but more can be done to improve the clustering. In particular, several features have been left out entirely because they aren't numeric. This is throwing away valuable information. Adding them back in some form should produce a better-informed clustering.

Earlier, three categorical features were excluded because nonnumeric features can't be used with the Euclidean distance function that K-means uses in MLlib. This is the reverse of the issue noted in Chapter 4, where numeric features were used to represent categorical values but a categorical feature was desired.

The categorical features can translate into several binary indicator features using one-hot encoding, which can be viewed as numeric dimensions. For example, the second column contains the protocol type: tcp, udp, or icmp. This feature could be thought of as *three* features, as if features "is TCP," "is UDP," and "is ICMP" were in the data set. The single feature value tcp might become 1,0,0; udp might be 0,1,0; and so on.

Here again, MLlib provides components that implement this transformation. In fact, one-hot-encoding string-valued features like protocol_type is actually a two-step process. First, the string values are converted to integer indices like 0, 1, 2, and so on using StringIndexer. Then these integer indices are encoded into a vector with One HotEncoder. These two steps can be thought of as a small Pipeline in themselves.

```
import org.apache.spark.ml.feature.{OneHotEncoder, StringIndexer}

def oneHotPipeline(inputCol: String): (Pipeline, String) = {
  val indexer = new StringIndexer().
    setInputCol(inputCol).
    setOutputCol(inputCol + "_indexed")
  val encoder = new OneHotEncoder().
    setInputCol(inputCol + "_indexed").
    setOutputCol(inputCol + "_vec")
  val pipeline = new Pipeline().setStages(Array(indexer, encoder))
  (pipeline, inputCol + "_vec") ❶
}
```

❶ Return Pipeline and name of output vector column

This method produces a Pipeline that can be added as a component in the overall clustering pipeline; pipelines can be composed. All that is left is to make sure to add the new vector output columns into VectorAssembler's output and proceed as before with scaling, clustering, and evaluation. The source code is omitted for brevity here, but can be found in the repository accompanying this chapter.

```
(60,39.739250062068685)
(90,15.814341529964691)
(120,3.5008631362395413)
(150,2.2151974068685547)
(180,1.587330730808905)
(210,1.3626704802348888)
(240,1.1202477806210747)
(270,0.9263659836264369)
```

These sample results suggest, possibly, $k=180$ as a value where the score flattens out a bit. At least the clustering is now using all input features.

Using Labels with Entropy

Earlier, we used the given label for each data point to create a quick sanity check of the quality of the clustering. This notion can be formalized further and used as an alternative means of evaluating clustering quality, and therefore, of choosing *k*.

The labels tell us something about the true nature of each data point. A good clustering, it seems, should agree with these human-applied labels. It should put together points that share a label frequently and not lump together points of many different labels. It should produce clusters with relatively homogeneous labels.

You may recall from Chapter 4 that we have metrics for homogeneity: Gini impurity and entropy. These are functions of the proportions of labels in each cluster, and produce a number that is low when the proportions are skewed toward few, or one, label. Entropy will be used here for illustration.

```
def entropy(counts: Iterable[Int]): Double = {
  val values = counts.filter(_ > 0)
  val n = values.map(_.toDouble).sum
  values.map { v =>
    val p = v / n
    -p * math.log(p)
  }.sum
}
```

A good clustering would have clusters whose collections of labels are homogeneous and so have low entropy. A weighted average of entropy can therefore be used as a cluster score:

```
val clusterLabel = pipelineModel.transform(data).
  select("cluster", "label").as[(Int, String)]   ❶

val weightedClusterEntropy = clusterLabel.
  groupByKey { case (cluster, _) => cluster }.   ❷
  mapGroups { case (_, clusterLabels) =>
    val labels = clusterLabels.map { case (_, label) => label }.toSeq
    val labelCounts = labels.groupBy(identity).values.map(_.size)   ❸
    labels.size * entropy(labelCounts)
  }.collect()

weightedClusterEntropy.sum / data.count()   ❹
```

❶ Predict cluster for each datum

❷ Extract collections of labels, per cluster

❸ Count labels in collections

❹ Average entropy weighted by cluster size

As before, this analysis can be used to obtain some idea of a suitable value of *k*. Entropy will not necessarily decrease as *k* increases, so it is possible to look for a local minimum value. Here again, results suggest *k*=180 is a reasonable choice because its score is actually lower than 150 *and* 210:

```
(60,0.03475331900669869)
(90,0.051512668026335535)
(120,0.02020028911919293)
(150,0.019962563512905682)
(180,0.01110240886325257)
(210,0.01259738444250231)
(240,0.01357435960663116)
(270,0.010119881917660544)
```

Clustering in Action

Finally, with confidence, we can cluster the full normalized data set with *k*=180. Again, we can print the labels for each cluster to get some sense of the resulting clustering. Clusters do seem to be dominated by one type of attack each, and contain only a few types.

```
val pipelineModel = fitPipeline4(data, 180) ❶
val countByClusterLabel = pipelineModel.transform(data).
  select("cluster", "label").
  groupBy("cluster", "label").count().
  orderBy("cluster", "label")
countByClusterLabel.show()
```

```
...
+-------+----------+------+
|cluster|     label| count|
+-------+----------+------+
|      0|     back.|   324|
|      0|   normal.| 42921|
|      1|  neptune.|  1039|
|      1|portsweep.|     9|
|      1|    satan.|     2|
|      2|  neptune.|365375|
|      2|portsweep.|   141|
|      3|portsweep.|     2|
|      3|    satan.| 10627|
|      4|  neptune.|  1033|
|      4|portsweep.|     6|
|      4|    satan.|     1|
...
```

❶ See accompanying source code for `fitPipeline4()` definition

Now we can make an actual anomaly detector. Anomaly detection amounts to measuring a new data point's distance to its nearest centroid. If this distance exceeds some threshold, it is anomalous. This threshold might be chosen to be the distance of, say, the 100th-farthest data point from among known data:

```
import org.apache.spark.ml.linalg.{Vector, Vectors}

val kMeansModel = pipelineModel.stages.last.asInstanceOf[KMeansModel]
val centroids = kMeansModel.clusterCenters

val clustered = pipelineModel.transform(data)
val threshold = clustered.
  select("cluster", "scaledFeatureVector").as[(Int, Vector)].
  map { case (cluster, vec) => Vectors.sqdist(centroids(cluster), vec) }.
  orderBy($"value".desc).take(100).last ❶
```

❶ Single output implicitly named "value"

The final step is to apply this threshold to all new data points as they arrive. For example, Spark Streaming can be used to apply this function to small batches of input data arriving from sources like Flume, Kafka, or files on HDFS. Data points exceeding the threshold might trigger an alert that sends an email or updates a database.

As an example, we will apply it to the original data set, to see some of the data points that are, we might believe, most anomalous within the input.

```
val originalCols = data.columns
val anomalies = clustered.filter { row =>
  val cluster = row.getAs[Int]("cluster")
  val vec = row.getAs[Vector]("scaledFeatureVector")
  Vectors.sqdist(centroids(cluster), vec) >= threshold
}.select(originalCols.head, originalCols.tail:_*) ❶

anomalies.first() ❷

...
[9,tcp,telnet,SF,307,2374,0,0,1,0,0,1,0,1,0,1,3,1,0,0,0,0,1,1,
 0.0,0.0,0.0,0.0,1.0,0.0,0.0,69,4,0.03,0.04,0.01,0.75,0.0,0.0,
 0.0,0.0,normal.]
```

❶ Note odd (`String`, `String*`) signature for selecting columns

❷ `show()` works; hard to read

This example shows a slightly different way of operating on data frames. Pure SQL can't express the computation of squared distance. A UDF could be used, as before, to define a function of two columns that returns a squared distance. However, it's also possible to interact with rows of data programmatically as a `Row` object, much like in JDBC.

A network security expert would be more able to interpret why this is or is not actually a strange connection. It appears unusual at least because it is labeled normal, but involves connections to 69 different hosts.

Where to Go from Here

The KMeansModel is, by itself, the essence of an anomaly detection system. The preceding code demonstrated how to apply it to data to detect anomalies. This same code could be used within Spark Streaming (*https://spark.apache.org/streaming/*) to score new data as it arrives in near real time, and perhaps trigger an alert or review.

MLlib also includes a variation called StreamingKMeans, which can update a clustering incrementally as new data arrives in a StreamingKMeansModel. We could use this to continue to learn, approximately, how new data affects the clustering, and not just to assess new data against existing clusters. It can be integrated with Spark Streaming as well. However, it has not been updated for the new DataFrame-based APIs.

This model is only a simplistic one. For example, Euclidean distance is used in this example because it is the only distance function supported by Spark MLlib at this time. In the future, it may be possible to use distance functions that can better account for the distributions of and correlations between features, such as the Mahalanobis distance (*http://bit.ly/2qYLZbx*).

There are also more sophisticated cluster-quality evaluation metrics (*http://bit.ly/2qYQlzf*) that could be applied (even without labels) to pick *k*, such as the Silhouette coefficient (*http://bit.ly/2qYQkLH*). These tend to evaluate not just closeness of points within one cluster, but closeness of points to other clusters. Finally, different models could be applied instead of simple K-means clustering; for example, a Gaussian mixture model (*https://bit.ly/1GzKhLJ*) or DBSCAN (*https://bit.ly/1GzKCOG*) could capture more subtle relationships between data points and the cluster centers. Spark MLlib already implements Gaussian mixture models (*http://bit.ly/2qYwxMu*); implementations of others may become available in Spark MLlib or other Spark-based libraries in the future.

Of course, clustering isn't just for anomaly detection. In fact, it's more often associated with use cases where the actual clusters matter! For example, clustering can also be used to group customers according to their behaviors, preferences, and attributes. Each cluster, by itself, might represent a usefully distinguishable type of customer. This is a more data-driven way to segment customers rather than leaning on arbitrary, generic divisions like "age 20–34" and "female."

## CHAPTER 6

Understanding Wikipedia with Latent Semantic Analysis

Sandy Ryza

Where are the Snowdens of yesteryear?
  —Capt. Yossarian

Most of the work in data engineering consists of assembling data into some sort of queryable format. We can query structured data with formal languages. For example, when this structured data is tabular, we can use SQL. While it is by no means an easy task in practice, at a high level, the work of making tabular data accessible is often straightforward—pull data from a variety of data sources into a single table, perhaps cleansing or fusing intelligently along the way. Unstructured text data presents a whole different set of challenges. The process of preparing data into a format that humans can interact with is not so much "assembly," but rather "indexing" in the nice case or "coercion" when things get ugly. A standard search index permits fast queries for the set of documents that contains a given set of terms. Sometimes, however, we want to find documents that relate to the *concepts* surrounding a particular word even if the documents do not contain that exact string. Standard search indexes often fail to capture the latent structure in the text's subject matter.

Latent semantic analysis (LSA) is a technique in natural language processing and information retrieval that seeks to better understand a corpus of documents and the relationships between the words in those documents. It attempts to distill the corpus into a set of relevant *concepts*. Each concept captures a thread of variation in the data and often corresponds to a topic that the corpus discusses. Without yet delving into the mathematics, each concept consists of three attributes: a level of affinity for each document in the corpus, a level of affinity for each term in the corpus, and an importance score reflecting how useful the concept is in describing variance in the data set. For example, LSA might discover a concept with high affinity for the terms "Asimov" and "robot," and high affinity for the documents "foundation series" and "science fiction." By selecting only the most important concepts, LSA can throw away some irrelevant noise and merge co-occurring strands to come up with a simpler representation of the data.

We can employ this concise representation in a variety of tasks. It can provide scores of similarity between terms and other terms, between documents and other documents, and between terms and documents. By encapsulating the patterns of variance in the corpus, it can base scores on a deeper understanding than simply on counting occurrences and co-occurrences of words. These similarity measures are ideal for tasks such as finding the set of documents relevant to query terms, grouping documents into topics, and finding related words.

LSA discovers this lower-dimensional representation using a linear algebra technique called SVD. SVD can be thought of as a more powerful version of the ALS factorization described in Chapter 3. It starts with a *document-term matrix* generated through counting word frequencies for each document. In this matrix, each document corresponds to a column, each term corresponds to a row, and each element represents the importance of a word to a document. SVD then factorizes this matrix into three matrices, one of which expresses concepts in regard to documents, one of which expresses concepts in regard to terms, and one of which contains the importance for each concept. The structure of these matrices can achieve a *low-rank approximation* of the original matrix by removing a set of rows and columns corresponding to the least important concepts. That is, the matrices in this low-rank approximation can be multiplied to produce a matrix close to the original, with increasing loss of fidelity as each concept is removed.

In this chapter, we'll embark upon the modest task of enabling queries against the full extent of human knowledge based on its latent semantic relationships. More specifically, we'll apply LSA to a corpus consisting of the full set of articles contained in Wikipedia, which is about 46 GB of raw text. We'll cover how to use Spark for preprocessing the data: reading it, cleansing it, and coercing it into a numerical form. We'll show how to compute the SVD and explain how to interpret and make use of it.

SVD has wide applications outside LSA. It appears in such diverse places as detecting climatological trends (Michael Mann's famous "hockey-stick" graph (*http://bit.ly/2qcHozy*)), face recognition, and image compression. Spark's implementation can perform the matrix factorization on enormous data sets, which opens up the technique to a whole new set of applications.

The Document-Term Matrix

Before performing any analysis, LSA requires transforming the raw text of the corpus into a document-term matrix. In this matrix, each column represents a term that occurs in the corpus, and each row represents a document. Loosely, the value at each position should correspond to the importance of the column's term to the row's document. A few weighting schemes have been proposed, but by far the most common is *term frequency* times *inverse document frequency*, or TF-IDF. Here's a representation in Scala code of the formula. We won't actually end up using this code because Spark provides its own implementation.

```
def termDocWeight(termFrequencyInDoc: Int, totalTermsInDoc: Int,
    termFreqInCorpus: Int, totalDocs: Int): Double = {
  val tf = termFrequencyInDoc.toDouble / totalTermsInDoc
  val docFreq = totalDocs.toDouble / termFreqInCorpus
  val idf = math.log(docFreq)
  tf * idf
}
```

TF-IDF captures two intuitions about the relevance of a term to a document. First, we would expect that the more often a term occurs in a document, the more important it is to that document. Second, not all terms are equal in a global sense. It is more meaningful to encounter a word that occurs rarely in the entire corpus than a word that appears in most of the documents, thus the metric uses the *inverse* of the word's appearance in documents in the full corpus.

The frequency of words in a corpus tends to be distributed exponentially. A common word will often appear ten times as often as a mildly common word, which in turn might appear ten or a hundred times as often as a rare word. Basing a metric on the raw inverse document frequency would give rare words enormous weight and practically ignore the impact of all other words. To capture this distribution, the scheme uses the *log* of the inverse document frequency. This mellows the differences in document frequencies by transforming the multiplicative gaps between them into additive gaps.

The model relies on a few assumptions. It treats each document as a "bag of words," meaning that it pays no attention to the ordering of words, sentence structure, or negations. By representing each term once, the model has difficulty dealing with *polysemy*, the use of the same word for multiple meanings. For example, the model can't distinguish between the use of "band" in "Radiohead is the best band ever" and "I broke a rubber band." If both sentences appear often in the corpus, it may come to associate "Radiohead" with "rubber."

The corpus has 10 million documents. Counting obscure technical jargon, the English language contains about a million terms, some subset in the tens of thousands of which is likely useful for understanding the corpus. Because the corpus contains far more documents than terms, it makes the most sense to generate the document-term matrix as a row matrix—a collection of sparse vectors—each corresponding to a document.

Getting from the raw Wikipedia dump into this form requires a set of preprocessing steps. First, the input consists of a single enormous XML file with documents delimited by <page> tags. This needs to be broken up to feed to the next step, turning Wiki-formatting into plain text. The plain text is then split into tokens, which are reduced from their different inflectional forms to a root term through a process called *lemmatization*. These tokens can then be used to compute term and document frequencies. A final step ties these frequencies together and builds the actual vector objects. In the book repo, all the code for performing these steps is encapsulated in the AssembleDocumentTermMatrix class.

The first steps can be performed for each document fully in parallel (which, in Spark, means as a set of map functions), but computing the inverse document frequencies requires aggregation across all the documents. A number of useful general NLP and Wikipedia-specific extraction tools exist that can aid in these tasks.

Getting the Data

Wikipedia makes dumps of all its articles available. The full dump comes in a single large XML file. These can be downloaded (*https://dumps.wikimedia.org/enwiki*) and then placed on HDFS. For example:

```
$ curl -s -L https://dumps.wikimedia.org/enwiki/latest/\
$ enwiki-latest-pages-articles-multistream.xml.bz2 \
$   | bzip2 -cd \
$   | hadoop fs -put - wikidump.xml
```

This will take a little while.

Chugging through this volume of data makes the most sense with a cluster of a few nodes to work with. To run this chapter's code on a local machine, a better option is to generate a smaller dump using Wikipedia's exports page (*https://en.wikipedia.org/wiki/Special:Export*). Try getting all the pages from a category that has many pages and few subcategories, such as Megafauna or Geometry. For the following code to work, download the dump into the *ch06-lsa/* directory and rename it to *wiki-dump.xml*.

Parsing and Preparing the Data

Here's a snippet at the beginning of the dump:

```
<page>
  <title>Anarchism</title>
  <ns>0</ns>
  <id>12</id>
  <revision>
    <id>584215651</id>
    <parentid>584213644</parentid>
```

```
          <timestamp>2013-12-02T15:14:01Z</timestamp>
          <contributor>
            <username>AnomieBOT</username>
            <id>7611264</id>
          </contributor>
          <comment>Rescuing orphaned refs (&quot;autogenerated1&quot; from rev
          584155010; &quot;bbc&quot; from rev 584155010)</comment>
          <text xml:space="preserve">{{Redirect|Anarchist|the fictional character|
          Anarchist (comics)}}
{{Redirect|Anarchists}}
{{pp-move-indef}}
{{Anarchism sidebar}}

'''Anarchism''' is a [[political philosophy]] that advocates [[stateless society|
stateless societies]] often defined as [[self-governance|self-governed]]
voluntary institutions,&lt;ref&gt;&quot;ANARCHISM, a social philosophy that
rejects authoritarian government and maintains that voluntary institutions are
best suited to express man's natural social tendencies.&quot; George Woodcock.
&quot;Anarchism&quot; at The Encyclopedia of Philosophy&lt;/ref&gt;&lt;ref&gt;
&quot;In a society developed on these lines, the voluntary associations which
already now begin to cover all the fields of human activity would take a still
greater extension so as to substitute
...
```

Let's fire up the Spark shell. In this chapter, we rely on several libraries to make our
lives easier. The GitHub repo contains a Maven project that can be used to build a
JAR file that packages all these dependencies together:

```
$ cd ch06-lsa/
$ mvn package
$ spark-shell --jars target/ch06-lsa-2.0.0-jar-with-dependencies.jar
```

To start operating on this dump, we'll need to strip out the formatting and get to the
content. A good start would be to produce a data set of (title, document content)
tuples that we can then run further processing on. The Cloud9 project provides a set
of APIs that are really helpful for this.

Cloud9 provides a class, `XMLInputFormat`, derived from the Apache Mahout project,
that can split up the enormous Wikipedia dump into documents. To create a data set
with it:

```
import edu.umd.cloud9.collection.XMLInputFormat
import org.apache.hadoop.conf.Configuration
import org.apache.hadoop.io._

val path = "wikidump.xml"
@transient val conf = new Configuration()
conf.set(XMLInputFormat.START_TAG_KEY, "<page>")
conf.set(XMLInputFormat.END_TAG_KEY, "</page>")
val kvs = spark.sparkContext.newAPIHadoopFile(path, classOf[XMLInputFormat],
  classOf[LongWritable], classOf[Text], conf)
val rawXmls = kvs.map(_._2.toString).toDS()
```

Turning the Wiki XML into the plain text of article contents could require a chapter of its own, but luckily the Cloud9 project provides APIs that handle this entirely:

```scala
import edu.umd.cloud9.collection.wikipedia.language._
import edu.umd.cloud9.collection.wikipedia._

def wikiXmlToPlainText(pageXml: String): Option[(String, String)] = {
  // Wikipedia has updated their dumps slightly since Cloud9 was written,
  // so this hacky replacement is sometimes required to get parsing to work.
  val hackedPageXml = pageXml.replaceFirst(
    "<text xml:space=\"preserve\" bytes=\"\\d+\">",
    "<text xml:space=\"preserve\">")

  val page = new EnglishWikipediaPage()
  WikipediaPage.readPage(page, hackedPageXml)
  if (page.isEmpty) None
  else Some((page.getTitle, page.getContent))
}

val docTexts = rawXmls.filter(_ != null).flatMap(wikiXmlToPlainText)
```

Lemmatization

With the plain text in hand, next we need to turn it into a bag of terms. This step requires care for a couple of reasons. First, common words like "the" and "is" take up space but at best offer no useful information to the model. Filtering out a list of *stop words* can both save space and improve fidelity. Second, terms with the same meaning can often take slightly different forms. For example, "monkey" and "monkeys" do not deserve to be separate terms. Nor do "nationalize" and "nationalization." Combining these different inflectional forms into single terms is called *stemming* or *lemmatization*. Stemming refers to heuristics-based techniques for chopping off characters at the ends of words, while lemmatization refers to more principled approaches. For example, the former might truncate "drew" to "dr," while the latter might more correctly output "draw." The Stanford Core NLP project provides an excellent lemmatizer with a Java API that Scala can take advantage of.

The following snippet takes the data set of plain-text documents and both lemmatizes it and filters out stop words. Note that this code relies on a file of stopwords called *stopwords.txt*, which is available in the accompanying source code repo (*http://bit.ly/2psi9Ms*) and should be downloaded into the current working directory first:

```scala
import scala.collection.JavaConverters._
import scala.collection.mutable.ArrayBuffer
import edu.stanford.nlp.pipeline._
import edu.stanford.nlp.ling.CoreAnnotations._
import java.util.Properties
import org.apache.spark.sql.Dataset

def createNLPPipeline(): StanfordCoreNLP = {
```

```
    val props = new Properties()
    props.put("annotators", "tokenize, ssplit, pos, lemma")
    new StanfordCoreNLP(props)
  }

  def isOnlyLetters(str: String): Boolean = {
    str.forall(c => Character.isLetter(c))
  }

  def plainTextToLemmas(text: String, stopWords: Set[String],
      pipeline: StanfordCoreNLP): Seq[String] = {
    val doc = new Annotation(text)
    pipeline.annotate(doc)

    val lemmas = new ArrayBuffer[String]()
    val sentences = doc.get(classOf[SentencesAnnotation])
    for (sentence <- sentences.asScala;
         token <- sentence.get(classOf[TokensAnnotation]).asScala) {
      val lemma = token.get(classOf[LemmaAnnotation])
      if (lemma.length > 2 && !stopWords.contains(lemma)
          && isOnlyLetters(lemma)) { ❶
        lemmas += lemma.toLowerCase
      }
    }
    lemmas
  }

  val stopWords = scala.io.Source.fromFile("stopwords.txt").getLines().toSet
  val bStopWords = spark.sparkContext.broadcast(stopWords) ❷

  val terms: Dataset[(String, Seq[String])] =
    docTexts.mapPartitions { iter =>
      val pipeline = createNLPPipeline()
      iter.map { case(title, contents) =>
        (title, plainTextToLemmas(contents, bStopWords.value, pipeline))
      }
    } ❸
```

❶ Specify some minimal requirements on lemmas to weed out garbage.

❷ Broadcast the stop words to save on memory in the executors.

❸ Use `mapPartitions` so that we only initialize the NLP pipeline object once per partition instead of once per document.

Computing the TF-IDFs

At this point, `terms` refers to a data set of sequences of terms, each corresponding to a document. The next step is to compute the frequencies for each term within each document and for each term within the entire corpus. The spark.ml package contains `Estimator` and `Transformer` implementations for doing exactly this.

To take advantage of them, first we'll need to convert our data set into a data frame:

```
val termsDF = terms.toDF("title", "terms")
```

Let's filter out all documents that have zero or one term:

```
val filtered = termsDF.where(size($"terms") > 1)
```

The `CountVectorizer` is an `Estimator` that can help compute the term frequencies for us. The `CountVectorizer` scans the data to build up a vocabulary, a mapping of integers to terms, encapsulated in the `CountVectorizerModel`, a `Transformer`. The `CountVectorizerModel` can then be used to generate a term frequency `Vector` for each document. The vector has a component for each term in the vocabulary, and the value for each component is the number of times the term appears in the document. Spark uses sparse vectors here, because documents typically only contain a small subset of the full vocabulary.

```
import org.apache.spark.ml.feature.CountVectorizer

val numTerms = 20000
val countVectorizer = new CountVectorizer().
  setInputCol("terms").setOutputCol("termFreqs").
  setVocabSize(numTerms)
val vocabModel = countVectorizer.fit(filtered)
val docTermFreqs = vocabModel.transform(filtered)
```

Notice the use of `setVocabSize`. The corpus contains millions of terms, but many are highly specialized words that only appear in one or two documents. Filtering out less frequent terms can both improve performance and remove noise. When we set a vocabulary size on the estimator, it leaves out all but the most frequent words.

The resulting DataFrame will be used at least twice after this point: to calculate the inverse document frequencies and the final document-term matrix. So caching it in memory is a good idea:

```
docTermFreqs.cache()
```

With the document frequencies in hand, we can compute the inverse document frequencies. For this, we use `IDF`, another `Estimator`, which counts the number of documents in which each term in the corpus appears and then uses these counts to compute the IDF scaling factor for each term. The `IDFModel` that it yields can then apply these scaling factors to each term in each vector in the data set.

```
import org.apache.spark.ml.feature.IDF

val idf = new IDF().setInputCol("termFreqs").setOutputCol("tfidfVec")
val idfModel = idf.fit(docTermFreqs)
val docTermMatrix = idfModel.transform(docTermFreqs).select("title", "tfidfVec")
```

As we descend from data frames into the world of vectors and matrices, we lose the ability to key by strings. Thus, if we want to trace what we learn back to recognizable entities, it's important for us to save a mapping of positions in the matrix to the terms and document titles in our original corpus. Positions in the term vectors are equivalent to columns in our document-term matrix. The mapping of these positions to term strings is already saved in our `CountVectorizerModel`. We can access it with:

```
val termIds: Array[String] = vocabModel.vocabulary
```

Creating a mapping of row IDs to document titles is a little more difficult. To achieve it, we can use the `zipWithUniqueId` function, which associates a unique deterministic ID with every row in the DataFrame. We rely on the fact that, if we call this function on a transformed version of the DataFrame, it will assign the same unique IDs to the transformed rows as long as the transformations don't change the number of rows or their partitioning. Thus, we can trace the rows back to their IDs in the DataFrame and, consequently, the document titles that they correspond to:

```
val docIds = docTermFreqs.rdd.map(_.getString(0)).
  zipWithUniqueId().
  map(_.swap).
  collect().toMap
```

Singular Value Decomposition

With the document-term matrix M in hand, the analysis can proceed to the factorization and dimensionality reduction. MLlib contains an implementation of the SVD that can handle enormous matrices. The singular value decomposition takes an $m \times n$ matrix and returns three matrices that approximately equal it when multiplied together:

$$M \approx U\ S\ V^T$$

The matrices are:

- U is an $m \times k$ matrix whose columns form an orthonormal basis for the document space.

- S is a $k \times k$ diagonal matrix, each of whose entries correspond to the strength of one of the concepts.

- V^T is a $k \times n$ matrix whose columns form an orthonormal basis for the term space.

In the LSA case, m is the number of documents and n is the number of terms. The decomposition is parameterized with a number k, less than or equal to n, which indicates how many concepts to keep around. When $k=n$, the product of the factor matrices reconstitutes the original matrix exactly. When $k<n$, the multiplication results in a low-rank approximation of the original matrix. k is typically chosen to be much

smaller than *n*. SVD ensures that the approximation will be the closest possible to the original matrix (as defined by the L2 Norm—that is, the sum of squares—of the difference), given the constraint that it needs to be expressible in only *k* concepts.

At the time of this writing, the spark.ml package, which operates on DataFrames, does not include an implementation of SVD. However, the older spark.mllib, which operates on RDDs, does. This means that to compute the SVD of our document-term matrix, we need to represent it as an RDD of vectors. On top of this, the spark.ml and spark.mllib packages each have their own Vector class. The spark.ml Transformers we used earlier yield spark.ml vectors but the SVD implementation only accepts spark.mllib vectors, so we need to perform a conversion. This is not the most elegant piece of code, but it gets the job done:

```
import org.apache.spark.mllib.linalg.{Vectors,
  Vector => MLLibVector}
import org.apache.spark.ml.linalg.{Vector => MLVector}


val vecRdd = docTermMatrix.select("tfidfVec").rdd.map { row =>
  Vectors.fromML(row.getAs[MLVector]("tfidfVec"))
}
```

To find the singular value decomposition, we simply wrap an RDD of row vectors in a RowMatrix and call computeSVD:

```
import org.apache.spark.mllib.linalg.distributed.RowMatrix

vecRdd.cache()
val mat = new RowMatrix(vecRdd)
val k = 1000
val svd = mat.computeSVD(k, computeU=true)
```

The RDD should be cached in memory beforehand because the computation requires multiple passes over the data. The computation requires *O(nk)* storage on the driver, *O(n)* storage for each task, and *O(k)* passes over the data.

As a reminder, a vector in *term space* means a vector with a weight on every term, a vector in *document space* means a vector with a weight on every document, and a vector in *concept space* means a vector with a weight on every concept. Each term, document, or concept defines an *axis* in its respective space, and the weight ascribed to the term, document, or concept means a length along that axis. Every term or document vector can be mapped to a corresponding vector in concept space. Every concept vector has possibly many term and document vectors that map to it, including a canonical term and document vector that it maps to when transformed in the reverse direction.

V is an *n* × *k* matrix in which each row corresponds to a term and each column corresponds to a concept. It defines a mapping between term space (the space where each point is an *n*-dimensional vector holding a weight for each term) and concept space (the space where each point is a k-dimensional vector holding a weight for each concept).

Similarly, U is an $m \times k$ matrix where each row corresponds to a document and each column corresponds to a concept. It defines a mapping between document space and concept space.

S is a $k \times k$ diagonal matrix that holds the singular values. Each diagonal element in S corresponds to a single concept (and thus a column in V and a column in U). The magnitude of each of these singular values corresponds to the importance of that concept: its power in explaining the variance in the data. An (inefficient) implementation of SVD could find the rank-k decomposition by starting with the rank-n decomposition and throwing away the $n–k$ smallest singular values until there are k left (along with their corresponding columns in U and V). A key insight of LSA is that only a small number of concepts is important to represent that data. The entries in the S matrix directly indicate the importance of each concept. They also happen to be the square roots of the eigenvalues (*http://bit.ly/2qcP6d3*) of MM^T.

Finding Important Concepts

So SVD outputs a bunch of numbers. How can we inspect these to verify they actually relate to anything useful? The V matrix represents concepts through the terms that are important to them. As discussed earlier, V contains a column for every concept and a row for every term. The value at each position can be interpreted as the relevance of that term to that concept. This means that the most relevant terms to each of the top concepts can be found with something like this:

```
import org.apache.spark.mllib.linalg.{Matrix,
  SingularValueDecomposition}
import org.apache.spark.mllib.linalg.distributed.RowMatrix

def topTermsInTopConcepts(
    svd: SingularValueDecomposition[RowMatrix, Matrix],
    numConcepts: Int,
    numTerms: Int, termIds: Array[String])
  : Seq[Seq[(String, Double)]] = {
  val v = svd.V
  val topTerms = new ArrayBuffer[Seq[(String, Double)]]()
  val arr = v.toArray
  for (i <- 0 until numConcepts) {
    val offs = i * v.numRows
    val termWeights = arr.slice(offs, offs + v.numRows).zipWithIndex
    val sorted = termWeights.sortBy(-_._1)
    topTerms += sorted.take(numTerms).map {
      case (score, id) => (termIds(id), score) ❶
    }
  }
```

```
        topTerms
    }
```

❶ This last step finds the actual terms that correspond to the positions in the term vectors. Recall that `termIds` is the integer->term mapping we got from the `Count Vectorizer`.

Note that *V* is a matrix in local memory in the driver process, and the computation occurs in a nondistributed manner. We can find the documents relevant to each of the top concepts in a similar manner using *U*, but the code looks a little bit different because *U* is stored as a distributed matrix:

```
def topDocsInTopConcepts(
    svd: SingularValueDecomposition[RowMatrix, Matrix],
    numConcepts: Int, numDocs: Int, docIds: Map[Long, String])
  : Seq[Seq[(String, Double)]] = {
  val u = svd.U
  val topDocs = new ArrayBuffer[Seq[(String, Double)]]()
  for (i <- 0 until numConcepts) {
    val docWeights = u.rows.map(_.toArray(i)).zipWithUniqueId()  ❶
    topDocs += docWeights.top(numDocs).map {
      case (score, id) => (docIds(id), score)
    }
  }
  topDocs
}
```

❶ `monotonically_increasing_id`/`zipWithUniqueId` trick discussed in the previous section of the chapter. This allows us to maintain continuity between rows in the matrix and rows in the DataFrame it is derived from, which also has the titles.

Let's inspect the first few concepts:

```
val topConceptTerms = topTermsInTopConcepts(svd, 4, 10, termIds)
val topConceptDocs = topDocsInTopConcepts(svd, 4, 10, docIds)
for ((terms, docs) <- topConceptTerms.zip(topConceptDocs)) {
  println("Concept terms: " + terms.map(_._1).mkString(", "))
  println("Concept docs: " + docs.map(_._1).mkString(", "))
  println()
}

Concept terms: summary, licensing, fur, logo, album, cover, rationale,
  gif, use, fair
Concept docs: File:Gladys-in-grammarland-cover-1897.png,
  File:Gladys-in-grammarland-cover-2010.png, File:1942ukrpoljudeakt4.jpg,
  File:Σακελλαρίδης.jpg, File:Baghdad-texas.jpg, File:Realistic.jpeg,
  File:DuplicateBoy.jpg, File:Garbo-the-spy.jpg, File:Joysagar.jpg,
  File:RizalHighSchoollogo.jpg

Concept terms: disambiguation, william, james, john, iran, australis,
  township, charles, robert, river
```

```
Concept docs: G. australis (disambiguation), F. australis (disambiguation),
    U. australis (disambiguation), L. maritima (disambiguation),
    G. maritima (disambiguation), F. japonica (disambiguation),
    P. japonica (disambiguation), Velo (disambiguation),
    Silencio (disambiguation), TVT (disambiguation)

Concept terms: licensing, disambiguation, australis, maritima, rawal,
    upington, tallulah, chf, satyanarayana, valérie
Concept docs: File:Rethymno.jpg, File:Ladycarolinelamb.jpg,
    File:KeyAirlines.jpg, File:NavyCivValor.gif, File:Vitushka.gif,
    File:DavidViscott.jpg, File:Bigbrother13cast.jpg, File:Rawal Lake1.JPG,
    File:Upington location.jpg, File:CHF SG Viewofaltar01.JPG

Concept terms: licensing, summarysource, summaryauthor, wikipedia,
    summarypicture, summaryfrom, summaryself, rawal, chf, upington
Concept docs: File:Rethymno.jpg, File:Wristlock4.jpg, File:Meseanlol.jpg,
    File:Sarles.gif, File:SuzlonWinMills.JPG, File:Rawal Lake1.JPG,
    File:CHF SG Viewofaltar01.JPG, File:Upington location.jpg,
    File:Driftwood-cover.jpg, File:Tallulah gorge2.jpg

Concept terms: establishment, norway, country, england, spain, florida,
    chile, colorado, australia, russia
Concept docs: Category:1794 establishments in Norway,
    Category:1838 establishments in Norway,
    Category:1849 establishments in Norway,
    Category:1908 establishments in Norway,
    Category:1966 establishments in Norway,
    Category:1926 establishments in Norway,
    Category:1957 establishments in Norway,
    Template:EstcatCountry1stMillennium,
    Category:2012 establishments in Chile,
    Category:1893 establishments in Chile
```

The documents in the first concept appear to all be image files, and the terms appear to be related to image attributes and licensing. The second concept appears to be disambiguation pages. It seems that perhaps this dump is not restricted to the raw Wikipedia articles and is cluttered by administrative pages as well as discussion pages. Inspecting the output of intermediate stages is useful for catching this kind of issue early. Luckily, it appears that Cloud9 provides some functionality for filtering these out. An updated version of the wikiXmlToPlainText method looks like the following:

```scala
def wikiXmlToPlainText(xml: String): Option[(String, String)] = {
  ...
  if (page.isEmpty || !page.isArticle || page.isRedirect ||
      page.getTitle.contains("(disambiguation)")) {
    None
  } else {
    Some((page.getTitle, page.getContent))
  }
}
```

Rerunning the pipeline on the filtered set of documents yields a much more reasonable result:

```
Concept terms: disambiguation, highway, school, airport, high, refer,
    number, squadron, list, may, division, regiment, wisconsin, channel,
    county
Concept docs: Tri-State Highway (disambiguation),
    Ocean-to-Ocean Highway (disambiguation), Highway 61 (disambiguation),
    Tri-County Airport (disambiguation), Tri-Cities Airport (disambiguation),
    Mid-Continent Airport (disambiguation), 99 Squadron (disambiguation),
    95th Squadron (disambiguation), 94 Squadron (disambiguation),
    92 Squadron (disambiguation)

Concept terms: disambiguation, nihilistic, recklessness, sullen, annealing,
    negativity, initialization, recapitulation, streetwise, pde, pounce,
    revisionism, hyperspace, sidestep, bandwagon
Concept docs: Nihilistic (disambiguation), Recklessness (disambiguation),
    Manjack (disambiguation), Wajid (disambiguation), Kopitar (disambiguation),
    Rocourt (disambiguation), QRG (disambiguation),
    Maimaicheng (disambiguation), Varen (disambiguation), Gvr (disambiguation)

Concept terms: department, commune, communes, insee, france, see, also,
    southwestern, oise, marne, moselle, manche, eure, aisne, isère
Concept docs: Communes in France, Saint-Mard, Meurthe-et-Moselle,
    Saint-Firmin, Meurthe-et-Moselle, Saint-Clément, Meurthe-et-Moselle,
    Saint-Sardos, Lot-et-Garonne, Saint-Urcisse, Lot-et-Garonne, Saint-Sernin,
    Lot-et-Garonne, Saint-Robert, Lot-et-Garonne, Saint-Léon, Lot-et-Garonne,
    Saint-Astier, Lot-et-Garonne

Concept terms: genus, species, moth, family, lepidoptera, beetle, bulbophyllum,
    snail, database, natural, find, geometridae, reference, museum, noctuidae
Concept docs: Chelonia (genus), Palea (genus), Argiope (genus), Sphingini,
    Cribrilinidae, Tahla (genus), Gigartinales, Parapodia (genus),
    Alpina (moth), Arycanda (moth)

Concept terms: province, district, municipality, census, rural, iran,
    romanize, population, infobox, azerbaijan, village, town, central,
    settlement, kerman
Concept docs: New York State Senate elections, 2012,
    New York State Senate elections, 2008,
    New York State Senate elections, 2010,
    Alabama State House of Representatives elections, 2010,
    Albergaria-a-Velha, Municipalities of Italy, Municipality of Malmö,
    Delhi Municipality, Shanghai Municipality, Göteborg Municipality

Concept terms: genus, species, district, moth, family, province, iran, rural,
    romanize, census, village, population, lepidoptera, beetle, bulbophyllum
Concept docs: Chelonia (genus), Palea (genus), Argiope (genus), Sphingini,
    Tahla (genus), Cribrilinidae, Gigartinales, Alpina (moth), Arycanda (moth),
    Arauco (moth)

Concept terms: protein, football, league, encode, gene, play, team, bear,
```

```
season, player, club, reading, human, footballer, cup
Concept docs: Protein FAM186B, ARL6IP1, HIP1R, SGIP1, MTMR3,
  Gem-associated protein 6, Gem-associated protein 7, C2orf30, OS9 (gene),
  RP2 (gene)
```

The first two concepts remain ambiguous, but the rest appear to correspond to mean-ingful categories. The third appears to be composed of locales in France, the fourth and sixth of animal and bug taxonomies. The fifth concerns elections, municipalities, and government. The articles in the seventh concern proteins, while some of the terms also reference football, perhaps with a crossover of fitness of performance-enhancing drugs? Even though unexpected words appear in each, all the concepts exhibit some thematic coherence.

Querying and Scoring with a Low-Dimensional Representation

How relevant is a term to a document? How relevant are two terms to each other? Which documents most closely match a set of query terms? The original document-term matrix provides a shallow way to answer these questions. We can achieve a rele-vance score between two terms by computing the *cosine similarity* between their two column vectors in the matrix. Cosine similarity measures the angle between two vec-tors. Vectors that point in the same direction in the high-dimensional document space are thought to be relevant to each other. This is computed as the dot product of the vectors divided by the product of their lengths.

Cosine similarity sees wide use as a similarity metric between vectors of term and document weights in natural language and information retrieval applications. Like-wise, for two documents, a relevance score can be computed as the cosine similarity between their two row vectors. A relevance score between a term and document can simply be the element in the matrix at the intersection of both.

However, these scores come from shallow knowledge about the relationships between these entities, relying on simple frequency counts. LSA provides the ability to base these scores on a deeper understanding of the corpus. For example, if the term "artil-lery" appears nowhere in a document on the "Normandy landings" article but it men-tions "howitzer" frequently, the LSA representation may be able to recover the relation between "artillery" and the article based on the co-occurrence of "artillery" and "howitzer" in other documents.

The LSA representation also offers benefits from an efficiency standpoint. It packs the important information into a lower-dimensional representation that can be operated on instead of the original document-term matrix. Consider the task of finding the set of terms most relevant to a particular term. The naive approach requires computing the dot product between that term's column vector and every other column vector in the document-term matrix. This involves a number of multiplications proportional to the number of terms times the number of documents. LSA can achieve the same by looking up its concept-space representation and mapping it back into term space, requiring a number of multiplications only proportional to the number of terms times k. The low-rank approximation encodes the relevant patterns in the data, so the full corpus need not be queried.

In this final section, we'll build a primitive query engine using the LSA representation of our data. In the book repo, the code for this section is encapsulated in the LSAQueryEngine class.

Term-Term Relevance

LSA understands the relation between two terms as the cosine similarity between their two columns in the reconstructed low-rank matrix; that is, the matrix that would be produced if the three approximate factors were multiplied back together. One of the ideas behind LSA is that this matrix offers a more useful representation of the data. It offers this in a few ways:

- Accounting for synonymy by condensing related terms
- Accounting for polysemy by placing less weight on terms that have multiple meanings
- Throwing out noise

However, we need not actually calculate the contents of this matrix to discover the cosine similarity. Some linear algebra manipulation reveals that the cosine similarity between two columns in the reconstructed matrix is exactly equal to the cosine similarity between the corresponding columns in SV^T. Consider the task of finding the set of terms most relevant to a particular term. Finding the cosine similarity between a term and all other terms is equivalent to normalizing each row in VS to length 1 and then multiplying the row corresponding to that term by it. Each element in the resulting vector will contain a similarity between a term and the query term.

For the sake of brevity, the implementations of the methods that compute VS and normalize its rows are omitted, but they can be found in the repository. We carry them out in the LSAQueryEngine class's initialization so that they can be reused:

```
import breeze.linalg.{DenseMatrix => BDenseMatrix}

class LSAQueryEngine(
    val svd: SingularValueDecomposition[RowMatrix, Matrix],
    ...
) {

  val VS: BDenseMatrix[Double] = multiplyByDiagonalMatrix(svd.V, svd.s)
```

```
    val normalizedVS: BDenseMatrix[Double] = rowsNormalized(VS)
    ...
```

In the initializer, we also compute invert our id-to-document and id-to-term map-
pings so that we can map query strings back into positions in our matrices:

```
val idTerms: Map[String, Int] = termIds.zipWithIndex.toMap
val idDocs: Map[String, Long] = docIds.map(_.swap)
```

Now, to find terms relevant to a term:

```
def topTermsForTerm(termId: Int): Seq[(Double, Int)] = {
  val rowVec = normalizedVS(termId, ::).t ❶

  val termScores = (normalizedVS * termRowVec).toArray.zipWithIndex ❷

  termScores.sortBy(-_._1).take(10) ❸
}

def printTopTermsForTerm(term: String): Unit = {
  val idWeights = topTermsForTerm(idTerms(term))
  println(idWeights.map { case (score, id) =>
    (termIds(id), score) ❹
  }.mkString(", "))
}
```

❶ Look up the row in VS corresponding to the given term ID

❷ Compute scores against every term

❸ Find the terms with the highest scores

❹ Compute a mapping of terms to term IDs

If you are following along in spark-shell, this functionality can be loaded using:

```
import com.cloudera.datascience.lsa.LSAQueryEngine

val termIdfs = idfModel.idf.toArray
val queryEngine = new LSAQueryEngine(svd, termIds, docIds, termIdfs)
```

Here are the highest-scored terms for a few example terms:

```
queryEngine.printTopTermsForTerm("algorithm")

(algorithm,1.000000000000002), (heuristic,0.8773199836391916),
(compute,0.8561015487853708), (constraint,0.8370707630657652),
(optimization,0.8331940333186296), (complexity,0.823738607119692),
(algorithmic,0.8227315888559854), (iterative,0.822364922633442),
(recursive,0.8176921180556759), (minimization,0.8160188481409465)

queryEngine.printTopTermsForTerm("radiohead")
```

```
(radiohead,0.9999999999999993), (lyrically,0.8837403315233519),
(catchy,0.8780717902060333), (riff,0.861326571452104),
(lyricsthe,0.8460798060853993), (lyric,0.8434937575368959),
(upbeat,0.8410212279939793), (song,0.8280655506697948),
(musically,0.8239497926624353), (anthemic,0.8207874883055177)

queryEngine.printTopTermsForTerm("tarantino")

(tarantino,1.0), (soderbergh,0.780999345687437),
(buscemi,0.7386998898933894), (screenplay,0.7347041267543623),
(spielberg,0.7342534745182226), (dicaprio,0.7279146798149239),
(filmmaking,0.7261103750076819), (lumet,0.7259812377657624),
(directorial,0.7195131565316943), (biopic,0.7164037755577743)
```

Document-Document Relevance

The same goes for computing relevance scores between documents. To find the similarity between two documents, compute the cosine similarity between $u_1^T S$ and $u_2^T S$, where u_i is the row in U corresponding to document i. To find the similarity between a document and all other documents, compute normalized(US) u_t.

Similar to normalized(VS), we compute normalized(US) in the initialization of the LSAQueryEngine class so the results can be reused. In this case, the implementation is slightly different because U is backed by an RDD, not a local matrix.

```
val US: RowMatrix = multiplyByDiagonalRowMatrix(svd.U, svd.s)
val normalizedUS: RowMatrix = distributedRowsNormalized(US)
```

Then, to find documents relevant to a document:

```
import org.apache.spark.mllib.linalg.Matrices

def topDocsForDoc(docId: Long): Seq[(Double, Long)] = {
  val docRowArr = normalizedUS.rows.zipWithUniqueId.map(_.swap)
    .lookup(docId).head.toArray  ❶
  val docRowVec = Matrices.dense(docRowArr.length, 1, docRowArr)

  val docScores = normalizedUS.multiply(docRowVec)  ❷

  val allDocWeights = docScores.rows.map(_.toArray(0)).
    zipWithUniqueId()  ❸

  allDocWeights.filter(!_._1.isNaN).top(10)  ❹
}

def printTopDocsForDoc(doc: String): Unit = {
  val idWeights = topDocsForDoc(idDocs(doc))
  println(idWeights.map { case (score, id) =>
    (docIds(id), score)
  }.mkString(", "))
}
```

❶ Look up the row in US corresponding to the given doc ID.

❷ Compute scores against every doc.

❸ Find the docs with the highest scores.

❹ Docs can end up with NaN score if their row in U is all zeros. Filter these out.

Here are the most similar documents for a few example documents:

```
queryEngine.printTopDocsForDoc("Romania")

(Romania,0.9999999999999994), (Roma in Romania,0.9229332158078395),
(Kingdom of Romania,0.9176138537751187),
(Anti-Romanian discrimination,0.9131983116426412),
(Timeline of Romanian history,0.9124093989500675),
(Romania and the euro,0.9123191881625798),
(History of Romania,0.9095848558045102),
(Romania–United States relations,0.9016913779787574),
(Wiesel Commission,0.9016106300096606),
(List of Romania-related topics,0.8981305676612493)

queryEngine.printTopDocsForDoc("Brad Pitt")

(Brad Pitt,0.9999999999999984), (Aaron Eckhart,0.8935447577397551),
(Leonardo DiCaprio,0.8930359829082504), (Winona Ryder,0.8903497762653693),
(Ryan Phillippe,0.8847178312465214), (Claudette Colbert,0.8812403821804665),
(Clint Eastwood,0.8785765085978459), (Reese Witherspoon,0.876540742663427),
(Meryl Streep in the 2000s,0.8751593996242115),
(Kate Winslet,0.873124888198288)

queryEngine.printTopDocsForDoc("Radiohead")

(Radiohead,1.0000000000000016), (Fightstar,0.9461712602479349),
(R.E.M.,0.9456251852095919), (Incubus (band),0.9434650141836163),
(Audioslave,0.9411291455765148), (Tonic (band),0.9374518874425788),
(Depeche Mode,0.9370085419199352), (Megadeth,0.9355302294384438),
(Alice in Chains,0.9347862053793862), (Blur (band),0.9347436350811016)
```

Document-Term Relevance

What about computing a relevance score between a term and a document? This is equivalent to finding the element corresponding to that term and document in the reduced-rank approximation of the document-term matrix. This is equal to $u_d^T S v_t$, where u_d is the row in U corresponding to the document, and v_t is the row in V corresponding to the term. Some simple linear algebra manipulation reveals that computing a similarity between a term and *every* document is equivalent to $US v_t$. Each element in the resulting vector will contain a similarity between a document and the query term. In the other direction, the similarity between a document and every term comes from $u_d^T SV$:

```
def topDocsForTerm(termId: Int): Seq[(Double, Long)] = {
  val rowArr = (0 until svd.V.numCols).
    map(i => svd.V(termId, i)).toArray
  val rowVec = Matrices.dense(termRowArr.length, 1, termRowArr)

  val docScores = US.multiply(rowVec) ❶

  val allDocWeights = docScores.rows.map(_.toArray(0)).
    zipWithUniqueId() ❷
  allDocWeights.top(10)
}

def printTopDocsForTerm(term: String): Unit = {
  val idWeights = topDocsForTerm(US, svd.V, idTerms(term))
  println(idWeights.map { case (score, id) =>
    (docIds(id), score)
  }.mkString(", "))
}
```

❶ Compute scores against every doc.

❷ Find the docs with the highest scores.

```
queryEngine.printTopDocsForTerm("fir")

(Silver tree,0.006292909647173194),
(See the forest for the trees,0.004785047583508223),
(Eucalyptus tree,0.004592837783089319),
(Sequoia tree,0.004497446632469554),
(Willow tree,0.004442871594515006),
(Coniferous tree,0.004429936059594164),
(Tulip Tree,0.004420469113273123),
(National tree,0.004381572286629475),
(Cottonwood tree,0.004374705020233878),
(Juniper Tree,0.004370895085141889)

queryEngine.printTopDocsForTerm("graph")

(K-factor (graph theory),0.07074443599385992),
(Mesh Graph,0.05843133228896666), (Mesh graph,0.05843133228896666),
(Grid Graph,0.05762071784234877), (Grid graph,0.05762071784234877),
(Graph factor,0.056799669054782564), (Graph (economics),0.05603848473056094),
(Skin graph,0.05512936759365371), (Edgeless graph,0.05507918292342141),
(Traversable graph,0.05507918292342141)
```

Multiple-Term Queries

Lastly, what about servicing queries with multiple terms? That is, finding documents relevant to a single term involved by selecting the row corresponding to that term from *V*. This is equivalent to multiplying *V* by a term vector with a single nonzero entry. To move to multiple terms, instead compute the concept-space vector by simply multiplying *V* by a term vector with nonzero entries for multiply terms. To maintain the weighting scheme used for the original document-term matrix, set the value for each term in the query to its inverse document frequency:

```
termIdfs = idfModel.idf.toArray
```

In one sense, querying in this way is like adding a new document to the corpus with just a few terms, finding its representation as a new row of the low-rank document-term matrix approximation, and then discovering the cosine similarity between it and the other entries in this matrix:

```
import breeze.linalg.{SparseVector => BSparseVector}

def termsToQueryVector(terms: Seq[String])
  : BSparseVector[Double] = {
  val indices = terms.map(idTerms(_)).toArray
  val values = terms.map(idfs(_)).toArray
  new BSparseVector[Double](indices, values, idTerms.size)
}

def topDocsForTermQuery(query: BSparseVector[Double])
  : Seq[(Double, Long)] = {
  val breezeV = new BDenseMatrix[Double](V.numRows, V.numCols,
    V.toArray)
  val termRowArr = (breezeV.t * query).toArray

  val termRowVec = Matrices.dense(termRowArr.length, 1, termRowArr)

  val docScores = US.multiply(termRowVec)  ❶

  val allDocWeights = docScores.rows.map(_.toArray(0)).
    zipWithUniqueId()  ❷
  allDocWeights.top(10)
}

def printTopDocsForTermQuery(terms: Seq[String]): Unit = {
  val queryVec = termsToQueryVector(terms)
  val idWeights = topDocsForTermQuery(queryVec)
  println(idWeights.map { case (score, id) =>
    (docIds(id), score)
  }.mkString(", "))
}
```

❶ Compute scores against every doc

❷ Find the docs with the highest scores

```
queryEngine.printTopDocsForTermQuery(Seq("factorization", "decomposition"))

(K-factor (graph theory),0.04335677416674133),
(Matrix Algebra,0.038074479507460755),
(Matrix algebra,0.038074479507460755),
```

```
(Zero Theorem,0.03758005783639301),
(Birkhoff-von Neumann Theorem,0.03594539874814679),
(Enumeration theorem,0.03498444607374629),
(Pythagoras' theorem,0.03489110483887526),
(Thales theorem,0.03481592682203685),
(Cpt theorem,0.03478175099368145),
(Fuss' theorem,0.034739350150484904)
```

Where to Go from Here

SVD and its sister technique, PCA, have a wide variety of applications outside of text analysis. A common method of recognizing human faces known as *eigenfaces* relies on it to understand the patterns of variation in human appearance. In climate research, it is used to find global temperature trends from disparate noisy data sources like tree rings. Michael Mann's famous "hockey stick" graph (*http://bit.ly/2qcHozy*), depicting the rise of temperatures throughout the 20th century, in fact depicts a *concept*. SVD and PCA are also useful in the visualization of high-dimensional data sets. When a data set is reduced down to its first two or three concepts, it can be plotted on a graph that humans can view.

A variety of other methods exist for understanding large corpora of text. For example, a technique known as latent dirichlet allocation (*http://bit.ly/2jxBq8h*) is useful in many similar applications. As a *topic model*, it infers a set of topics from a corpus and assigns each document a level of participation in each topic.

## CHAPTER 7

Analyzing Co-Occurrence Networks with GraphX

Josh Wills

It's a small world. It keeps recrossing itself.
—David Mitchell

Data scientists come in all shapes and sizes from a remarkably diverse set of academic backgrounds. Although many have some training in disciplines like computer science, mathematics, and physics, others have studied neuroscience, sociology, and political science. Although these fields study different things (e.g., brains, people, political institutions) and have not traditionally required students to learn how to program, they all share two important characteristics that have made them fertile training ground for data scientists.

First, all of these fields are interested in understanding *relationships* between entities, whether between neurons, individuals, or countries, and how these relationships affect the observed behavior of the entities. Second, the explosion of digital data over the past decade has given researchers access to vast quantities of information about these relationships and required that they develop new skills in order to acquire and manage these data sets.

As these researchers began to collaborate with each other and with computer scientists, they also discovered that many of the techniques they were using to analyze relationships could be applied to problems across domains, and the field of *network science* was born. Network science applies tools from *graph theory*, the mathematical discipline that studies the properties of pairwise relationships (called *edges*) between a set of entities (called *vertices*). Graph theory is also widely used in computer science to study everything from data structures to computer architecture to the design of networks like the internet.

Graph theory and network science have had a significant impact in the business world as well. Almost every major internet company derives a significant fraction of its value from its ability to build and analyze an important network of relationships better than any of its competitors: the recommendation algorithms used at Amazon and Netflix rely on the networks of consumer-item purchases (Amazon) and user-movie ratings (Netflix) that each company creates and controls. Facebook and LinkedIn have built graphs of relationships between people that they analyze in order to organize content feeds, promote advertisements, and broker new connections. And perhaps most famously of all, Google used the PageRank algorithm that the founders developed to create a fundamentally better way to search the web.

The computational and analytical needs of these network-centric companies helped drive the creation of distributed processing frameworks like MapReduce as well as the hiring of data scientists who were capable of using these new tools to analyze and create value from the ever-expanding volume of data. One of the earliest use cases for MapReduce was to create a scalable and reliable way to solve the equation at the heart of PageRank. Over time, as the graphs became larger and data scientists needed to analyze them faster, new graph-parallel processing frameworks—like Pregel at Google, Giraph at Yahoo!, and GraphLab at Carnegie Mellon—were developed. These frameworks supported fault-tolerant, in-memory, iterative, and graph-centric processing, and were capable of performing certain types of graph computations orders of magnitude faster than the equivalent data-parallel MapReduce jobs.

In this chapter, we're going to introduce a Spark library called GraphX, which extends Spark to support many of the graph-parallel processing tasks that Pregel, Giraph, and GraphLab support. Although it cannot handle every graph computation as quickly as the custom graph frameworks do, the fact that it is a Spark library means that it is relatively easy to bring GraphX into your normal data analysis workflow whenever you want to analyze a network-centric data set. With it, you can combine graph-parallel programming with the familiar Spark abstractions you are used to working with.

GraphX and GraphFrames

GraphX was created prior to the introduction of DataFrames in Spark 1.3, and its APIs are all designed to work with RDDs. More recently, effort is being made to port GraphX to the new APIs developed around DataFrames; it is called (appropriately enough) GraphFrames. GraphFrames promises a number of benefits over the legacy GraphX API, including richer support for reading and writing graphs to serialized data formats via the DataFrame API and expressive graph queries.

At the time we were writing the second edition of the book, not all of the analyses that we conduct in this chapter were possible against the GraphFrames API on Spark 2.1, so we decided to continue using the fully functional GraphX API for this chapter. The

---

good news is that the GraphFrames API takes a lot of inspiration from GraphX, so all the methods and concepts we introduce in this chapter have a one-to-one mapping to GraphFrames. We're looking forward to migrating to GraphFrames for the (currently purely hypothetical) next edition of this book; you can follow the status of the project (*http://graphframes.github.io*).

The MEDLINE Citation Index: A Network Analysis

MEDLINE (Medical Literature Analysis and Retrieval System Online) is a database of academic papers that have been published in journals covering the life sciences and medicine. It is managed and released by the US National Library of Medicine (NLM), a division of the National Institutes of Health (NIH). Its citation index, which tracks the publication of articles across thousands of journals, can trace its history back to 1879, and it has been available online to medical schools since 1971 and to the general public via the web since 1996. The main database contains more than 20 million articles going back to the early 1950s and is updated 5 days a week.

Due to the volume of citations and the frequency of updates, the research community developed an extensive set of semantic tags, called MeSH (Medical Subject Headings), that are applied to all of the citations in the index. These tags provide a meaningful framework that can be used to explore relationships between documents to facilitate literature reviews, and they have also been used as the basis for building data products: in 2001, PubGene demonstrated one of the first production applications of biomedical text mining by launching a search engine that allowed users to explore the graph of MeSH terms that connect related documents together.

In this chapter, we're going to use Scala, Spark, and GraphX to acquire, transform, and then analyze the network of MeSH terms on a recently published subset of citation data from MEDLINE. The network analysis we'll be performing was inspired by the paper "Large-Scale Structure of a Network of Co-Occurring MeSH Terms: Statistical Analysis of Macroscopic Properties" (*https://www.ncbi.nlm.nih.gov/pmc/articles/PMC4090190/*), by Kastrin et al. (2014), although we'll be using a different subset of the citation data and performing the analysis with GraphX instead of the R packages and C++ code used in that paper.

Our goal will be to get a feel for the shape and properties of the citation graph. We'll attack this from a few different angles to get a full view of the data set. First, we'll get our feet wet by looking at the major topics and their co-occurrences—a simpler analysis that doesn't require using GraphX. Then we'll look for *connected components*—can one follow a path of citations from any topic to any other topic, or is the data actually a set of separate smaller graphs? We'll move on to look at the *degree distribution* of the graph, which gives a sense of how the relevance of topics can vary, and find the topics that are connected to the most other topics. Last, we'll compute a couple of slightly more advanced graph statistics: the *clustering coefficient* and the *average path length*. Among other uses, these allow us to understand how similar the citation graph is to other common real-world graphs like the web and Facebook's social network.

Getting the Data

We can retrieve a sample of the citation index data from the NIH's FTP server:

```
$ mkdir medline_data
$ cd medline_data
$ wget ftp://ftp.nlm.nih.gov/nlmdata/sample/medline/*.gz
```

Let's uncompress the citation data and examine it before we load it into HDFS:

```
$ gunzip *.gz
$ ls -ltr
...
total 1814128
-rw-r--r--  1 jwills  staff  145188012 Dec  3  2015 medsamp2016h.xml
-rw-r--r--  1 jwills  staff  133663105 Dec  3  2015 medsamp2016g.xml
-rw-r--r--  1 jwills  staff  131298588 Dec  3  2015 medsamp2016f.xml
-rw-r--r--  1 jwills  staff  156910066 Dec  3  2015 medsamp2016e.xml
-rw-r--r--  1 jwills  staff  112711106 Dec  3  2015 medsamp2016d.xml
-rw-r--r--  1 jwills  staff  105189622 Dec  3  2015 medsamp2016c.xml
-rw-r--r--  1 jwills  staff   72705330 Dec  3  2015 medsamp2016b.xml
-rw-r--r--  1 jwills  staff   71147066 Dec  3  2015 medsamp2016a.xml
```

The sample files contain about 600 MB of XML-formatted data, uncompressed. Each entry in the sample files is a `MedlineCitation` record, which contains information about the publication of an article in a biomedical journal, including the journal name, issue, publication date, the names of the authors, the abstract, and the set of MeSH keywords that are associated with the article. In addition, each of the MeSH keywords has an attribute to indicate whether or not the concept the keyword refers to was a major topic of the article. Let's take a look at the first citation record in *medsamp2016a.xml*:

```
<MedlineCitation Owner="PIP" Status="MEDLINE">
<PMID Version="1">12255379</PMID>
<DateCreated>
  <Year>1980</Year>
  <Month>01</Month>
  <Day>03</Day>
</DateCreated>
...
<MeshHeadingList>
...
  <MeshHeading>
    <DescriptorName MajorTopicYN="N">Humans</DescriptorName>
  </MeshHeading>
```

```
<MeshHeading>
  <DescriptorName MajorTopicYN="Y">Intelligence</DescriptorName>
</MeshHeading>
<MeshHeading>
  <DescriptorName MajorTopicYN="Y">Rorschach Test</DescriptorName>
</MeshHeading>
...
</MeshHeadingList>
...
</MedlineCitation>
```

In our latent semantic analysis of Wikipedia articles, we were primarily interested in the unstructured article text contained in each of the XML records. But for our co-occurrence analysis, we're going to want to extract the values contained within the DescriptorName tags by parsing the structure of the XML directly. Fortunately, Scala comes with an excellent library called *scala-xml* for parsing and querying XML documents directly, which we can use to help us out.

Let's get started by loading the citation data into HDFS:

```
$ hadoop fs -mkdir medline
$ hadoop fs -put *.xml medline
```

Now we can start up an instance of the Spark shell. The chapter relies on the code described in Chapter 6 for parsing XML-formatted data. To compile this code into a JAR so that we can make use of it, go into the *ch07-graph/* directory in the Git repo and build it with Maven:

```
$ cd ch07-graph/
$ mvn package
$ cd target
$ spark-shell --jars ch07-graph-2.0.0-jar-with-dependencies.jar
```

Let's write a function to read the XML-formatted MEDLINE data into the shell:

```
import edu.umd.cloud9.collection.XMLInputFormat
import org.apache.spark.sql.{Dataset, SparkSession}
import org.apache.hadoop.io.{Text, LongWritable}
import org.apache.hadoop.conf.Configuration

def loadMedline(spark: SparkSession, path: String) = {
  import spark.implicits._
  @transient val conf = new Configuration()
  conf.set(XMLInputFormat.START_TAG_KEY, "<MedlineCitation ")
  conf.set(XMLInputFormat.END_TAG_KEY, "</MedlineCitation>")
  val sc = spark.sparkContext
  val in = sc.newAPIHadoopFile(path, classOf[XMLInputFormat],
    classOf[LongWritable], classOf[Text], conf)
  in.map(line => line._2.toString).toDS()
}
val medlineRaw = loadMedline(spark, "medline")
```

We are setting the value of the START_TAG_KEY configuration parameter to be the prefix of the MedlineCitation start tag, because the values of the tag's attributes may change from record to record. The XmlInputFormat will include these varying attributes in the record values that are returned.

Parsing XML Documents with Scala's XML Library

Scala has an interesting history with XML. Since version 1.2, Scala has treated XML as a first-class data type. This means that the following code is syntactically valid:

```
import scala.xml._

val cit = <MedlineCitation>data</MedlineCitation>
```

This support for XML literals has always been somewhat unusual among major programming languages, especially as other serialization formats such as JSON have come into widespread use. In 2012, Martin Odersky published the following note to the Scala language mailing list:

> [XML literals] Seemed a great idea at the time, now it sticks out like a sore thumb. I believe with the new string interpolation scheme we will be able to put all of XML processing in the libraries, which should be a big win.

As of Scala 2.11, the scala.xml package is no longer a part of the core Scala libraries. After you upgrade, you will need to explicitly include the scala-xml dependency to use the Scala XML libraries in your projects.

With that caveat in mind, Scala's support for parsing and querying XML documents is truly excellent, and we will be availing ourselves of it to help extract the information we want from the MEDLINE citations. Let's get started by pulling the unparsed first citation record into our Spark shell:

```
val rawXml = medlineRaw.take(1)(0)
val elem = XML.loadString(rawXml)
```

The elem variable is an instance of the scala.xml.Elem class, which is how Scala represents an individual node in an XML document. The class contains a number of built-in functions for retrieving information about the node and its contents, such as:

```
elem.label
elem.attributes
```

It also contains a small set of operators for finding the children of a given XML node; the first one, for retrieving a node's direct children by name, is called \:

```
elem \ "MeshHeadingList"
...
NodeSeq(<MeshHeadingList>
<MeshHeading>
<DescriptorName MajorTopicYN="N">Behavior</DescriptorName>
```

```
</MeshHeading>
...
```

The \ operator only works on *direct* children of the node; if we execute `elem \ "Mesh
Heading"`, the result is an empty `NodeSeq`. To extract nondirect children of a given
node, we need to use the \\ operator:

```
elem \\ "MeshHeading"
...
NodeSeq(<MeshHeading>
<DescriptorName MajorTopicYN="N">Behavior</DescriptorName>
</MeshHeading>,
...
```

We can also use the \\ operator to get at the `DescriptorName` entries directly, and
then retrieve the MeSH tags within each node by calling the `text` function on each
element of the `NodeSeq`:

```
(elem \\ "DescriptorName").map(_.text)
...
List(Behavior, Congenital Abnormalities, ...
```

Finally, note that each of the `DescriptorName` entries has an attribute called `MajorTo
picYN` that indicates whether or not this MeSH tag was a major topic of the cited arti-
cle. We can look up the value of attributes of XML tags using the \ and \\ operators if
we preface the attribute name with an @ symbol. We can use this to create a filter that
only returns the names of the major MeSH tags for each article:

```
def majorTopics(record: String): Seq[String] = {
  val elem = XML.loadString(record)
  val dn = elem \\ "DescriptorName"
  val mt = dn.filter(n => (n \ "@MajorTopicYN").text == "Y")
  mt.map(n => n.text)
}
majorTopics(elem)
```

Now that we have our XML parsing code working locally, let's apply it to parse the
MeSH codes for each citation record in our RDD and cache the result:

```
val medline = medlineRaw.map(majorTopics)
medline.cache()
medline.take(1)(0)
```

Analyzing the MeSH Major Topics and Their Co-Occurrences

Now that we've extracted the MeSH tags we want from the MEDLINE citation
records, let's get a feel for the overall distribution of tags in our data set by calculating
some basic summary statistics using Spark SQL, such as the number of records and a
histogram of the frequencies of various major MeSH topics:

```
medline.count()
val topics = medline.flatMap(mesh => mesh).toDF("topic")
topics.createOrReplaceTempView("topics")
val topicDist = spark.sql("""
  SELECT topic, COUNT(*) cnt
  FROM topics
  GROUP BY topic
  ORDER BY cnt DESC""")
topicDist.count()
...
res: Long = 14548
topicDist.show()
...
+--------------------+----+
|               topic| cnt|
+--------------------+----+
|            Research|1649|
|             Disease|1349|
|           Neoplasms|1123|
|        Tuberculosis|1066|
|       Public Policy| 816|
|        Jurisprudence| 796|
|           Demography| 763|
| Population Dynamics| 753|
|           Economics| 690|
|            Medicine| 682|
...
```

The most frequently occurring major topics are, unsurprisingly, some of the most general ones, like the uber-generic Research and Disease, or the slightly less generic Neoplasms and Tuberculosis. Fortunately, there are more than 13,000 different major topics in our data set, and given that the most frequently occurring major topic only occurs in a tiny fraction of all the documents (1,649/240,000 ~ 0.7%), we would expect that the overall distribution of the number of documents containing a topic has a relatively long tail. We can verify this by creating a frequency count of the values of the topicDist DataFrame:

```
topicDist.createOrReplaceTempView("topic_dist")
spark.sql("""
  SELECT cnt, COUNT(*) dist
  FROM topic_dist
  GROUP BY cnt
  ORDER BY dist DESC
  LIMIT 10""").show()
...
+---+----+
|cnt|dist|
+---+----+
|  1|3106|
|  2|1699|
|  3|1207|
```

```
|  4|  902|
|  5|  680|
|  6|  571|
|  7|  490|
|  8|  380|
|  9|  356|
| 10|  296|
+---+----+
```

Of course, our primary interest is in co-occurring MeSH topics. Each entry in the `medline` data set is a list of strings that are the names of topics that are mentioned in each citation record. To get the co-occurrences, we need to generate all of the two-element subsets of this list of strings. Fortunately, Scala's Collections library has a built-in method called `combinations` to make generating these sublists extremely easy. `combinations` returns an `Iterator`, meaning that the combinations need not all be held in memory at the same time:

```
val list = List(1, 2, 3)
val combs = list.combinations(2)
combs.foreach(println)
```

When using this function to generate sublists that we are going to aggregate with Spark, we need to be careful that all of the lists are sorted in the same way. This is because the lists returned from the `combinations` function depend on the order of the input elements, and lists with the same elements in a different order are not equal to one another:

```
val combs = list.reverse.combinations(2)
combs.foreach(println)
List(3, 2) == List(2, 3)
```

Therefore, when we generate the two-element sublists for each citation record, we'll ensure that the list of topics is sorted before we call `combinations`:

```
val topicPairs = medline.flatMap(t => {
  t.sorted.combinations(2)
}).toDF("pairs")
topicPairs.createOrReplaceTempView("topic_pairs")
val cooccurs = spark.sql("""
  SELECT pairs, COUNT(*) cnt
  FROM topic_pairs
  GROUP BY pairs""")
cooccurs.cache()
cooccurs.count()
```

Because there are 14,548 topics in our data, there are potentially 14,548*14,547/2 = 105,814,878 unordered co-occurrence pairs. However, the count of co-occurrences reveals that only 213,745 pairs actually appear in the data set, a tiny fraction of the possible pairs. If we look at the most frequently appearing co-occurrence pairs in the data, we see this:

```
cooccurs.createOrReplaceTempView("cooccurs")
spark.sql("""
  SELECT pairs, cnt
  FROM cooccurs
  ORDER BY cnt DESC
  LIMIT 10""").collect().foreach(println)
...
[WrappedArray(Demography, Population Dynamics),288]
[WrappedArray(Government Regulation, Social Control, Formal),254]
[WrappedArray(Emigration and Immigration, Population Dynamics),230]
[WrappedArray(Acquired Immunodeficiency Syndrome, HIV Infections),220]
[WrappedArray(Antibiotics, Antitubercular, Dermatologic Agents),205]
[WrappedArray(Analgesia, Anesthesia),183]
[WrappedArray(Economics, Population Dynamics),181]
[WrappedArray(Analgesia, Anesthesia and Analgesia),179]
[WrappedArray(Anesthesia, Anesthesia and Analgesia),177]
[WrappedArray(Population Dynamics, Population Growth),174]
```

As we might have suspected from the counts of the most frequently occurring major topics, the most frequently occurring co-occurrence pairs are also relatively uninteresting. Most of the top pairs, such as (Demography, Population Dynamics), are either the product of two of the most frequently occurring individual topics, or terms that occur together so frequently that they are nearly synonyms, like (Analgesia, Anesthesia). There's nothing surprising or informative about the fact that these topic pairs exist in the data.

Constructing a Co-Occurrence Network with GraphX

As we saw in the preceding section, when we're studying co-occurrence networks, our standard tools for summarizing data don't provide us much insight. The overall summary statistics we can calculate, like raw counts, don't give us a feel for the overall structure of the relationships in the network, and the co-occurrence pairs that we can see at the extremes of the distribution are usually the ones that we care about least.

What we really want to do is analyze the co-occurrence network: by thinking of the topics as vertices in a graph, and the existence of a citation record that features both topics as an edge between those two vertices. Then, we could compute network-centric statistics that would help us understand the overall structure of the network and identify interesting local outlier vertices that are worthy of further investigation.

We can also use co-occurrence networks to identify meaningful interactions between entities that are worthy of further investigation. Figure 7-1 shows part of a co-occurrence graph for combinations of cancer drugs that were associated with adverse events in the patients who were taking them. We can use the information in these graphs to help us design clinical trials to study these interactions.

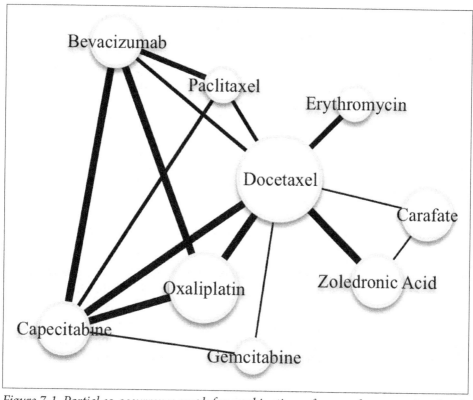

Figure 7-1. Partial co-occurrence graph for combinations of cancer drugs associated with adverse events in patients

In the same way that MLlib provides a set of patterns and algorithms for creating machine learning models in Spark, GraphX is a Spark library that is designed to help us analyze various kinds of networks using the language and tools of graph theory. Because GraphX builds on top of Spark, it inherits all of Spark's scalability properties, which means that it is capable of carrying out analyses on extremely large graphs that are distributed across multiple machines. GraphX also integrates well with the rest of the Spark platform and, as we will see, makes it easy for data scientists to move from writing data-parallel ETL routines against RDDs to executing graph-parallel algorithms against a graph, to analyzing and summarizing the output of the graph computation in a data-parallel fashion again. It is the seamless way that GraphX allows us to introduce graph-style processing into our analytic workflow, which makes it so powerful.

Like the Dataset API, GraphX is built on top of Spark's fundamental data primitive, the RDD. Specifically, GraphX is based on two custom RDD implementations that are optimized for working with graphs. The `VertexRDD[VD]` is a specialized implementation of `RDD[(VertexId, VD)]`, in which the `VertexID` type is an instance of `Long` and is required for every vertex, while the VD can be any other type of data associated with the vertex, and is called the *vertex attribute*. The EdgeRDD[ED] is a specialized implementation of RDD[Edge[ED]], where Edge is a case class that contains two VertexId values and an *edge attribute* of type ED. Both the VertexRDD and the EdgeRDD have internal indices within each partition of the data that are designed to facilitate fast joins and attribute updates. Given both a VertexRDD and an associated EdgeRDD, we can create an instance of the Graph class, which contains a number of methods for efficiently performing graph computations.

The first requirement in creating a graph is to have a Long value that can be used as an identifier for each vertex in the graph. This is a bit of a problem for us in constructing our co-occurrence network, because all of our topics are identified as strings. We need a way to come up with a unique 64-bit value that can be associated with each topic string, and ideally, we'd like to do it in a distributed fashion so that it can be done quickly across all of our data.

One option would be to use the built-in hashCode method, which will generate a 32-bit integer for any given Scala object. For our problem, which only has 13,000 vertices in the graph, the hash code trick will probably work. But for graphs that have millions or tens of millions of vertices, the probability of a hash code collision might be unacceptably high. For this reason, we're going to copy a hashing implementation from Google's Guava Library to create a unique 64-bit identifier for each topic using the MD5 hashing algorithm:

```
import java.nio.charset.StandardCharsets
import java.security.MessageDigest

def hashId(str: String): Long = {
 val bytes = MessageDigest.getInstance("MD5").
   digest(str.getBytes(StandardCharsets.UTF_8))
  (bytes(0) & 0xFFL) |
  ((bytes(1) & 0xFFL) << 8) |
  ((bytes(2) & 0xFFL) << 16) |
  ((bytes(3) & 0xFFL) << 24) |
  ((bytes(4) & 0xFFL) << 32) |
  ((bytes(5) & 0xFFL) << 40) |
  ((bytes(6) & 0xFFL) << 48) |
  ((bytes(7) & 0xFFL) << 56)
}
```

We can apply this hashing function to our MEDLINE data to generate a data frame that will be the basis for the set of vertices in our co-occurrence graph. We can also do a simple verification check to ensure that the hash value was unique for each topic:

```
import org.apache.spark.sql.Row
val vertices = topics.map{ case Row(topic: String) =>
(hashId(topic), topic) }.toDF("hash", "topic")
val uniqueHashes = vertices.agg(countDistinct("hash")).take(1)
```

```
...
res: Array[Row] = Array([14548])
```

We will generate the edges for the graph from the co-occurrence counts that we created in the previous section, using the hashing function to map each topic name to its
corresponding vertex ID. A good habit to get into when generating edges is to ensure
that the left side VertexId (which GraphX refers to as the src) is *less* than the right
side VertexId (which GraphX refers to as the dst). Although most of the algorithms
in the GraphX library do not assume anything about the relationship between src
and dst, there are a few that do, so it's a good idea to implement this pattern early so
that you don't have to think about it later on:

```
import org.apache.spark.graphx._

val edges = cooccurs.map{ case Row(topics: Seq[_], cnt: Long) =>
  val ids = topics.map(_.toString).map(hashId).sorted
  Edge(ids(0), ids(1), cnt)
}
```

Now that we have both the vertices and the edges, we can create our Graph instance
and mark it as cached so we can keep it around for subsequent processing:

```
val vertexRDD = vertices.rdd.map{
  case Row(hash: Long, topic: String) => (hash, topic)
}
val topicGraph = Graph(vertexRDD, edges.rdd)
topicGraph.cache()
```

The vertexRDD and edges arguments that we used to construct the Graph instance
were regular RDDs—we didn't even deduplicate the entries in the vertices so that
there was only a single instance of each topic. Fortunately, the Graph API does this
for us, converting the RDDs we passed in to a VertexRDD and an EdgeRDD, so that the
vertex counts are now unique:

```
vertexRDD.count()
...
280464

topicGraph.vertices.count()
...
14548
```

Note that if there are duplicate entries in the EdgeRDD for a given pair of vertices, the
Graph API will not deduplicate them: GraphX allows us to create *multigraphs*, which
can have multiple edges with different values between the same pair of vertices. This
can be useful in applications where the vertices in the graph represent rich objects,
like people or businesses, that may have many different kinds of relationships among
them (e.g., friends, family members, customers, partners, etc.). It also allows us to
treat the edges as either directed or undirected, depending on the context.

Understanding the Structure of Networks

When we explore the contents of a table, there are a number of summary statistics about the columns that we want to calculate right away so that we can get a feel for the structure of the data and explore any problem areas. The same principle applies when we are investigating a new graph, although the summary statistics we are interested in are slightly different. The Graph class provides built-in methods for calculating a number of these statistics and, in combination with the regular Spark RDD APIs, makes it easy for us to quickly get a feel for the structure of a graph to guide our exploration.

Connected Components

One of the most basic things we want to know about a graph is whether or not it is *connected*. In a connected graph, it is possible for any vertex to reach any other vertex by following a *path*, which is simply a sequence of edges that lead from one vertex to another. If the graph isn't connected, it may be divided into a smaller set of connected subgraphs that we can investigate individually.

Connectedness is a fundamental graph property, so it shouldn't be surprising that GraphX includes a built-in method for identifying the connected components in a graph. You'll note that as soon as you call the connectedComponents method on the graph, a number of Spark jobs will be launched, and then you'll finally see the result of the computation:

```
val connectedComponentGraph = topicGraph.connectedComponents()
```

Look at the type of the object returned by the connectedComponents method: it's another instance of the Graph class, but the type of the vertex attribute is a VertexId that is used as a unique identifier for the component that each vertex belongs to. To get a count of the number of connected components and their size, we can convert the VertexRDD back into a data frame and then use our standard toolkit:

```
val componentDF = connectedComponentGraph.vertices.toDF("vid", "cid")
val componentCounts = componentDF.groupBy("cid").count()
componentCounts.count()
...
878
```

Let's look a bit closer at some of the largest connected components:

```
componentCounts.orderBy(desc("count")).show()
...
+--------------------+-----+
|                 cid|count|
+--------------------+-----+
|-9218306090261648869|13610|
|-8193948242717911820|    5|
```

```
|-2062883918534425492|    4|
|-8679136035911620397|    3|
| 1765411469112156596|    3|
|-7016546051037489808|    3|
|-7685954109876710390|    3|
| -784187332742198415|    3|
| 2742772755763603550|    3|
...
```

The largest component includes more than 90% of the vertices, while the second larg-est contains only 4 vertices—a vanishingly small fraction of the graph. It's worthwhile to take a look at the topics for some of these smaller components, if only to under-stand why they were not connected to the largest component. To see the names of the topics associated with these smaller components, we'll need to join the VertexRDD for the connected components graph with the vertices from our original concept graph. VertexRDD provides an innerJoin transformation that can take advantage of the way GraphX lays out data for much better performance than Spark's regular join trans-formation. The innerJoin method requires that we provide a function on the Ver texID and the data contained inside each of the two VertexRDDs that returns a value that will be used as the new data type for the resulting VertexRDD. In this case, we want to understand the names of the concepts for each connected component, so we'll return a data frame that contains both the topic name and the component ID:

```
val topicComponentDF = topicGraph.vertices.innerJoin(
  connectedComponentGraph.vertices) {
  (topicId, name, componentId) => (name, componentId.toLong)
}.toDF("topic", "cid")
```

Let's take a look at the topic names for the largest connected component that wasn't a part of the giant component:

```
topicComponentDF.where("cid = -2062883918534425492").show()
...
+--------------------+--------------------+
|               topic|                 cid|
+--------------------+--------------------+
|          Serotyping|-2062883918534425492|
|Campylobacter jejuni|-2062883918534425492|
|Campylobacter Inf...|-2062883918534425492|
|  Campylobacter coli|-2062883918534425492|
+--------------------+--------------------+
```

A bit of Google searching reveals that "Campylobacter" is a genus of bacteria that is one of the most common causes of food poisoning, and "serotyping" is a technique used for classifying bacteria based on their cell surface "antigens," which is a toxin that induces an immune response in the body. (It's this kind of research work that leads your average data scientist to spend at least two hours a day wandering around Wikipedia.)

Let's take a look at the original topic distribution to see if there are any similarly named topics in the data set that did not end up in this cluster:

```
val campy = spark.sql("""
  SELECT *
  FROM topic_dist
  WHERE topic LIKE '%ampylobacter%'""")
campy.show()
...
+--------------------+---+
|               topic|cnt|
+--------------------+---+
|Campylobacter jejuni|  3|
|Campylobacter Inf...|  2|
|  Campylobacter coli|  1|
|       Campylobacter|  1|
| Campylobacter fetus|  1|
+--------------------+---+
```

The "Campylobacter fetus" topic sounds similar to the topic of our Campylobacter cluster, but was not connected to it via a paper in the MEDLINE citation data. A bit of additional internet searching reveals that this subspecies of Campylobacter primarily occurs in cattle and sheep, not humans, hence the disconnection in the research literature in spite of its similar name.

The broader pattern we see in this data is that the topic co-occurrence network is tending toward being fully connected as we add more citations to it over time, and there do not appear to be structural reasons that we would expect it to become disconnected into distinct subgraphs.

Under the covers, the connectedComponents method is performing a series of iterative computations on our graph in order to identify the component that each vertex belongs to, taking advantage of the fact that the VertexId is a unique numeric identifier for each vertex. During each phase of the computation, each vertex broadcasts the smallest VertexID value that it has seen to each of its neighbors. During the first iteration, this will simply be the vertex's own ID, but this will generally be updated in subsequent iterations. Each vertex keeps track of the smallest VertexID it has seen, and when none of these smallest IDs changes during an iteration, the connected component computation is complete, with each vertex assigned to the component that is represented by the smallest VertexID value for a vertex that was a part of that component. These kinds of iterative computations on graphs are common, and later in this chapter, we will see how we can use this iterative pattern to compute other graph metrics that illuminate the structure of the graph.

Degree Distribution

A connected graph can be structured in many different ways. For example, there might be a single vertex that is connected to all of the other vertices, but none of those other vertices connect to each other. If we eliminated that single central vertex, the graph would shatter into individual vertices. We might also have a situation in which every vertex in the graph was connected to exactly two other vertices, so that the entire connected component formed a giant loop.

Figure 7-2 illustrates how connected graphs may have radically different degree distributions.

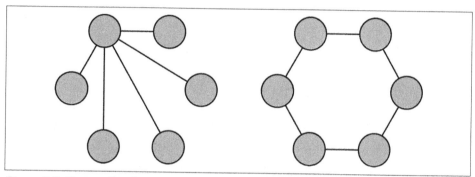

Figure 7-2. Degree distributions in connected graphs

To gain additional insight into how the graph is structured, it's helpful to look at the *degree* of each vertex, which is simply the number of edges that a particular vertex belongs to. In a graph without loops (i.e., an edge that connects a vertex to itself), the sum of the degrees of the vertices will be equal to twice the number of edges, because each edge will contain two distinct vertices.

In GraphX, we can get the degree of each vertex by calling the `degrees` method on the `Graph` object. This method returns a `VertexRDD` of integers that is the degree at each vertex. Let's get the degree distribution and some basic summary statistics on it for our concept network:

```
val degrees: VertexRDD[Int] = topicGraph.degrees.cache()
degrees.map(_._2).stats()
...
(count: 13721, mean: 31.155892,
 stdev: 65.497591, max: 2596.000000,
 min: 1.000000)
```

There are a few interesting bits of information in the degree distribution. First, note that the number of entries in the `degrees` RDD is less than the number of vertices in the graph: while the graph contains 13,034 vertices, the `degrees` RDD only has 12,065 entries. Some vertices have no edges that touch them. This is probably caused by citations in the MEDLINE data that only had a single major topic, which means that they would not have had any other topics to co-occur within our data. We can confirm that this is the case by revisiting the original medline data set:

```
val sing = medline.filter(x => x.size == 1)
sing.count()
...
44509

val singTopic = sing.flatMap(topic => topic).distinct()
singTopic.count()
...
8243
```

There are 8,243 distinct topics that occur as singletons inside of 44,509 MEDLINE documents. Let's remove the instances of those topics that already occur in the topic Pairs data set:

```
val topic2 = topicPairs.flatMap(_.getAs[Seq[String]](0))
singTopic.except(topic2).count()
...
827
```

This leaves 827 topics that only occur as singletons inside MEDLINE documents, and 14,548–827 is 13,721, the number of entries in the degrees RDD.

Next, note that although the mean is relatively small, indicating that the average vertex in the graph is only connected to a small fraction of the other nodes, the maximum value indicates that there is at least one highly connected node in the graph that is connected to almost a third of the other nodes in the graph.

Let's take a closer look at the concepts for these high-degree vertices by joining the degrees VertexRDD to the vertices in the concept graph using GraphX's innerJoin method and an associated function for combining the name of a concept and the degree of the vertex into a tuple. Remember, the innerJoin method only returns vertices that are present in *both* of the VertexRDDs, so the concepts that do not have any co-occurring concepts will be filtered out.

```
val namesAndDegrees = degrees.innerJoin(topicGraph.vertices) {
  (topicId, degree, name) => (name, degree.toInt)
}.values.toDF("topic", "degree")
```

When we print the top 20 elements of the namesAndDegrees DataFrame ordered by the value of the degree, we get this:

```
namesAndDegrees.orderBy(desc("degree")).show()
...
+--------------------+------+
|               topic|degree|
+--------------------+------+
|            Research|  2596|
```

```
|          Disease|  1746|
|        Neoplasms|  1202|
|            Blood|   914|
|     Pharmacology|   882|
|     Tuberculosis|   815|
|       Toxicology|   694|
|     Drug Therapy|   678|
|     Jurisprudence|  661|
|Biomedical Research|  633|
```

Unsurprisingly, most of the high-degree vertices refer to the same generic concepts that we've been seeing throughout this analysis. In the next section, we'll use some new functionality of the GraphX API and a bit of old-fashioned statistics to filter out some of the less interesting co-occurrence pairs from the graph.

Filtering Out Noisy Edges

In the current co-occurrence graph, the edges are weighted based on the count of how often a pair of concepts appears in the same paper. The problem with this simple weighting scheme is that it doesn't distinguish concept pairs that occur together because they have a meaningful semantic relationship from concept pairs that occur together because they happen to both occur frequently for any type of document. We need to use a new edge-weighting scheme that takes into account how "interesting" or "surprising" a particular pair of concepts is for a document given the overall prevalence of those concepts in the data. We will use Pearson's *chi-squared test* to calculate this "interestingness" in a principled way—that is, to test whether the occurrence of a particular concept is independent from the occurrence of another concept.

For any pair of concepts A and B, we can create a 2×2 contingency table that contains the counts of how those concepts co-occur in MEDLINE documents:

	Yes B	No B	A Total
Yes A	YY	YN	YA
No A	NY	NN	NA
B Total	YB	NB	T

In this table, the entries YY, YN, NY, and NN represent the raw counts of presence/absence for concepts A and B. The entries YA and NA are the row sums for concept A, YB and NB are the column sums for concept B, and the value T is the total number of documents.

For the chi-squared test, we think of YY, YN, NY, and NN as sampled from an unknown distribution. We can compute a *chi-squared statistic* from these values with:

$$\chi^2 = T\frac{(|YY*NN - YN*NY| - T/2)^2}{YA*NA*YB*NB}$$

Note that this formulation of the chi-squared statistic includes a term "- T / 2". This is Yates's continuity correction (*http://bit.ly/2qKl0RM*) and it is not included in some formulations.

If our samples are in fact independent, we would expect the value of this statistic to be drawn from a *chi-squared distribution* with the appropriate degrees of freedom. Where r and c are the cardinalities of the two random variables being compared, the degrees of freedom are calculated as $(r-1)(c-1)=1$. A large chi-squared statistic indicates that the variables are less likely to be independent, and thus we find the pair of concepts more interesting. More specifically, the CDF of the one-degree chi-squared distribution yields a *p*-value that is the level of confidence with which we can reject the null hypothesis that the variables are independent.

In this section, we'll compute the value of the chi-squared statistic for each pair of concepts in our co-occurrence graph using GraphX.

Processing EdgeTriplets

The easiest part of the chi-squared statistic to count is T, which is the total number of documents under consideration. We can get this easily by simply counting the number of entries in the medline RDD:

```
val T = medline.count()
```

It's also relatively easy for us to get the counts of how many documents feature each concept. We already did this analysis to create the topicDist DataFrame earlier in this chapter, but now we'll get the hashed versions of the topic and their counts as an RDD:

```
val topicDistRdd = topicDist.map{
  case Row(topic: String, cnt: Long) => (hashId(topic), cnt)
}.rdd
```

Once we have this VertexRDD of counts, we can create a new graph using it as the vertex set, along with the existing edges RDD:

```
val topicDistGraph = Graph(topicDistRdd, topicGraph.edges)
```

Now we have all of the information we need to compute the chi-squared statistic for each edge in the topicDistGraph. To do the calculation, we need to combine data that is stored at both the vertices (i.e., the count of how often each concept appears in a document) as well as the edges (i.e., the count of how often each pair of concepts occurs in the same document). GraphX supports this kind of computation via a data structure called an EdgeTriplet[VD,ED], which has information about the attributes

---

of both the vertices and the edges contained within a single object, as well as the IDs of both of the vertices. Given an `EdgeTriplet` over our `topicDistGraph`, we can calculate the chi-squared statistic as follows:

```
def chiSq(YY: Long, YB: Long, YA: Long, T: Long): Double = {
  val NB = T - YB
  val NA = T - YA
  val YN = YA - YY
  val NY = YB - YY
  val NN = T - NY - YN - YY
  val inner = math.abs(YY * NN - YN * NY) - T / 2.0
  T * math.pow(inner, 2) / (YA * NA * YB * NB)
}
```

We can then apply this method to transform the value of the graph edges via the `map Triplets` operator, which returns a new graph whose edge attributes will be the value of the chi-squared statistic for each co-occurrence pair, and then get an idea of the distribution of the values for this statistic across the edges:

```
val chiSquaredGraph = topicDistGraph.mapTriplets(triplet => {
  chiSq(triplet.attr, triplet.srcAttr, triplet.dstAttr, T)
})
chiSquaredGraph.edges.map(x => x.attr).stats()
...
(count: 213745, mean: 877.96,
 stdev: 5094.94, max: 198668.41,
 min: 0.0)
```

Having calculated the chi-squared statistic value, we want to use it to filter out edges that don't appear to have any meaningful relationship between the co-occurring concepts. As we can see from the distribution of the edge values, there is an enormous range of values for the chi-squared statistic across the data, which should make us feel comfortable experimenting with an aggressive filtering criterion to eliminate noisy edges. For a 2×2 contingency table in which there is no relationship between the variables, we expect that the value of the chi-squared metric will follow the chi-squared distribution with one degree of freedom. The 99.999th percentile of the chi-squared distribution with one degree of freedom is approximately 19.5, so let's try this value as a cutoff to eliminate edges from the graph, leaving us with only those edges where we are *extremely* confident that they represent an interesting co-occurrence relationship. We'll perform this filtering on the graph with the `subgraph` method, which takes a boolean function of an `EdgeTriplet` to determine which edges to include in the subgraph:

```
val interesting = chiSquaredGraph.subgraph(
  triplet => triplet.attr > 19.5)
interesting.edges.count
...
140575
```

Our extremely strict filtering rule removed about one third of the edges in the original co-occurrence graph. It isn't a bad thing that the rule didn't remove more of the edges because we expect that most of the co-occurring concepts in the graph are actually semantically related to one another, so they would co-occur more often than they would simply by chance. In the next section, we'll analyze the connectedness and overall degree distribution of the subgraph, to see if there was any major impact to the structure of the graph when we removed the noisy edges.

Analyzing the Filtered Graph

We'll start by rerunning the connected component algorithm on the subgraph and checking the component counts and sizes, using the function we wrote earlier for the original graph:

```
val interestingComponentGraph = interesting.connectedComponents()
val icDF = interestingComponentGraph.vertices.toDF("vid", "cid")
val icCountDF = icDF.groupBy("cid").count()
icCountDF.count()
...
878

icCountDF.orderBy(desc("count")).show()
...
+--------------------+-----+
|                 cid|count|
+--------------------+-----+
|-9218306090261648869|13610|
|-8193948242717911820|    5|
|-2062883918534425492|    4|
|-7016546051037489808|    3|
|-7685954109876710390|    3|
| -784187332742198415|    3|
| 1765411469112156596|    3|
| 2742772755763603550|    3|
|-8679136035911620397|    3|
```

Filtering out a third of the edges in the graph had no impact on the connectedness of the overall graph, nor did it change the size of the largest connected component; removing the "uninteresting" edges in the graph left the overall connectedness of the topic graph intact. When we look at the degree distribution for the filtered graph, we see a similar story:

```
val interestingDegrees = interesting.degrees.cache()
interestingDegrees.map(_._2).stats()
...
(count: 13721, mean: 20.49,
 stdev: 29.86, max: 863.0, min: 1.0)
```

The mean degree for the original graph was about 43, and the mean degree for the filtered graph has fallen a bit, to about 28. More interesting, however, is the precipitous drop in the size of the largest degree vertex, which has fallen from 3,753 in the original graph to 1,603 in the filtered graph. If we look at the association between concept and degree in the filtered graph, we see this:

```
interestingDegrees.innerJoin(topicGraph.vertices) {
  (topicId, degree, name) => (name, degree)
}.values.toDF("topic", "degree").orderBy(desc("degree")).show()
...
+--------------------+------+
|               topic|degree|
+--------------------+------+
|            Research|   863|
|             Disease|   637|
|        Pharmacology|   509|
|           Neoplasms|   453|
|          Toxicology|   381|
|          Metabolism|   321|
|        Drug Therapy|   304|
|               Blood|   302|
|       Public Policy|   279|
|       Social Change|   277|
...
```

Our chi-squared filtering criterion appears to have the desired effect: it's eliminating edges in our graph related to generic concepts, while preserving the edges in the rest of the graph that represent meaningful and interesting semantic relationships between concepts. We can continue to experiment with different chi-squared filtering criteria to see how it impacts the connectedness and degree distribution in the graph; it would be interesting to find out what value of the chi-squared distribution would cause the large connected component in the graph to break up into smaller pieces, or if the largest component would simply continue to "melt," like a giant iceberg slowly losing tiny pieces over time.

Small-World Networks

The connectedness and degree distribution of a graph can give us a basic idea of its overall structure, and GraphX makes it easy to calculate and analyze these properties. In this section, we'll go a bit deeper into the GraphX APIs and show how we can use them to calculate some more advanced properties of a graph that do not have built-in support in GraphX.

With the rise of computer networks like the web and social networks like Facebook and Twitter, data scientists now have rich data sets that describe the structure and formation of real-world networks versus the idealized networks that mathematicians and graph theorists have traditionally studied. One of the first papers to describe the properties of these real-world networks and how they differed from the idealized models was published in 1998 by Duncan Watts and Steven Strogatz and was titled

"Collective Dynamics of 'Small-World' Networks" (*http://bit.ly/2pshNFH*). It was a seminal paper that outlined the first mathematical model for how to generate graphs that exhibited the two "small-world" properties that we see in real-world graphs:

- Most of the nodes in the network have a small degree and belong to a relatively dense cluster of other nodes; that is, a high fraction of a node's neighbors are also connected to each other.
- Despite the small degree and dense clustering of most nodes in the graph, it is possible to reach any node in the network from any other network relatively quickly by traversing a small number of edges.

For each of these properties, Watts and Strogatz defined a metric that could be used to rank graphs based on how strongly they expressed these properties. In this section, we will use GraphX to compute these metrics for our concept network, and compare the values we get to the values we would get for an idealized random graph in order to test whether our concept network exhibits the small-world property.

Cliques and Clustering Coefficients

A graph is *complete* if every vertex is connected to every other vertex by an edge. In a given graph, there may be many subsets of vertices that are complete, and we call these complete subgraphs *cliques*. The presence of many large cliques in a graph indicates that the graph has the kind of locally dense structure that we see in real small-world networks.

Unfortunately, finding cliques in a given graph turns out to be very difficult to do. The problem of detecting whether or not a given graph has a clique of a given size is NP-complete, which means that finding cliques in even small graphs can be computationally intensive.

Computer scientists have developed a number of simple metrics that give us a good feel for the local density of a graph without the computational costs of finding all of the cliques of a given size. One of these metrics is the *triangle count* at a vertex. A *triangle* is a complete graph on three vertices, and the triangle count at a vertex V is simply the number of triangles that contain V. The triangle count is a measure of how many neighbors of V are also connected to each other. Watts and Strogatz defined a new metric, called the *local clustering coefficient*, that is the ratio of the actual triangle count at a vertex to the number of possible triangles at that vertex based on how many neighbors it has. For an undirected graph, the local clustering coefficient C for a vertex that has k neighbors and t triangles is:

$$C = \frac{2t}{k(k-1)}$$

Let's use GraphX to compute the local clustering coefficients for each node in the filtered concept network. GraphX has a built-in method called `triangleCount` that returns a `Graph` whose `VertexRDD` contains the number of triangles at each vertex:

```
val triCountGraph = interesting.triangleCount()
triCountGraph.vertices.map(x => x._2).stats()
...
(count: 14548, mean: 74.66, stdev: 295.33, max: 11023.0, min: 0.0)
```

To compute the local clustering coefficient, we'll need to normalize these triangle counts by the total number of possible triangles at each vertex, which we can compute from the `interestingDegrees` RDD:

```
val maxTrisGraph = interestingDegrees.mapValues(d => d * (d - 1) / 2.0)
```

Now we'll join the `VertexRDD` of triangle counts from `triCountGraph` to the `VertexRDD` of normalization terms we calculated and compute the ratio of the two, being careful to avoid dividing by zero for any vertices that only have a single edge:

```
val clusterCoef = triCountGraph.vertices.
  innerJoin(maxTrisGraph) { (vertexId, triCount, maxTris) => {
    if (maxTris == 0) 0 else triCount / maxTris
  }
}
```

Computing the average value of the local clustering coefficient for all of the vertices in the graph gives us the *network average clustering coefficient*:

```
clusterCoef.map(_._2).sum() / interesting.vertices.count()
...
0.30624625605188605
```

Computing Average Path Length with Pregel

The second property of small-world networks is that the length of the shortest path between any two randomly chosen nodes tends to be small. In this section, we'll compute the average path length for nodes contained in the large connected component of our filtered graph.

Computing the path length between vertices in a graph is an iterative process that is similar to the iterative process we use to find the connected components. At each phase of the process, each vertex will maintain a collection of the vertices that it knows about and how far away each vertex is. Each vertex will then query its neighbors about the contents of their lists, and it will update its own list with any new vertices that are contained in its neighbors' lists that were not contained in its own list. This process of querying neighbors and updating lists will continue across the entire graph until none of the vertices are able to add any new information to their lists.

This iterative, vertex-centric method of parallel programming on large, distributed graphs is based on a paper that Google published in 2009 called "Pregel: a system for large-scale graph processing" (*http://bit.ly/2qKTfbL*). Pregel is based on a model of distributed computation that predates MapReduce called *bulk-synchronous parallel* (BSP). BSP programs divide parallel processing stages into two phases: *computation* and *communication*. During the computation phase, each vertex in the graph examines its own internal state and decides to send zero or more *messages* to other vertices in the graph. During the communication phase, the Pregel framework handles routing the messages that resulted from the previous communication phase to the appropriate vertices, which then process those messages, updates their internal state, and potentially generates new messages during the next computation phase. The sequence of computation and communication steps continues until all of the vertices in the graph vote to halt, at which point the computation is finished.

BSP was one of the first parallel programming frameworks that was both fairly general purpose as well as fault tolerant: it was possible to design BSP systems in such a way that the state of the system at any computation phase could be captured and stored so that if a particular machine failed, the state of that machine could be replicated on another machine, the overall computation could be rolled back to the earlier state before the failure occurred, and then the computation could continue.

Since Google published its paper on Pregel, a number of open source projects have been developed that replicate aspects of the BSP programming model on top of HDFS, such as Apache Giraph and Apache Hama. These systems have proven very useful for specialized problems that fit nicely into the BSP computational model, such as large-scale PageRank computations, but they are not widely deployed as part of the analysis toolkit for regular data scientists because it is relatively difficult to integrate them into a standard data-parallel workflow. GraphX solves this problem by allowing data scientists to easily bring graphs into a data-parallel workflow when it is convenient for representing data and implementing algorithms, and it provides a built-in `pregel` operator for expressing BSP computations on top of graphs.

In this section, we'll demonstrate how to use this operator to implement the iterative, graph-parallel computations we need to compute the average path length for a graph:

1. Figure out what state we need to keep track of at each vertex.
2. Write a function that takes the current state into account and evaluates each pair of linked vertices to determine which messages to send at the next phase.
3. Write a function that merges the messages from all of the different vertices before we pass the output of the function to the vertex for updating.

There are three major decisions we need to make in order to implement a distributed algorithm using Pregel. First, we need to decide what data structure we're going to use to represent the state of each vertex, and what data structure we're going to use to represent the messages passed between vertices. For the average path length problem, we want each vertex to have a lookup table that contains the IDs of the vertices it currently knows about and how far away from those vertices it is. We'll store this information inside of a Map[VertexId, Int] that we maintain for each vertex. Similarly, the messages that are passed to each vertex should be a lookup table of vertex IDs and distances that are based on information that the vertex receives from its neighbors, and we can use a Map[VertexId, Int] to represent this information as well.

Once we know the data structures that we'll use for representing the state of the vertices and the content of the messages, we need to write two functions. The first one, which we'll call mergeMaps, is used to merge the information from the new messages into the state of the vertex. In this case, both the state and the message are of type Map[VertexId, Int], so we need to merge the contents of these two maps while retaining the smallest value associated with any VertexId entries that occur in both maps:

```
def mergeMaps(m1: Map[VertexId, Int], m2: Map[VertexId, Int])
  : Map[VertexId, Int] = {
  def minThatExists(k: VertexId): Int = {
    math.min(
      m1.getOrElse(k, Int.MaxValue),
      m2.getOrElse(k, Int.MaxValue))
  }

  (m1.keySet ++ m2.keySet).map {
    k => (k, minThatExists(k))
  }.toMap
}
```

The vertex update function also includes the VertexId value as an argument, so we'll define a trivial update function that takes the VertexId along with the Map[VertexId, Int] arguments, but delegates all of the actual work to mergeMaps:

```
def update(
    id: VertexId,
    state: Map[VertexId, Int],
    msg: Map[VertexId, Int]) = {
  mergeMaps(state, msg)
}
```

Because the messages we will pass during the algorithm are also of type Map[VertexId, Int], and we want to merge them and keep the minimal value of each key they possess, we will be able to use the mergeMaps function for the reduce phase of the Pregel run as well.

The final step is usually the most involved: we need to write the code that constructs the message that will be sent to each vertex based on the information it receives from its neighbors at each iteration. The basic idea here is that each vertex should increment the value of each key in its current Map[VertexId, Int] by one, combine the incremented map values with the values from its neighbor using the mergeMaps method, and send the result of the `mergeMaps` function to the neighboring vertex if it differs from the neighbor's internal `Map[VertexId, Int]`. The code for performing this sequence of operations looks like this:

```
def checkIncrement(
    a: Map[VertexId, Int],
    b: Map[VertexId, Int],
    bid: VertexId) = {
  val aplus = a.map { case (v, d) => v -> (d + 1) }
  if (b != mergeMaps(aplus, b)) {
    Iterator((bid, aplus))
  } else {
    Iterator.empty
  }
}
```

With the `checkIncrement` function in hand, we can define the `iterate` function that we will use for performing the message updates at each Pregel iteration for both the `src` and `dst` vertices inside of an `EdgeTriplet`:

```
def iterate(e: EdgeTriplet[Map[VertexId, Int], _]) = {
  checkIncrement(e.srcAttr, e.dstAttr, e.dstId) ++
  checkIncrement(e.dstAttr, e.srcAttr, e.srcId)
}
```

During each iteration, we need to determine the path lengths that need to be communicated to each of the vertices based on the path lengths that they already know about, and then we need to return an `Iterator` that contains a tuple of (`VertexId`, `Map[VertexId, Int]`), where the first `VertexId` indicates where the message should be routed and the `Map[VertexId, Int]` is the message itself.

If a vertex does not receive any messages during an iteration, the `pregel` operator assumes that this vertex is finished computing, and it will be excluded from subsequent processing. As soon as no more messages are sent to any vertex from the `iterate` method, the algorithm is complete.

> The implementation of the `pregel` operator in GraphX has a limitation compared to BSP systems like Giraph: GraphX can only send messages between vertices that are connected by an edge, whereas Giraph can send messages between *any* two vertices in a graph.

Now that our functions are complete, let's prepare the data for the BSP run. Given a large enough cluster and plenty of memory, we could compute the path lengths between every pair of vertices using a Pregel-style algorithm with GraphX. However, this isn't necessary for us to get an idea of the general distribution of path lengths in the graph; instead, we can randomly sample a small subset of the vertices and then compute the path lengths for each vertex to just that subset. Using the RDD `sample` method, let's select 2% of the `VertexId` values for our sample without replacement, using the value 1729L as the seed for the random number generator:

```
val fraction = 0.02
val replacement = false
val sample = interesting.vertices.map(v => v._1).
  sample(replacement, fraction, 1729L)
val ids = sample.collect().toSet
```

Now we'll create a new `Graph` object whose vertex `Map[VertexId, Int]` values are only nonempty if the vertex is a member of the sampled IDs:

```
val mapGraph = interesting.mapVertices((id, _) => {
  if (ids.contains(id)) {
    Map(id -> 0)
  } else {
    Map[VertexId, Int]()
  }
})
```

Finally, to kick off the run, we need an initial message to send to the vertices. For this algorithm, that initial message is an empty `Map[VertexId, Int]`. We can then call the `pregel` method, followed by the `update`, `iterate`, and `mergeMaps` functions to execute during each iteration:

```
val start = Map[VertexId, Int]()
val res = mapGraph.pregel(start)(update, iterate, mergeMaps)
```

This should run for a few minutes; the number of iterations of the algorithm will be one plus the length of the longest path in our sample. Once it completes, we can `flat Map` the vertices to extract the tuples of (`VertexId, VertexId, Int`) values that represent the unique path lengths that were computed:

```
val paths = res.vertices.flatMap { case (id, m) =>
  m.map { case (k, v) =>
    if (id < k) {
      (id, k, v)
    } else {
      (k, id, v)
    }
  }
}.distinct()
paths.cache()
```

We can now compute summary statistics for the nonzero path lengths and compute the histogram of path lengths in our sample:

```
paths.map(_._3).filter(_ > 0).stats()
...
(count: 3197372, mean: 3.63, stdev: 0.78, max: 8.0, min: 1.0)

val hist = paths.map(_._3).countByValue()
```

```
hist.toSeq.sorted.foreach(println)
...
(0,255)
(1,4336)
(2,159813)
(3,1238373)
(4,1433353)
(5,335461)
(6,24961)
(7,1052)
(8,23)
```

The average path length of our sample was 3.63, while the clustering coefficient that we calculated in the last section was 0.306. Table 7-1 shows the values of these statistics for three different small-world networks as well as for random graphs that were generated on the same number of vertices and edges as each of the real-world networks, and is taken from a paper titled "Multiscale Visualization of Small World Networks" (*https://dl.acm.org/citation.cfm?id=1947385*) by Auber et al. (2003).

Table 7-1. Example small-world networks

Graph	Avg path length (APL)	Clustering coefficient (CC)	Random APL	Random CC
IMDB	3.20	0.967	2.67	0.024
macOS 9	3.28	0.388	3.32	0.018
.edu sites	4.06	0.156	4.048	0.001

The IMDB graph was built from actors who had appeared in the same movies—the macOS 9 network referred to header files that were likely coincluded in the same source files in the OS 9 source code, and *.edu* sites refer to sites in the *.edu* top-level domain that linked to one another and are drawn from a paper by Adamic (1999) (*https://bit.ly/1wuHgfB*). Our analysis shows that the network of MeSH tags in the MEDLINE citation index fits naturally into the same range of average path length and clustering coefficient values that we see in other well-known small-world networks, with a much higher clustering coefficient value than we would expect given the relatively low average path length.

Where to Go from Here

At first, small-world networks were a curiosity; it was interesting that so many different types of real-world networks, from sociology and political science to neuroscience and cell biology, had such similar and peculiar structural properties. More recently, however, it seems that deviances from small-world structure in these networks can be indicative of the potential for functional problems. Dr. Jeffrey Petrella at Duke University gathered research (*https://bit.ly/1wuHi7f*) that indicates that the network of neurons in the brain exhibits a small-world structure, and that deviance from this structure occurs in patients who have been diagnosed with Alzheimer's disease, schizophrenia, depression, and attention-deficit disorders. In general, real-world graphs should exhibit the small-world property; if they do not, that may be evidence of a problem, such as fraudulent activity in a small-world graph of transactions or trust relationships between businesses.

## CHAPTER 8

Geospatial and Temporal Data Analysis on New York City Taxi Trip Data

Josh Wills

Nothing puzzles me more than time and space;
and yet nothing troubles me less, as I never think about them.
  —Charles Lamb

New York City is widely known for its yellow taxis, and hailing one is just as much a part of the experience of visiting the city as eating a hot dog from a street vendor or riding the elevator to the top of the Empire State Building.

Residents of New York City have all kinds of tips based on their anecdotal experiences about the best times and places to catch a cab, especially during rush hour and when it's raining. But there is one time of day when everyone will recommend that you simply take the subway instead: during the shift change that happens between 4 and 5PM every day. During this time, yellow taxis have to return to their dispatch centers (often in Queens) so that one driver can quit for the day and the next one can start, and drivers who are late to return have to pay fines.

In March of 2014, the New York City Taxi and Limousine Commission shared an infographic on its Twitter account, @nyctaxi (*https://twitter.com/nyctaxi*), that showed the number of taxis on the road and the fraction of those taxis that was occupied at any given time. Sure enough, there was a noticeable dip of taxis on the road from 4 to 6PM, and two-thirds of the taxis that were driving were occupied.

This tweet caught the eye of self-described urbanist, mapmaker, and data junkie Chris Whong, who sent a tweet to the @nyctaxi account to find out if the data it used in its infographic was publicly available. The taxi commission replied that he could have the data if he filed a Freedom of Information Law (FOIL) request and provided the commission with hard drives that they could copy the data on to. After filling out one

PDF form, buying two new 500 GB hard drives, and waiting two business days, Chris had access to all of the data on taxi rides from January 1 through December 31, 2013. Even better, he posted all of the fare data online, where it has been used as the basis for a number of beautiful visualizations of transportation in New York City.

One statistic that is important to understanding the economics of taxis is *utilization*: the fraction of time that a cab is on the road and is occupied by one or more passengers. One factor that impacts utilization is the passenger's destination: a cab that drops off passengers near Union Square at midday is much more likely to find its next fare in just a minute or two, whereas a cab that drops someone off at 2AM on Staten Island may have to drive all the way back to Manhattan before it finds its next fare. We'd like to quantify these effects and find out the average time it takes for a cab to find its next fare as a function of the borough in which it dropped its passengers off—Manhattan, Brooklyn, Queens, the Bronx, Staten Island, or none of the above (e.g., if it dropped the passenger off somewhere outside of the city, like Newark International Airport).

To carry out this analysis, we need to deal with two types of data that come up all the time: *temporal data*, such as dates and times, and *geospatial information*, like points of longitude and latitude and spatial boundaries. Since the first edition of this book was released, there have been a number of improvements in the ways that we can work with temporal data in Spark, such as the new `java.time` package that was released in Java 8 and the incorporation of UDFs from the Apache Hive project in SparkSQL; these include many functions that deal with time, like `date_add` and `from_timestamp`, which make it much easier to work with time in Spark 2 than it was in Spark 1. Geospatial data, on the other hand, is still a fairly specialized kind of analysis, and we will need to work with third-party libraries and write our own custom UDFs in order to be able to effectively work with this data inside Spark.

Getting the Data

For this analysis, we're only going to consider the fare data from January 2013, which will be about 2.5 GB of data after we uncompress it. You can access the data for each month of 2013 (*http://www.andresmh.com/nyctaxitrips/*), and if you have a sufficiently large Spark cluster at your disposal, you can re-create the following analysis against all of the data for the year. For now, let's create a working directory on our client machine and take a look at the structure of the fare data:

```
$ mkdir taxidata
$ cd taxidata
$ curl -O https://nyctaxitrips.blob.core.windows.net/data/trip_data_1.csv.zip
$ unzip trip_data_1.csv.zip
$ head -n 10 trip_data_1.csv
```

Each row of the file after the header represents a single taxi ride in CSV format. For each ride, we have some attributes of the cab (a hashed version of the medallion number) as well as the driver (a hashed version of the *hack license*, which is what licenses to drive taxis are called), some temporal information about when the trip started and ended, and the longitude/latitude coordinates for where the passenger(s) were picked up and dropped off.

Working with Third-Party Libraries in Spark

One of the great features of the Java platform is the sheer volume of code that has been developed for it over the years: for any kind of data type or algorithm you might need to use, it's likely that someone else has written a Java library that you can use to solve your problem, and there's also a good chance that an open source version of that library exists that you can download and use without having to purchase a license.

Of course, just because a library exists and is freely available doesn't mean you necessarily want to rely on it to solve your problem. Open source projects have a lot of variation in terms of their quality, state of development in terms of bug fixes and new features, and ease-of-use in terms of API design and the presence of useful documentation and tutorials.

Our decision-making process is a bit different than that of a developer choosing a library for an application; we want something that will be pleasant to use for interactive data analysis and that is easy to use in a distributed application. In particular, we want to be sure that the main data types we will be working with in our RDDs implement the Serializable interface and/or can be easily serialized using libraries like Kryo.

Additionally, we would like the libraries we use for interactive data analysis to have as few external dependencies as possible. Tools like Maven and SBT can help application developers deal with complex dependencies when building applications, but for interactive data analysis, we would much rather simply grab a JAR file with all of the code we need, load it into the Spark shell, and start our analysis. Additionally, bringing in libraries with lots of dependencies can cause version conflicts with other libraries that Spark depends on, which can cause difficult-to-diagnose error conditions that developers refer to as *JAR hell*.

Finally, we would like our libraries to have relatively simple and rich APIs that do not make extensive use of Java-oriented design patterns like abstract factories and visitors. Although these patterns can be very useful for application developers, they tend to add a lot of complexity to our code that is unrelated to our analysis. Even better, many Java libraries have Scala wrappers that take advantage of Scala's power to reduce the amount of boilerplate code required to use them.

Geospatial Data with the Esri Geometry API and Spray

Working with temporal data on the JVM has become significantly easier in Java 8 thanks to the `java.time` package, whose design is based on the highly successful JodaTime library. For geospatial data, the answer isn't nearly so simple; there are many different libraries and tools that have different functions, states of development, and maturity levels, so there is not a dominant Java library for all geospatial use cases.

The first thing you must consider when choosing a library is determine what kind of geospatial data you will need to work with. There are two major kinds—vector and raster—and there are different tools for working with each type. In our case, we have latitude and longitude for our taxi trip records, and vector data stored in the GeoJSON format that represents the boundaries of the different boroughs of New York. So we need a library that can parse GeoJSON data and can handle spatial relationships, like detecting whether a given longitude/latitude pair is contained inside a polygon that represents the boundaries of a particular borough.

Unfortunately, there isn't an open source library that fits our needs exactly. There is a GeoJSON parser library that can convert GeoJSON records into Java objects, but there isn't an associated geospatial library that can analyze spatial relationships on the generated objects. There is the GeoTools project, but it has a long list of components and dependencies—exactly the kind of thing we try to avoid when choosing a library to work with from the Spark shell. Finally, there is the Esri Geometry API for Java, which has few dependencies and can analyze spatial relationships but can only parse a subset of the GeoJSON standard, so it won't be able to parse the GeoJSON data we downloaded without us doing some preliminary data munging.

For a data analyst, this lack of tooling might be an insurmountable problem. But we are data scientists: if our tools don't allow us to solve a problem, we build new tools. In this case, we will add Scala functionality for parsing *all* of the GeoJSON data, including the bits that aren't handled by the Esri Geometry API, by leveraging one of the many Scala projects that support parsing JSON data. The code that we will be discussing in the next few sections is available in the book's Git repo, but has also been made available as a standalone library on GitHub (*https://github.com/jwills/geojson*), where it can be used for any kind of geospatial analysis project in Scala.

Exploring the Esri Geometry API

The core data type of the Esri library is the `Geometry` object. A `Geometry` describes a shape, accompanied by a geolocation where that shape resides. The library contains a set of spatial operations that allows analyzing geometries and their relationships. These operations can do things like tell us the area of a geometry and whether two geometries overlap, or compute the geometry formed by the union of two geometries.

In our case, we'll have `Geometry` objects representing dropoff points for cab rides (longitude and latitude), and `Geometry` objects that represent the boundaries of a borough in NYC. The spatial relationship we're interested in is containment: is a given point in space located inside one of the polygons associated with a borough of Manhattan?

The Esri API provides a convenience class called `GeometryEngine` that contains static methods for performing all of the spatial relationship operations, including a `con tains` operation. The `contains` method takes three arguments: two `Geometry` objects, and one instance of the `SpatialReference` class, which represents the coordinate system used to perform the geospatial calculations. For maximum precision, we need to analyze spatial relationships relative to a coordinate plane that maps each point on the misshapen spheroid that is planet Earth into a 2D coordinate system. Geospatial engineers have a standard set of well-known identifiers (referred to as WKIDs) that can be used to reference the most commonly used coordinate systems. For our purposes, we will be using WKID 4326, which is the standard coordinate system used by GPS.

As Scala developers, we're always on the lookout for ways to reduce the amount of typing we need to do as part of our interactive data analysis in the Spark shell, where we don't have access to development environments like Eclipse and IntelliJ that can automatically complete long method names for us and provide some syntactic sugar to make it easier to read certain kinds of operations. Following the naming convention we saw in the NScalaTime library, which defined wrapper classes like `RichDate Time` and `RichDuration`, we'll define our own `RichGeometry` class that extends the Esri `Geometry` object with some useful helper methods:

```scala
import com.esri.core.geometry.Geometry
import com.esri.core.geometry.GeometryEngine
import com.esri.core.geometry.SpatialReference

class RichGeometry(val geometry: Geometry,
    val spatialReference: SpatialReference =
      SpatialReference.create(4326)) {
  def area2D() = geometry.calculateArea2D()

  def contains(other: Geometry): Boolean = {
    GeometryEngine.contains(geometry, other, spatialReference)
  }

  def distance(other: Geometry): Double = {
    GeometryEngine.distance(geometry, other, spatialReference)
  }
}
```

We'll also declare a companion object for `RichGeometry` that provides support for implicitly converting instances of the `Geometry` class into `RichGeometry` instances:

```
object RichGeometry {
  implicit def wrapRichGeo(g: Geometry) = {
    new RichGeometry(g)
  }
}
```

Remember, to be able to take advantage of this conversion, we need to import the implicit function definition into the Scala environment, like this:

```
import RichGeometry._
```

Intro to GeoJSON

The data we'll use for the boundaries of boroughs in New York City comes written in a format called *GeoJSON*. The core object in GeoJSON is called a *feature*, which is made up of a *geometry* instance and a set of key-value pairs called *properties*. A geometry is a shape like a point, line, or polygon. A set of features is called a FeatureCol lection. Let's pull down the GeoJSON data for the NYC borough maps and take a look at its structure.

In the *taxidata* directory on your client machine, download the data and rename the file to something a bit shorter:

```
$ curl -O https://nycdatastables.s3.amazonaws.com/2013-08-19T18:15:35.172Z/
  nyc-borough-boundaries-polygon.geojson
$ mv nyc-borough-boundaries-polygon.geojson nyc-boroughs.geojson
```

Open the file and look at a feature record. Note the properties and the geometry objects—in this case, a polygon representing the boundaries of the borough, and the properties containing the name of the borough and other related information.

The Esri Geometry API will help us parse the Geometry JSON inside each feature but won't help us parse the id or the properties fields, which can be arbitrary JSON objects. To parse these objects, we need to use a Scala JSON library, of which there are many to choose from.

Spray, an open source toolkit for building web services with Scala, provides a JSON library that is up to the task. *spray-json* allows us to convert any Scala object to a corresponding JsValue by calling an implicit toJson method. It also allows us to convert any String that contains JSON to a parsed intermediate form by calling parseJson, and then converting it to a Scala type T by calling convertTo[T] on the intermediate type. Spray comes with built-in conversion implementations for the common Scala primitive types as well as tuples and collection types, and it also has a formatting library that allows us to declare the rules for converting custom types like our RichGe ometry class to and from JSON.

First, we'll need to create a case class for representing GeoJSON features. According to the specification, a feature is a JSON object that is required to have one field named "geometry" that corresponds to a GeoJSON `Geometry` type, and one field named "properties" that is a JSON object with any number of key-value pairs of any type. A feature may also have an optional "id" field that may be any JSON identifier. Our `Feature` case class will define corresponding Scala fields for each of the JSON fields, and will add some convenience methods for looking up values from the map of properties:

```
import spray.json.JsValue

case class Feature(
    val id: Option[JsValue],
    val properties: Map[String, JsValue],
    val geometry: RichGeometry) {
  def apply(property: String) = properties(property)
  def get(property: String) = properties.get(property)
}
```

We're representing the `Geometry` field in `Feature` using an instance of our `RichGeometry` class, which we'll create with the help of the GeoJSON geometry parsing functions from the Esri Geometry API.

We'll also need a case class that corresponds to the GeoJson `FeatureCollection`. To make the `FeatureCollection` class a bit easier to use, we will have it extend the `IndexedSeq[Feature]` trait by implementing the appropriate `apply` and `length` methods so that we can call the standard Scala Collections API methods like `map`, `filter`, and `sortBy` directly on the `FeatureCollection` instance itself, without having to access the underlying `Array[Feature]` value that it wraps:

```
case class FeatureCollection(features: Array[Feature])
    extends IndexedSeq[Feature] {
  def apply(index: Int) = features(index)
  def length = features.length
}
```

After we have defined the case classes for representing the GeoJSON data, we need to define the formats that tell Spray how to convert between our domain objects (`RichGeometry`, `Feature`, and `FeatureCollection`) and a corresponding `JsValue` instance. To do this, we need to create Scala singleton objects that extend the `RootJsonFormat[T]` trait, which defines abstract `read(jsv: JsValue): T` and `write(t: T): JsValue` methods. For the `RichGeometry` class, we can delegate most of the parsing and formatting logic to the Esri Geometry API, particularly the `geometryToGeoJson` and `geometryFromGeoJson` methods on the `GeometryEngine` class. But for our case classes, we need to write the formatting code ourselves. Here's the formatting code for the `Feature` case class, including some special logic to handle the optional id field:

```
implicit object FeatureJsonFormat extends
    RootJsonFormat[Feature] {
  def write(f: Feature) = {
```

```
val buf = scala.collection.mutable.ArrayBuffer(
  "type" -> JsString("Feature"),
  "properties" -> JsObject(f.properties),
  "geometry" -> f.geometry.toJson)
f.id.foreach(v => { buf += "id" -> v})
JsObject(buf.toMap)
}

def read(value: JsValue) = {
  val jso = value.asJsObject
  val id = jso.fields.get("id")
  val properties = jso.fields("properties").asJsObject.fields
  val geometry = jso.fields("geometry").convertTo[RichGeometry]
  Feature(id, properties, geometry)
}
}
```

The `FeatureJsonFormat` object uses the `implicit` keyword so that the Spray library can look it up when the `convertTo[Feature]` method is called on an instance of `JsValue`. You can see the rest of the `RootJsonFormat` implementations in the source code for the GeoJSON library on GitHub.

Preparing the New York City Taxi Trip Data

With the GeoJSON and JodaTime libraries in hand, it's time to begin analyzing the NYC taxi trip data interactively using Spark. Let's create a *taxidata* directory in HDFS and copy the trip data into the cluster:

```
$ hadoop fs -mkdir taxidata
$ hadoop fs -put trip_data_1.csv taxidata/
```

Now start the Spark shell, using the `--jars` argument to make the libraries we need available in the REPL:

```
$ mvn package
$ spark-shell --jars ch08-geotime-2.0.0-jar-with-dependencies.jar
```

Once the Spark shell has loaded, we can create a data set from the taxi data and examine the first few lines, just as we have in other chapters:

```
val taxiRaw = spark.read.option("header", "true").csv("taxidata")
taxiRaw.show()
```

The taxi data appears to be a well-formatted CSV file with clearly defined data types. In Chapter 2, we used the built-in type inference library included in `spark-csv` to automatically convert our CSV data from strings to column-specific types. The cost of this automatic conversion is two-fold. First, we need to do an extra pass over the data so that the converter can infer the type of each column. Second, if we only want to use a subset of the columns in the data set for our analysis, we will need to spend extra resources to do type inference on columns that we will end up dropping immediately when we begin our analysis. For smaller data sets, like the record linkage data we analyzed in Chapter 2, these costs are relatively inconsequential. But for very large data sets that we're planning on analyzing again and again, it may be a better use of our time to create code for performing custom type conversions on just the subset of columns we know we're going to need. In this chapter, we're going to opt to do the conversion ourselves via custom code.

Let's begin by defining a case class that contains just the information about each taxi trip that we want to use in our analysis. Since we're going to use this case class as the basis for a data set, we need to be mindful of the fact that a data set can only be optimized for a relatively small set of data types, including `Strings`, primitives (like `Int`, `Double`, etc.), and certain special Scala types like `Option`. If we want to take advantage of the performance enhancements and analysis utilities that the `Dataset` class provides, our case class can only contain fields that belong to this small set of supported types. (Note that the code listings below are only illustrative extracts from the complete code that you will need to execute to follow along with this chapter. Please refer to the accompanying Chapter 8 source code repository (*http://bit.ly/2qj8oRr*), in particular *GeoJson.scala*.)

```
case class Trip(
  license: String,
  pickupTime: Long,
  dropoffTime: Long,
  pickupX: Double,
  pickupY: Double,
  dropoffX: Double,
  dropoffY: Double)
```

We are representing the `pickupTime` and `dropoffTime` fields as `Longs` that are the number of milliseconds since the Unix epoch, and storing the individual xy coordinates of the pickup and dropoff locations in their own fields, even though we will typically work with them by converting these values to instances of the `Point` class in the Esri API.

To parse the `Rows` from the `taxiRaw` data set into instances of our case class, we will need to create some helper objects and functions. First, we need to be mindful of the fact that it's likely that some of the fields in a row may be missing from the data, so it's possible that when we go to retrieve them from the `Row`, we'll first need to check to see if they are `null` before we retrieve them or else we'll get an error. We can write a small helper class to handle this problem for any kind of `Row` we need to parse:

```
class RichRow(row: org.apache.spark.sql.Row) {
  def getAs[T](field: String): Option[T] = {
    if (row.isNullAt(row.fieldIndex(field))) {
      None
    } else {
      Some(row.getAs[T](field))
```

```
      }
    }
  }
```

In the RichRow class, the getAs[T] method always returns an Option[T] instead of the raw value directly so that we can explicitly handle a situation in which a field is missing when we parse a Row. In this case, all of the fields in our data set are Strings, so we'll be working with values of type Option[String].

Next, we'll need to process the pickup and dropoff times using an instance of Java's SimpleDateFormat class with an appropriate formatting string to get the time in milliseconds:

```
def parseTaxiTime(rr: RichRow, timeField: String): Long = {
  val formatter = new SimpleDateFormat(
      "yyyy-MM-dd HH:mm:ss", Locale.ENGLISH)
  val optDt = rr.getAs[String](timeField)
  optDt.map(dt => formatter.parse(dt).getTime).getOrElse(0L)
}
```

Then we will parse the longitude and latitude of the pickup and dropoff locations from Strings to Doubles using Scala's implicit toDouble method, defaulting to a value of 0.0 if the coordinate is missing:

```
def parseTaxiLoc(rr: RichRow, locField: String): Double = {
  rr.getAs[String](locField).map(_.toDouble).getOrElse(0.0)
}
```

Putting these functions together, our resulting parse method looks like this:

```
def parse(row: org.apache.spark.sql.Row): Trip = {
  val rr = new RichRow(row)
  Trip(
    license = rr.getAs[String]("hack_license").orNull,
    pickupTime = parseTaxiTime(rr, "pickup_datetime"),
    dropoffTime = parseTaxiTime(rr, "dropoff_datetime"),
    pickupX = parseTaxiLoc(rr, "pickup_longitude"),
    pickupY = parseTaxiLoc(rr, "pickup_latitude"),
    dropoffX = parseTaxiLoc(rr, "dropoff_longitude"),
    dropoffY = parseTaxiLoc(rr, "dropoff_latitude")
  )
}
```

We can test the parse function on several records from the head of the taxiRaw data to verify that it can correctly handle a sample of the data.

Handling Invalid Records at Scale

Anyone who has been working with large-scale, real-world data sets knows that they invariably contain at least a few records that do not conform to the expectations of the person who wrote the code to handle them. Many MapReduce jobs and Spark pipelines have failed because of invalid records that caused the parsing logic to throw an exception.

Typically, we handle these exceptions one at a time by checking the logs for the individual tasks, figuring out which line of code threw the exception, and then figuring out how to tweak the code to ignore or correct the invalid records. This is a tedious process, and it often feels like we're playing whack-a-mole: just as we get one exception fixed, we discover another one on a record that came later within the partition.

One strategy that experienced data scientists deploy when working with a new data set is to add a try-catch block to their parsing code so that any invalid records can be written out to the logs without causing the entire job to fail. If there are only a handful of invalid records in the entire data set, we might be okay with ignoring them and continuing with our analysis. With Spark, we can do even better: we can adapt our parsing code so that we can interactively analyze the invalid records in our data just as easily as we would perform any other kind of analysis.

For any individual record in an RDD or data set, there are two possible outcomes for our parsing code: it will either parse the record successfully and return meaningful output, or it will fail and throw an exception, in which case we want to capture both the value of the invalid record and the exception that was thrown. Whenever an operation has two mutually exclusive outcomes, we can use Scala's Either[L, R] type to represent the return type of the operation. For us, the "left" outcome is the successfully parsed record and the "right" outcome is a tuple of the exception we hit and the input record that caused it.

The safe function takes an argument named f of type S => T and returns a new S => Either[T, (S, Exception)] that will return either the result of calling f or, if an exception is thrown, a tuple containing the invalid input value and the exception itself:

```scala
def safe[S, T](f: S => T): S => Either[T, (S, Exception)] = {
  new Function[S, Either[T, (S, Exception)]] with Serializable {
    def apply(s: S): Either[T, (S, Exception)] = {
      try {
        Left(f(s))
      } catch {
        case e: Exception => Right((s, e))
      }
    }
  }
}
```

We can now create a safe wrapper function called safeParse by passing our parse function (of type String => Trip) to the safe function, and then applying safeParse to the backing RDD of the taxiRaw data set:

```
val safeParse = safe(parse)
val taxiParsed = taxiRaw.rdd.map(safeParse)
```

(Note that we cannot apply safeParse to the taxiRaw data set directly because the Either[L, R] type isn't supported by the Dataset API.)

If we want to determine how many of the input lines were parsed successfully, we can use the isLeft method on Either[L, R] in combination with the countByValue action:

```
taxiParsed.map(_.isLeft).
countByValue().
foreach(println)
...
(true,14776615)
```

What luck—none of the records threw exceptions during parsing! We can now convert the taxiParsed RDD into a Dataset[Trip] instance by getting the left element of the Either value:

```
val taxiGood = taxiParsed.map(_.left.get).toDS
taxiGood.cache()
```

Even though the records in the taxiGood data set parsed correctly, they may still have data quality problems that we want to uncover and handle. To find the remaining data quality problems, we can start to think of conditions that we expect to be true for any correctly recorded trip.

Given the temporal nature of our trip data, one reasonable invariant that we can expect is that the dropoff time for any trip will be sometime after the pickup time. We might also expect that trips will not take more than a few hours to complete, although it's certainly possible that long trips, trips that take place during rush hour, or trips that are delayed by accidents could go on for several hours. We're not exactly sure what the cutoff should be for a trip that takes a "reasonable" amount of time.

Let's define a helper function named hours that uses Java's TimeUnit helper method to convert the difference of the pickup and dropoff times in milliseconds to hours:

```
val hours = (pickup: Long, dropoff: Long) => {
  TimeUnit.HOURS.convert(dropoff - pickup, TimeUnit.MILLISECONDS)
}
```

We would like to be able to use our hours function to compute a histogram of the number of trips that lasted at least a given number of hours. This sort of calculation is exactly what the Dataset API and Spark SQL are designed to do, but by default, we can only use these methods on the columns of a Dataset instance, whereas the hour UDF is computed from two of these columns—the pickupTime and the dropoffTime. We need a mechanism that allows us to apply the hours functions to the columns of a data set and then perform the normal filtering and grouping operations that we are familiar with to the results.

This is exactly the use case that Spark SQL UDFs are designed to address. By wrapping a Scala function in an instance of Spark's UserDefinedFunction class, we can apply the function to the columns of a data set and analyze the results. Let's start by wrapping hours in a UDF and computing our histogram:

```
import org.apache.spark.sql.functions.udf
val hoursUDF = udf(hours)
taxiGood.
  groupBy(hoursUDF($"pickupTime", $"dropoffTime").as("h")).
  count().
  sort("h").
  show()
...
+---+--------+
|  h|   count|
+---+--------+
| -8|       1|
|  0|22355710|
|  1|   22934|
|  2|     843|
|  3|     197|
|  4|      86|
|  5|      55|
...
```

Everything looks fine here, except for one trip that took a -8 hours to complete! Perhaps the DeLorean from *Back to the Future* is moonlighting as an NYC taxi? Let's examine this record:

```
taxiGood.
  where(hoursUDF($"pickupTime", $"dropoffTime") < 0).
  collect().
  foreach(println)
```

This reveals the one odd record—a trip that began around 6PM on January 25 and finished just before 10AM the same day. It isn't obvious what went wrong with the recording of this trip but because it only seemed to happen for a single record, it should be okay to exclude it from our analysis for now.

Looking at the remainder of the trips that went on for a nonnegative number of hours, it appears that the vast majority of taxi rides last for no longer than three hours. We'll apply a filter to the taxiGood RDD so that we can focus on the distribution of these "typical" rides and ignore the outliers for now. Because it's a bit easier to express this filtering condition in Spark SQL, let's register our hours function with Spark SQL under the name "hours", so that we can use it inside SQL expressions:

```
spark.udf.register("hours", hours)
val taxiClean = taxiGood.where(
  "hours(pickupTime, dropoffTime) BETWEEN 0 AND 3"
)
```

To UDF or Not to UDF?

Spark SQL makes it very easy to inline business logic into functions that can be used from standard SQL, as we did here with the hours function. Given this, you might think that it would be a good idea to move all of your business logic into UDFs in order to make it easy to reuse, test, and maintain. However, there are a few caveats for using UDFs that you should be mindful of before you start sprinkling them throughout your code.

First, UDFs are opaque to Spark's SQL query planner and execution engine in a way that standard SQL query syntax is not, so moving logic into a UDF instead of using a literal SQL expression could hurt query performance.

Second, handling null values in Spark SQL can get complicated quickly, especially for UDFs that take multiple arguments. To properly handle nulls, you need to use Scala's Option[T] type or write your UDFs using the Java wrapper types, like java.lang.Integer and java.lang.Double, instead of the primitive types Int and Double in Scala.

Geospatial Analysis

Let's start examining the geospatial aspects of the taxi data. For each trip, we have longitude/latitude pairs representing where the passenger was picked up and dropped off. We would like to be able to determine which borough each of these longitude/latitude pairs belongs to, and identify any trips that did not start or end in any of the five boroughs. For example, if a taxi took passengers from Manhattan to Newark International Airport, that would be a valid ride that would be interesting to analyze, even though it would not end within one of the five boroughs. However, if it looks as if a taxi took a passenger to the South Pole, we can be reasonably confident that the record is invalid and should be excluded from our analysis.

To perform our borough analysis, we need to load the GeoJSON data we downloaded earlier and stored in the *nyc-boroughs.geojson* file. The Source class in the scala.io package makes it easy to read the contents of a text file or URL into the client as a single String:

```
val geojson = scala.io.Source.
  fromFile("nyc-boroughs.geojson").
  mkString
```

Now we need to import the GeoJSON parsing tools we reviewed earlier in the chapter using Spray and Esri into the Spark shell so that we can parse the geojson string into an instance of our FeatureCollection case class:

```
import com.cloudera.datascience.geotime._
import GeoJsonProtocol._
import spray.json._

val features = geojson.parseJson.convertTo[FeatureCollection]
```

We can create a sample point to test the functionality of the Esri Geometry API and verify that it can correctly identify which borough a particular xy coordinate belongs to:

```
import com.esri.core.geometry.Point
val p = new Point(-73.994499, 40.75066)
val borough = features.find(f => f.geometry.contains(p))
```

Before we use the features on the taxi trip data, we should take a moment to think about how to organize this geospatial data for maximum efficiency. One option would be to research data structures that are optimized for geospatial lookups, such as quad trees, and then find or write our own implementation. But let's see if we can come up with a quick heuristic that will allow us to bypass that bit of work.

The find method will iterate through the FeatureCollection until it finds a feature whose geometry contains the given Point of longitude/latitude. Most taxi rides in NYC begin and end in Manhattan, so if the geospatial features that represent Manhattan are earlier in the sequence, most of the find calls will return relatively quickly. We can use the fact that the boroughCode property of each feature can be used as a sorting key, with the code for Manhattan equal to 1 and the code for Staten Island equal to 5. Within the features for each borough, we want the features associated with the largest polygons to come before the smaller polygons, because most trips will be to and from the "major" region of each borough. Sorting the features by the combination of the borough code and the area2D() of each feature's geometry should do the trick:

```
val areaSortedFeatures = features.sortBy(f => {
  val borough = f("boroughCode").convertTo[Int]
  (borough, -f.geometry.area2D())
})
```

Note that we're sorting based on the negation of the area2D() value because we want the largest polygons to come first, and Scala sorts in ascending order by default.

Now we can broadcast the sorted features in the areaSortedFeatures sequence to the cluster and write a function that uses these features to find out in which of the five boroughs (if any) a particular trip ended:

```
val bFeatures = sc.broadcast(areaSortedFeatures)

val bLookup = (x: Double, y: Double) => {
  val feature: Option[Feature] = bFeatures.value.find(f => {
    f.geometry.contains(new Point(x, y))
  })
  feature.map(f => {
    f("borough").convertTo[String]
  }).getOrElse("NA")
}
val boroughUDF = udf(bLookup)
```

We can apply boroughUDF to the trips in the taxiClean RDD to create a histogram of trips by borough:

```
taxiClean.
  groupBy(boroughUDF($"dropoffX", $"dropoffY")).
  count().
  show()
...
+-----------------------+--------+
|UDF(dropoffX, dropoffY)|   count|
+-----------------------+--------+
|                 Queens|  672192|
|                     NA| 7942421|
|               Brooklyn|  715252|
|          Staten Island|    3338|
|              Manhattan|12979047|
|                  Bronx|   67434|
+-----------------------+--------+
```

As we expected, the vast majority of trips end in the borough of Manhattan, while relatively few trips end in Staten Island. One surprising observation is the number of trips that end outside of any borough; the number of NA records is substantially larger than the number of taxi rides that end in the Bronx. Let's grab some examples of this kind of trip from the data:

```
taxiClean.
  where(boroughUDF($"dropoffX", $"dropoffY") === "NA").
  show()
```

When we print out these records, we see that a substantial fraction of them start and end at the point (0.0, 0.0), indicating that the trip location is missing for these records. We should filter these events out of our data set because they won't help us with our analysis:

```
val taxiDone = taxiClean.where(
  "dropoffX != 0 and dropoffY != 0 and pickupX != 0 and pickupY != 0"
).cache()
```

When we rerun our borough analysis on the taxiDone RDD, we see this:

```
taxiDone.
  groupBy(boroughUDF($"dropoffX", $"dropoffY")).
  count().
  show()
...
+------------------------+--------+
|UDF(dropoffX, dropoffY)|   count|
+------------------------+--------+
|                 Queens|  670912|
|                     NA|   62778|
|               Brooklyn|  714659|
|          Staten Island|    3333|
|              Manhattan|12971314|
|                  Bronx|   67333|
+------------------------+--------+
```

Our zero-point filter removed a small number of observations from the output boroughs, but it removed a large fraction of the NA entries, leaving a much more reasonable number of observations that had dropoffs outside the city.

Sessionization in Spark

Our goal, from many pages ago, was to investigate the relationship between the borough in which a driver drops his passenger off and the amount of time it takes to acquire another fare. At this point, the taxiDone data set contains all of the individual trips for each taxi driver in individual records distributed across different partitions of the data. To compute the length of time between the end of one ride and the start of the next one, we need to aggregate all of the trips from a shift by a single driver into a single record, and then sort the trips within that shift by time. The sort step allows us to compare the dropoff time of one trip to the pickup time of the next trip. This kind of analysis, in which we want to analyze a single entity as it executes a series of events over time, is called *sessionization*, and is commonly performed over web logs to analyze the behavior of the users of a website.

Sessionization can be a very powerful technique for uncovering insights in data and building new data products that can be used to help people make better decisions. For example, Google's spell-correction engine is built on top of the sessions of user activity that Google builds each day from the logged records of every event (searches, clicks, maps visits, etc.) occurring on its web properties. To identify likely spell-correction candidates, Google processes those sessions looking for situations where a user typed a query, didn't click anything, typed a slightly different query a few seconds later, and then clicked a result and didn't come back to Google. Then it counts how often this pattern occurs for any pair of queries. If it occurs frequently enough (e.g., if every time we see the query "untied stats," it's followed a few seconds later by the query "united states"), then we assume that the second query is a spell correction of the first.

This analysis takes advantage of the patterns of human behavior that are represented in the event logs to build a spell-correction engine from data that is more powerful than any engine that could be created from a dictionary. The engine can be used to perform spell correction in any language, and can correct words that might not be included in any dictionary (e.g., the name of a new startup), and can even correct queries like "untied stats" where none of the words are misspelled! Google uses similar techniques to show recommended and related searches, as well as to decide which queries should return a OneBox result that gives the answer to a query on the search page itself, without requiring that the user click through to a different page. There are OneBoxes for weather, scores from sports games, addresses, and lots of other kinds of queries.

So far, information about the set of events that occurs to each entity is spread out across the RDD's partitions, so, for analysis, we need to place these relevant events next to each other and in chronological order. In the next section, we'll show how to efficiently construct and analyze sessions using advanced functionality that was introduced in Spark 2.0.

Building Sessions: Secondary Sorts in Spark

The naive way to create sessions in Spark is to perform a `groupBy` on the identifier we want to create sessions for and then sort the events postshuffle by a timestamp identifier. If we only have a small number of events for each entity, this approach will work reasonably well. However, because this approach requires all the events for any particular entity to be in memory at the same time, it will not scale as the number of events for each entity gets larger and larger. We need a way of building sessions that does not require all of the events for a particular entity to be held in memory at the same time for sorting.

In MapReduce, we can build sessions by performing a *secondary sort*, where we create a composite key made up of an identifier and a timestamp value, sort all of the records on the composite key, and then use a custom partitioner and grouping function to ensure that all of the records for the same identifier appear in the same output partition. Fortunately, Spark can also support this same secondary sort pattern by combining its `repartition` and a `sortWithinPartitions` transformation; in Spark 2.0, sessionizing a data set can be done in three lines of code:

```
val sessions = taxiDone.
  repartition($"license").
  sortWithinPartitions($"license", $"pickupTime")
```

First, we use the `repartition` method to ensure that all of the `Trip` records that have the same value for the `license` column end up in the same partition. Then, within each of these partitions, we sort the records by their `license` value (so all trips by the same driver appear together) and then by their `pickupTime`, so that the sequence of trips appear in sorted order within the partition. Now when we process the trip records using a method like mapPartitions, we can be sure that the trips are ordered in a way that is optimal for sessions analysis. Because this operation triggers a shuffle and a fair bit of computation, and we'll need to use the results more than once, we cache them:

```
sessions.cache()
```

Executing a sessionization pipeline is an expensive operation, and the sessionized data is often useful for many different analysis tasks that we might want to perform. In settings where one might want to pick up on the analysis later or collaborate with other data scientists, it's a good idea to amortize the cost of sessionizing a large data set by only performing the sessionization once, and then writing the sessionized data to HDFS so that it can be used to answer lots of different questions. Performing sessionization once is also a good way to enforce standard rules for session definitions across the entire data science team, which has the same benefits for ensuring apples-to-apples comparisons of results.

At this point, we are ready to analyze our sessions data to see how long it takes for a driver to find his next fare after a dropoff in a particular borough. We will create a boroughDuration method that takes two instances of the Trip class and computes both the borough of the first trip and the duration in seconds between the dropoff time of the first trip and the pickup time of the second:

```
def boroughDuration(t1: Trip, t2: Trip): (String, Long) = {
  val b = bLookup(t1.dropoffX, t1.dropoffY)
  val d = (t2.pickupTime - t1.dropoffTime) / 1000
  (b, d)
}
```

We want to apply our new function to all sequential pairs of trips inside our sessions data set. Although we could write a for loop to do this, we can also use the sliding method of the Scala Collections API to get the sequential pairs in a more functional way:

```
val boroughDurations: DataFrame =
  sessions.mapPartitions(trips => {
    val iter: Iterator[Seq[Trip]] = trips.sliding(2)
    val viter = iter.
      filter(_.size == 2).
      filter(p => p(0).license == p(1).license)
    viter.map(p => boroughDuration(p(0), p(1)))
  }).toDF("borough", "seconds")
```

The filter call on the result of the sliding method ensures that we ignore any sessions that contain only a single trip, or any trip pairs that have different values of the license field. The result of our mapPartitions over the sessions is a data frame of borough/duration pairs that we can now examine. First, we should do a validation check to ensure that most of the durations are nonnegative:

```
boroughDurations.
  selectExpr("floor(seconds / 3600) as hours").
  groupBy("hours").
  count().
  sort("hours").
  show()
...
+-----+--------+
|hours|   count|
+-----+--------+
|   -3|       2|
|   -2|      16|
|   -1|    4253|
|    0|13359033|
|    1|  347634|
|    2|   76286|
|    3|   24812|
|    4|   10026|
|    5|    4789|
```

Only a few of the records have a negative duration, and when we examine them more closely, there don't seem to be any common patterns to them that we could use to understand the source of the erroneous data. If we exclude these negative duration records from our input data set and look at the average and standard deviation of the pickup times by borough, we see this:

```
boroughDurations.
  where("seconds > 0 AND seconds < 60*60*4").
  groupBy("borough").
  agg(avg("seconds"), stddev("seconds")).
  show()
...
+-------------+------------------+-------------------+
|      borough|      avg(seconds)|stddev_samp(seconds)|
+-------------+------------------+-------------------+
|       Queens|2380.6603554494727|  2206.6572799118035|
|           NA|  2006.53571169866|  1997.0891370324784|
|     Brooklyn| 1365.394576250576|  1612.9921698951398|
|Staten Island|         2723.5625|  2395.7745475546385|
|    Manhattan| 631.8473780726746|   1042.919915477234|
|        Bronx|1975.9209786770646|   1704.006452085683|
+-------------+------------------+-------------------+
```

As we would expect, the data shows that dropoffs in Manhattan have the shortest amount of downtime for drivers, at around 10 minutes. Taxi rides that end in Brooklyn have a downtime of more than twice that, and the relatively few rides that end in Staten Island take a driver an average of almost 45 minutes to get to his next fare.

As the data demonstrates, taxi drivers have a major financial incentive to discriminate among passengers based on their final destination; dropoffs in Staten Island, in particular, involve an extensive amount of downtime for a driver. The NYC Taxi and Limousine Commission has made a major effort over the years to identify this discrimination and has fined drivers who have been caught rejecting passengers because of where they wanted to go. It would be interesting to attempt to examine the data for unusually short taxi rides that could be indicative of a dispute between the driver and the passenger about where the passenger wanted to be dropped off.

Where to Go from Here

Imagine using this same technique on the taxi data to build an application that could recommend the best place for a cab to go after a dropoff based on current traffic patterns and the historical record of next-best locations contained within this data. You could also look at the information from the perspective of someone trying to catch a cab: given the current time, place, and weather data, what is the probability that I will be able to hail a cab from the street within the next five minutes? This sort of information could be incorporated into applications like Google Maps to help travelers decide when to leave and which travel option they should take.

The Esri API is one of a few different tools that can help us interact with geospatial data from JVM-based languages. Another is GeoTrellis, a geospatial library written in Scala, that seeks to be easily accessible from Spark. A third is GeoTools, a Java-based GIS toolkit.

Estimating Financial Risk Through Monte Carlo Simulation

Sandy Ryza

If you want to understand geology, study earthquakes.
If you want to understand the economy, study the Depression.
　　—Ben Bernanke

Under reasonable circumstances, how much can you expect to lose? This is the quantity that the financial statistic *Value at Risk* (VaR) seeks to measure. Since its development soon after the stock market crash of 1987, VaR has seen widespread use across financial services organizations. The statistic plays a vital role in the management of these institutions by helping to determine how much cash they must hold to meet the credit ratings they seek. In addition, some use it to more broadly understand the risk characteristics of large portfolios, and others compute it before executing trades to help inform immediate decisions.

Many of the most sophisticated approaches to estimating this statistic rely on computationally intensive simulation of markets under random conditions. The technique behind these approaches, called *Monte Carlo simulation*, involves posing thousands or millions of random market scenarios and observing how they tend to affect a portfolio. Spark is an ideal tool for Monte Carlo simulation, because the technique is naturally massively parallelizable. Spark can leverage thousands of cores to run random trials and aggregate their results. As a general-purpose data transformation engine, it is also adept at performing the pre- and postprocessing steps that surround the simulations. It can transform raw financial data into the model parameters needed to carry out the simulations, as well as support ad hoc analysis of the results. Its simple programming model can drastically reduce development time compared to more traditional approaches that use HPC environments.

Let's define "how much can you expect to lose" a little more rigorously. VaR is a simple measure of investment risk that tries to provide a reasonable estimate of the maximum probable loss in value of an investment portfolio over a particular time period. A VaR statistic depends on three parameters: a portfolio, a time period, and a probability. A VaR of $1 million with a 5% probability and two weeks indicates the belief that the portfolio stands only a 5% chance of losing more than $1 million over two weeks.

We'll also discuss how to compute a related statistic called *Conditional Value at Risk* (CVaR), sometimes known as expected shortfall, which the Basel Committee on Banking Supervision has recently proposed as a better risk measure than VaR. A CVaR statistic has the same three parameters as a VaR statistic, but considers the expected loss instead of the cutoff value. A CVaR of $5 million with a 5% *q-value* and two weeks indicates the belief that the average loss in the worst 5% of outcomes is $5 million.

In service of modeling VaR, we'll introduce a few different concepts, approaches, and packages. We'll cover kernel density estimation and plotting using the *breeze-viz* package, sampling using the multivariate normal distribution, and statistics functions using the Apache Commons Math package.

Terminology

This chapter makes use of a set of terms specific to the finance domain. We'll briefly define them here:

Instrument
A tradable asset, such as a bond, loan, option, or stock investment. At any particular time, an instrument is considered to have a *value*, which is the price for which it could be sold.

Portfolio
A collection of instruments owned by a financial institution.

Return
The change in an instrument or portfolio's value over a time period.

Loss
A negative return.

Index
An imaginary portfolio of instruments. For example, the NASDAQ Composite Index includes about 3,000 stocks and similar instruments for major US and international companies.

Market factor

> A value that can be used as an indicator of macroaspects of the financial climate at a particular time—for example, the value of an index, the gross domestic product of the United States, or the exchange rate between the dollar and the euro. We will often refer to market factors as just *factors*.

Methods for Calculating VaR

So far, our definition of VaR has been fairly open-ended. Estimating this statistic requires proposing a model for how a portfolio functions and choosing the probability distribution its returns are likely to take. Institutions employ a variety of approaches for calculating VaR, all of which tend to fall under a few general methods.

Variance-Covariance

Variance-covariance is by far the simplest and least computationally intensive method. Its model assumes that the return of each instrument is normally distributed, which allows deriving a estimate analytically.

Historical Simulation

Historical simulation extrapolates risk from historical data by using its distribution directly instead of relying on summary statistics. For example, to determine a 95% VaR for a portfolio, we might look at that portfolio's performance for the last 100 days and estimate the statistic as its value on the fifth-worst day. A drawback of this method is that historical data can be limited and fails to include what-ifs. For example, what if the history we have for the instruments in our portfolio lacks market collapses, and we want to model what happens to our portfolio in these situations. Techniques exist for making historical simulation robust to these issues, such as introducing "shocks" into the data, but we won't cover them here.

Monte Carlo Simulation

Monte Carlo simulation, which the rest of this chapter will focus on, tries to weaken the assumptions in the previous methods by simulating the portfolio under random conditions. When we can't derive a closed form for a probability distribution analytically, we can often estimate its probability density function (PDF) by repeatedly sampling simpler random variables that it depends on and seeing how it plays out in aggregate. In its most general form, this method:

- Defines a relationship between market conditions and each instrument's returns. This relationship takes the form of a model fitted to historical data.

- Defines distributions for the market conditions that are straightforward to sample from. These distributions are fitted to historical data.

- Poses *trials* consisting of random market conditions.

- Calculates the total portfolio loss for each trial, and uses these losses to define an empirical distribution over losses. This means that, if we run 100 trials and want to estimate the 5% VaR, we would choose it as the loss from the trial with the fifth-greatest loss. To calculate the 5% CVaR, we would find the average loss over the five worst trials.

Of course, the Monte Carlo method isn't perfect either. It relies on models for generating trial conditions and for inferring instrument performance, and these models must make simplifying assumptions. If these assumptions don't correspond to reality, then neither will the final probability distribution that comes out.

Our Model

A Monte Carlo risk model typically phrases each instrument's return in terms of a set of *market factors*. Common market factors might be the value of indexes like the S&P 500, the US GDP, or currency exchange rates. We then need a model that predicts the return of each instrument based on these market conditions. In our simulation, we'll use a simple linear model. By our previous definition of return, a *factor return* is a change in the value of a market factor over a particular time. For example, if the value of the S&P 500 moves from 2,000 to 2,100 over a time interval, its return would be 100. We'll derive a set of features from simple transformations of the factor returns. That is, the market factor vector m_t for a trial t is transformed by some function φ to produce a feature vector of possible different length f_t:

$$f_t = \phi(m_t)$$

For each instrument, we'll train a model that assigns a weight to each feature. To calculate r_{it}, the return of instrument i in trial t, we use c_i, the intercept term for the instrument; w_{ij}, the regression weight for feature j on instrument i; and f_{tj}, the randomly generated value of feature j in trial t:

$$r_{it} = c_i + \sum_{j=1}^{|w_i|} w_{ij} * f_{tj}$$

This means that the return of each instrument is calculated as the sum of the returns of the market factor features multiplied by their weights for that instrument. We can fit the linear model for each instrument using historical data (also known as doing linear regression). If the horizon of the VaR calculation is two weeks, the regression treats every (overlapping) two-week interval in history as a labeled point.

It's also worth mentioning that we could have chosen a more complicated model. For example, the model need not be linear: it could be a regression tree or explicitly incorporate domain-specific knowledge.

Now that we have our model for calculating instrument losses from market factors, we need a process for simulating the behavior of market factors. A simple assumption is that each market factor return follows a normal distribution. To capture the fact that market factors are often correlated—when NASDAQ is down, the Dow is likely to be suffering as well—we can use a multivariate normal distribution with a non-diagonal covariance matrix:

$$m_t \sim \mathcal{N}(\mu, \Sigma)$$

where μ is a vector of the empirical means of the returns of the factors and Σ is the empirical covariance matrix of the returns of the factors.

As before, we could have chosen a more complicated method of simulating the market or assumed a different type of distribution for each market factor, perhaps using distributions with fatter tails.

Getting the Data

It can be difficult to find large volumes of nicely formatted historical price data, but Yahoo! has a variety of stock data available for download in CSV format. The following script, located in the *risk/data* directory of the repo, will make a series of REST calls to download histories for all the stocks included in the NASDAQ index and place them in a *stocks/* directory:

```
$ ./download-all-symbols.sh
```

We also need historical data for risk factors. For our factors, we'll use the values of the S&P 500 and NASDAQ indexes, as well as the prices of 5-year and 30-year US Treasury bonds. These can all be downloaded from Yahoo! as well:

```
$ mkdir factors/
$ ./download-symbol.sh ^GSPC factors
$ ./download-symbol.sh ^IXIC factors
$ ./download-symbol.sh ^TYX factors
$ ./download-symbol.sh ^FVX factors
```

Preprocessing

The first few rows of the Yahoo!-formatted data for GOOGL looks like:

```
Date,Open,High,Low,Close,Volume,Adj Close
2014-10-24,554.98,555.00,545.16,548.90,2175400,548.90
2014-10-23,548.28,557.40,545.50,553.65,2151300,553.65
2014-10-22,541.05,550.76,540.23,542.69,2973700,542.69
2014-10-21,537.27,538.77,530.20,538.03,2459500,538.03
2014-10-20,520.45,533.16,519.14,532.38,2748200,532.38
```

Let's fire up the Spark shell. In this chapter, we rely on several libraries to make our lives easier. The GitHub repo contains a Maven project that can be used to build a JAR file that packages all these dependencies together:

```
$ cd ch09-risk/
$ mvn package
$ cd data/
$ spark-shell --jars ../target/ch09-risk-2.0.0-jar-with-dependencies.jar
```

For each instrument and factor, we want to derive a list of (date, closing price) tuples. The `java.time` library contains useful functionality for representing and manipulating dates. We can represent our dates as `LocalDate` objects. We can use the `DateTimeFormatter` to parse dates in the Yahoo date format:

```
import java.time.LocalDate
import java.time.format.DateTimeFormatter

val format = DateTimeFormatter.ofPattern("yyyy-MM-dd")
LocalDate.parse("2014-10-24")
res0: java.time.LocalDate = 2014-10-24
```

The 3,000-instrument histories and 4-factor histories are small enough to read and process locally. This remains the case even for larger simulations with hundreds of thousands of instruments and thousands of factors. The need arises for a distributed system like Spark when we're actually running the simulations, which can require massive amounts of computation on each instrument.

To read a full Yahoo history from local disk:

```
import java.io.File

def readYahooHistory(file: File): Array[(LocalDate, Double)] = {
  val formatter = DateTimeFormatter.ofPattern("yyyy-MM-dd")
  val lines = scala.io.Source.fromFile(file).getLines().toSeq
  lines.tail.map { line =>
    val cols = line.split(',')
    val date = LocalDate.parse(cols(0), formatter)
    val value = cols(1).toDouble
    (date, value)
  }.reverse.toArray
}
```

Notice that `lines.tail` is useful for excluding the header row. We load all the data and filter out instruments with less than five years of history:

```
val start = LocalDate.of(2009, 10, 23)
val end = LocalDate.of(2014, 10, 23)

val stocksDir = new File("stocks/")
val files = stocksDir.listFiles()
val allStocks = files.iterator.flatMap { file =>> ❶
  try {
    Some(readYahooHistory(file))
  } catch {
    case e: Exception => None
  }
}
val rawStocks = allStocks.filter(_.size >= 260 * 5 + 10)

val factorsPrefix = "factors/"
val rawFactors = Array(
  "^GSPC.csv", "^IXIC.csv", "^TYX.csv", "^FVX.csv").
  map(x => new File(factorsPrefix + x)).
  map(readYahooHistory)
```

❶ Using `iterator` here allows us to stream over the files instead of loading their full contents in memory all at once.

Different types of instruments may trade on different days, or the data may have missing values for other reasons, so it is important to make sure that our different histories align. First, we need to trim all of our time series to the same region in time. Then we need to fill in missing values. To deal with time series that are missing values at the start and end dates in the time region, we simply fill in those dates with nearby values in the time region:

```
def trimToRegion(history: Array[(LocalDate, Double)],
    start: LocalDate, end: LocalDate)
  : Array[(LocalDate, Double)] = {
  var trimmed = history.dropWhile(_._1.isBefore(start)).
    takeWhile(x => x._1.isBefore(end) || x._1.isEqual(end))
  if (trimmed.head._1 != start) {
    trimmed = Array((start, trimmed.head._2)) ++ trimmed
  }
  if (trimmed.last._1 != end) {
    trimmed = trimmed ++ Array((end, trimmed.last._2))
  }
  trimmed
}
```

To deal with missing values within a time series, we use a simple imputation strategy that fills in an instrument's price as its most recent closing price before that day. Because there is no pretty Scala Collections method that can do this for us, we write it on our own. The spark-ts (*https://github.com/sryza/spark-timeseries*) and flint (*https://github.com/twosigma/flint*) libraries are alternatives that contain an array of useful time series manipulations functions.

```
import scala.collection.mutable.ArrayBuffer

def fillInHistory(history: Array[(DateTime, Double)],
    start: DateTime, end: DateTime): Array[(DateTime, Double)] = {
  var cur = history
  val filled = new ArrayBuffer[(DateTime, Double)]()
  var curDate = start
  while (curDate < end) {
    if (cur.tail.nonEmpty && cur.tail.head._1 == curDate) {
      cur = cur.tail
    }

    filled += ((curDate, cur.head._2))

    curDate += 1.days
    // Skip weekends
    if (curDate.dayOfWeek().get > 5) curDate += 2.days
  }
  filled.toArray
}
```

We apply `trimToRegion` and `fillInHistory` to the data:

```
val stocks = rawStocks.
  map(trimToRegion(_, start, end)).
  map(fillInHistory(_, start, end))

val factors = (factors1 ++ factors2).
  map(trimToRegion(_, start, end)).
  map(fillInHistory(_, start, end))
```

Keep in mind that, even though the Scala APIs used here look very similar to Spark's API, these operations are executing locally. Each element of `stocks` is an array of values at different time points for a particular stock. `factors` has the same structure. All these arrays should have equal length, which we can verify with:

```
(stocks ++ factors).forall(_.size == stocks(0).size)
res17: Boolean = true
```

Determining the Factor Weights

Recall that VaR deals with losses *over a particular time horizon*. We are not concerned with the absolute prices of instruments but how those prices move over a given length of time. In our calculation, we will set that length to two weeks. The following function makes use of the Scala Collections' `sliding` method to transform time series of prices into an overlapping sequence of price movements over two-week intervals. Note that we use 10 instead of 14 to define the window because financial data does not include weekends:

```
def twoWeekReturns(history: Array[(LocalDate, Double)])
  : Array[Double] = {
```

```
history.sliding(10).
  map { window =>
    val next = window.last._2
    val prev = window.head._2
    (next - prev) / prev
  }.toArray
}

val stocksReturns = stocks.map(twoWeekReturns).toArray.toSeq  ❶
val factorsReturns = factors.map(twoWeekReturns)
```

❶ Because of our earlier use of `iterator`, `stocks` is an iterator. `.toArray.toSeq` runs through it and collects the elements in memory into a sequence.

With these return histories in hand, we can turn to our goal of training predictive models for the instrument returns. For each instrument, we want a model that predicts its two-week return based on the returns of the factors over the same time period. For simplicity, we will use a linear regression model.

To model the fact that instrument returns may be nonlinear functions of the factor returns, we can include some additional features in our model that we derive from nonlinear transformations of the factor returns. We will try adding two additional features for each factor return: square and square root. Our model is still a linear model in the sense that the response variable is a linear function of the features. Some of the features just happen to be determined by nonlinear functions of the factor returns. Keep in mind that this particular feature transformation is meant to demonstrate some of the options available—it shouldn't be perceived as a state-of-the-art practice in predictive financial modeling.

Even though we will be carrying out many regressions—one for each instrument—the number of features and data points in each regression is small, meaning that we don't need to make use of Spark's distributed linear modeling capabilities. Instead, we'll use the ordinary least squares regression offered by the Apache Commons Math package. While our factor data is currently a `Seq` of histories (each an array of (`Date Time, Double`) tuples), `OLSMultipleLinearRegression` expects data as an array of sample points (in our case a two-week interval), so we need to transpose our factor matrix:

```
def factorMatrix(histories: Seq[Array[Double]])
  : Array[Array[Double]] = {
  val mat = new Array[Array[Double]](histories.head.length)
  for (i <- histories.head.indices) {
    mat(i) = histories.map(_(i)).toArray
  }
  mat
}

val factorMat = factorMatrix(factorsReturns)
```

Then we can tack on our additional features:

```
def featurize(factorReturns: Array[Double]): Array[Double] = {
  val squaredReturns = factorReturns.
    map(x => math.signum(x) * x * x)
  val squareRootedReturns = factorReturns.
    map(x => math.signum(x) * math.sqrt(math.abs(x)))
  squaredReturns ++ squareRootedReturns ++ factorReturns
}

val factorFeatures = factorMat.map(featurize)
```

And then we can fit the linear models. In addition, to find the model parameters for each instrument, we can use the `OLSMultipleLinearRegression`'s `estimateRegres sionParameters` method:

```
import org.apache.commons.math3.stat.regression.OLSMultipleLinearRegression

def linearModel(instrument: Array[Double],
    factorMatrix: Array[Array[Double]])
  : OLSMultipleLinearRegression = {
  val regression = new OLSMultipleLinearRegression()
  regression.newSampleData(instrument, factorMatrix)
  regression
}

val factorWeights = stocksReturns.
  map(linearModel(_, factorFeatures)).
  map(_.estimateRegressionParameters()).
  toArray
```

We now have a 1,867×8 matrix where each row is the set of model parameters (coefficients, weights, covariants, regressors, or whatever you wish to call them) for an instrument.

We will elide this analysis for brevity, but at this point in any real-world pipeline it would be useful to understand how well these models fit the data. Because the data points are drawn from time series, and especially because the time intervals are overlapping, it is very likely that the samples are autocorrelated. This means that common measures like R^2 are likely to overestimate how well the models fit the data. The Breusch-Godfrey (*http://bit.ly/2psAwB7*) test is a standard test for assessing these effects. One quick way to evaluate a model is to separate a time series into two sets, leaving out enough data points in the middle so that the last points in the earlier set are not autocorrelated with the first points in the later set. Then train the model on one set and look at its error on the other.

Sampling

With our models that map factor returns to instrument returns in hand, we now need a procedure for simulating market conditions by generating random factor returns. That is, we need to decide on a probability distribution over factor return vectors and sample from it. What distribution does the data actually take? It can often be useful to start answering this kind of question visually. A nice way to visualize a probability distribution over continuous data is a density plot that plots the distribution's domain versus its PDF. Because we don't know the distribution that governs the data, we don't have an equation that can give us its density at an arbitrary point, but we can approximate it through a technique called *kernel density estimation*. In a loose way, kernel density estimation is a way of smoothing out a histogram. It centers a probability distribution (usually a normal distribution) at each data point. So a set of two-week-return samples would result in 200 normal distributions, each with a different mean. To estimate the probability density at a given point, it evaluates the PDFs of all the normal distributions at that point and takes their average. The smoothness of a kernel density plot depends on its *bandwidth*, the standard deviation of each of the normal distributions. The GitHub repository comes with a kernel density implementation that works both over RDDs and local collections. For brevity, it is elided here.

breeze-viz is a Scala library that makes it easy to draw simple plots. The following snippet creates a density plot from a set of samples:

```
import org.apache.spark.mllib.stat.KernelDensity
import org.apache.spark.util.StatCounter
import breeze.plot._

def plotDistribution(samples: Array[Double]): Figure = {
  val min = samples.min
  val max = samples.max
  val stddev = new StatCounter(samples).stdev
  val bandwidth = 1.06 * stddev * math.pow(samples.size, -0.2) ❶

  val domain = Range.Double(min, max, (max - min) / 100).
    toList.toArray
  val kd = new KernelDensity().
    setSample(samples.toSeq.toDS.rdd).
    setBandwidth(bandwidth)
  val densities = kd.estimate(domain)
  val f = Figure()
  val p = f.subplot(0)
  p += plot(domain, densities)
  p.xlabel = "Two Week Return ($)"
  p.ylabel = "Density"
  f
}
```

```
plotDistribution(factorsReturns(0))
plotDistribution(factorsReturns(2))
```

❶ We use what is known as "Silverman's rule of thumb," named after the British statistician Bernard Silverman, to pick a reasonable bandwidth.

Figure 9-1 shows the distribution (probability density function) of two-week returns for the S&P 500 in our history.

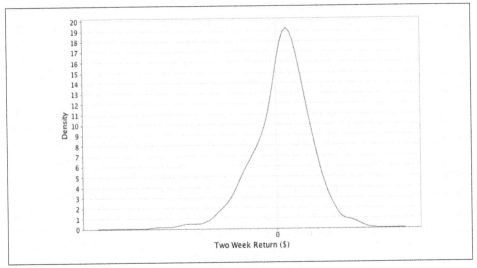

Figure 9-1. Two-week S&P 500 returns distribution

Figure 9-2 shows the same for two-week returns of 30-year Treasury bonds.

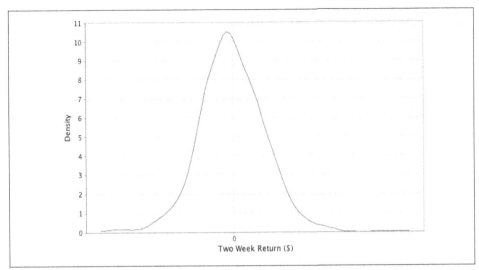

Figure 9-2. Two-week 30-year Treasury bond returns distribution

We will fit a normal distribution to the returns of each factor. Looking for a more exotic distribution, perhaps with fatter tails, that more closely fits the data is often worthwhile. However, for the sake of simplicity, we will avoid tuning our simulation in this way.

The simplest way to sample factors' returns would be to fit a normal distribution to each of the factors and sample from these distributions independently. However, this ignores the fact that market factors are often correlated. If the S&P is down, the Dow is likely to be down as well. Failing to take these correlations into account can give us a much rosier picture of our risk profile than its reality. Are the returns of our factors correlated? The Pearson's correlation implementation from Commons Math can help us find out:

```
import org.apache.commons.math3.stat.correlation.PearsonsCorrelation

val factorCor =
  new PearsonsCorrelation(factorMat).getCorrelationMatrix().getData()
println(factorCor.map(_.mkString("\t")).mkString("\n"))
1.0      -0.3472  0.4424   0.4633  ❶
-0.3472  1.0      -0.4777  -0.5096
0.4424   -0.4777  1.0      0.9199
0.4633   -0.5096  0.9199   1.0
```

❶ Digits truncated to fit within the margins

Because we have nonzero elements off the diagonals, it doesn't look like it.

The Multivariate Normal Distribution

The multivariate normal distribution can help here by taking the correlation information between the factors into account. Each sample from a multivariate normal is a vector. Given values for all of the dimensions but one, the distribution of values along that dimension is normal. But, in their joint distribution, the variables are not independent.

The multivariate normal is parameterized with a mean along each dimension and a matrix describing the covariances between each pair of dimensions. With N dimensions, the covariance matrix is N by N because we want to capture the covariances between each pair of dimensions. When the covariance matrix is diagonal, the multivariate normal reduces to sampling along each dimension independently, but placing nonzero values in the off-diagonals helps capture the relationships between variables.

The VaR literature often describes a step in which the factor weights are transformed (decorrelated) so that sampling can proceed. This is normally accomplished with a Cholesky decomposition or eigendecomposition. The Apache Commons Math `Multi variateNormalDistribution` takes care of this step for us under the covers using an eigendecomposition.

To fit a multivariate normal distribution to our data, first we need to find its sample means and covariances:

```
import org.apache.commons.math3.stat.correlation.Covariance

val factorCov = new Covariance(factorMat).getCovarianceMatrix().
  getData()

val factorMeans = factorsReturns.
  map(factor => factor.sum / factor.size).toArray
```

Then we can simply create a distribution parameterized with them:

```
import org.apache.commons.math3.distribution.MultivariateNormalDistribution

val factorsDist = new MultivariateNormalDistribution(factorMeans,
  factorCov)
```

To sample a set of market conditions from it:

```
factorsDist.sample()
res1: Array[Double] = Array(-0.05782773255967754, 0.01890770078427768,
  0.029344325473062878, 0.04398266164298203)

factorsDist.sample()
res2: Array[Double] = Array(-0.009840154244155741, -0.01573733572551166,
  0.029140934507992572, 0.028227818241305904)
```

Running the Trials

With the per-instrument models and a procedure for sampling factor returns, we now have the pieces we need to run the actual trials. Because running the trials is very computationally intensive, we will finally turn to Spark to help us parallelize them. In each trial, we want to sample a set of risk factors, use them to predict the return of each instrument, and sum all those returns to find the full trial loss. To achieve a representative distribution, we want to run thousands or millions of these trials.

We have a few choices for how to parallelize the simulation. We can parallelize along trials, instruments, or both. To parallelize along both, we would create a data set of instruments and a data set of trial parameters, and then use the crossJoin transformation to generate a data set of all the pairs. This is the most general approach, but it has a couple of disadvantages. First, it requires explicitly creating an RDD of trial parameters, which we can avoid by using some tricks with random seeds. Second, it requires a shuffle operation.

Partitioning along instruments would look something like this:

```
val randomSeed = 1496
val instrumentsDS = ...
def trialLossesForInstrument(seed: Long, instrument: Array[Double])
  : Array[(Int, Double)] = {
  ...
}
instrumentsDS.flatMap(trialLossesForInstrument(randomSeed, _)).
  reduceByKey(_ + _)
```

With this approach, the data is partitioned across an RDD of instruments, and for each instrument a flatMap transformation computes and yields the loss against every trial. Using the same random seed across all tasks means that we will generate the same sequence of trials. A reduceByKey sums together all the losses corresponding to the same trials. A disadvantage of this approach is that it still requires shuffling $O(|$ instruments$| * |$trials$|)$ data.

Our model data for our few thousand instruments data is small enough to fit in memory on every executor, and some back-of-the-envelope calculations reveal that this is probably still the case even with a million or so instruments and hundreds of factors. A million instruments times 500 factors times the 8 bytes needed for the double that stores each factor weight equals roughly 4 GB, small enough to fit in each executor on most modern-day cluster machines. This means that a good option is to distribute the instrument data in a broadcast variable. The advantage of each executor having a full copy of the instrument data is that total loss for each trial can be computed on a single machine. No aggregation is necessary.

With the partition-by-trials approach (which we will use), we start out with an RDD of seeds. We want a different seed in each partition so that each partition generates different trials:

```
val parallelism = 1000
val baseSeed = 1496

val seeds = (baseSeed until baseSeed + parallelism)
val seedDS = seeds.toDS().repartition(parallelism)
```

Random number generation is a time-consuming and CPU-intensive process. While we don't employ this trick here, it can often be useful to generate a set of random numbers in advance and use it across multiple jobs. The same random numbers should *not* be used within a single job, because this would violate the Monte Carlo assumption that the random values are independently distributed. If we were to go this route, we would replace toDS with textFile and load randomNumbersDS.

For each seed, we want to generate a set of trial parameters and observe the effects of these parameters on all the instruments. Let's start from the ground up by writing a function that calculates the return of a single instrument underneath a single trial. We simply apply the linear model that we trained earlier for that instrument. The length of the instrument array of regression parameters is one greater than the length of the trial array, because the first element of the instrument array contains the intercept term:

```
def instrumentTrialReturn(instrument: Array[Double],
    trial: Array[Double]): Double = {
  var instrumentTrialReturn = instrument(0)
  var i = 0
  while (i < trial.length) {  ❶
    instrumentTrialReturn += trial(i) * instrument(i+1)
    i += 1
  }
  instrumentTrialReturn
}
```

❶ We use a while loop here instead of a more functional Scala construct because this is a performance-critical region.

Then, to calculate the full return for a single trial, we simply average over the returns of all the instruments. This assumes that we're holding an equal value of each instrument in the portfolio. A weighted average would be used if we held different amounts of each stock.

```
def trialReturn(trial: Array[Double],
    instruments: Seq[Array[Double]]): Double = {
  var totalReturn = 0.0
  for (instrument <- instruments) {
    totalReturn += instrumentTrialReturn(instrument, trial)
```

```
        }
        totalReturn / instruments.size
    }
```

Lastly, we need to generate a bunch of trials in each task. Because choosing random numbers is a big part of the process, it is important to use a strong random number generator that will take a very long time to repeat itself. Commons Math includes a Mersenne Twister implementation that is good for this. We use it to sample from a multivariate normal distribution as described previously. Note that we are applying the `featurize` method that we defined before on the generated factor returns in order to transform them into the feature representation used in our models:

```
import org.apache.commons.math3.random.MersenneTwister

def trialReturns(seed: Long, numTrials: Int,
    instruments: Seq[Array[Double]], factorMeans: Array[Double],
    factorCovariances: Array[Array[Double]]): Seq[Double] = {
  val rand = new MersenneTwister(seed)
  val multivariateNormal = new MultivariateNormalDistribution(
    rand, factorMeans, factorCovariances)

  val trialReturns = new Array[Double](numTrials)
  for (i <- 0 until numTrials) {
    val trialFactorReturns = multivariateNormal.sample()
    val trialFeatures = featurize(trialFactorReturns)
    trialReturns(i) = trialReturn(trialFeatures, instruments)
  }
  trialReturns
}
```

With our scaffolding complete, we can use it to compute an RDD where each element is the total return from a single trial. Because the instrument data (matrix including a weight on each factor feature for each instrument) is large, we use a broadcast variable for it. This ensures that it only needs to be deserialized once per executor:

```
val numTrials = 10000000

val trials = seedDS.flatMap(
  trialReturns(_, numTrials / parallelism,
    factorWeights, factorMeans, factorCov))

trials.cache()
```

If you recall, the whole reason we've been messing around with all these numbers is to calculate VaR. `trials` now forms an empirical distribution over portfolio returns. To calculate 5% VaR, we need to find a return that we expect to underperform 5% of the time, and a return that we expect to outperform 5% of the time. With our empirical distribution, this is as simple as finding the value that 5% of trials are worse than and 95% of trials are better than. We can accomplish this using the `takeOrdered` action to pull the worst 5% of trials into the driver. Our VaR is the return of the best trial in this subset:

```
def fivePercentVaR(trials: Dataset[Double]): Double = {
  val quantiles = trials.stat.approxQuantile("value",
    Array(0.05), 0.0)
  quantiles.head
}

val valueAtRisk = fivePercentVaR(trials)
valueAtRisk: Double = -0.010831826593164014
```

We can find the CVaR with a nearly identical approach. Instead of taking the best trial return from the worst 5% of trials, we take the average return from that set of trials:

```
def fivePercentCVaR(trials: Dataset[Double]): Double = {
  val topLosses = trials.orderBy("value").
    limit(math.max(trials.count().toInt / 20, 1))
  topLosses.agg("value" -> "avg").first()(0).asInstanceOf[Double]
}

val conditionalValueAtRisk = fivePercentCVaR(trials)
conditionalValueAtRisk: Double = -0.09002629251426077
```

Visualizing the Distribution of Returns

In addition to calculating VaR at a particular confidence level, it can be useful to look at a fuller picture of the distribution of returns. Are they normally distributed? Do they spike at the extremities? As we did for the individual factors, we can plot an estimate of the probability density function for the joint probability distribution using kernel density estimation (see Figure 9-3). Again, the supporting code for calculating the density estimates in a distributed fashion (over RDDs) is included in the GitHub repository accompanying this book:

```
import org.apache.spark.sql.functions

def plotDistribution(samples: Dataset[Double]): Figure = {
  val (min, max, count, stddev) = samples.agg(
    functions.min($"value"),
    functions.max($"value"),
    functions.count($"value"),
    functions.stddev_pop($"value")
  ).as[(Double, Double, Long, Double)].first()
  val bandwidth = 1.06 * stddev * math.pow(count, -0.2) ❶

  // Using toList before toArray avoids a Scala bug
  val domain = Range.Double(min, max, (max - min) / 100).
    toList.toArray
  val kd = new KernelDensity().
    setSample(samples.rdd).
    setBandwidth(bandwidth)
```

```
val densities = kd.estimate(domain)
val f = Figure()
val p = f.subplot(0)
p += plot(domain, densities)
p.xlabel = "Two Week Return ($)"
p.ylabel = "Density"
f
}

plotDistribution(trials)
```

❶ Again, Silverman's rule of thumb.

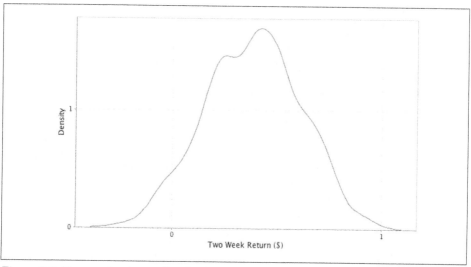

Figure 9-3. Two-week returns distribution

Evaluating Our Results

How do we know whether our estimate is a good estimate? How do we know whether we should simulate with a larger number of trials? In general, the error in a Monte Carlo simulation should be proportional to $1/\sqrt{n}$. This means that, in general, quadrupling the number of trials should approximately cut the error in half.

A nice way to get a confidence interval on our VaR statistic is through bootstrapping. We achieve a bootstrap distribution over the VaR by repeatedly sampling with replacement from the set of portfolio return results of our trials. Each time, we take a number of samples equal to the full size of the trials set and compute a VaR from those samples. The set of VaRs computed from all the times form an empirical distribution, and we can get our confidence interval by simply looking at its quantiles.

The following is a function that will compute a bootstrapped confidence interval for any statistic (given by the computeStatistic argument) of an RDD. Notice its use of Spark's sample where we pass true for its first argument withReplacement, and 1.0 for its second argument to collect a number of samples equal to the full size of the data set:

```
def bootstrappedConfidenceInterval(
    trials: Dataset[Double],
    computeStatistic: Dataset[Double] => Double,
    numResamples: Int,
    probability: Double): (Double, Double) = {
  val stats = (0 until numResamples).map { i =>
    val resample = trials.sample(true, 1.0)
    computeStatistic(resample)
  }.sorted
  val lowerIndex = (numResamples * probability / 2 - 1).toInt
  val upperIndex = math.ceil(numResamples * (1 - probability / 2))
    .toInt
  (stats(lowerIndex), stats(upperIndex))
}
```

Then we call this function, passing in the fivePercentVaR function we defined earlier that computes the VaR from an RDD of trials:

```
bootstrappedConfidenceInterval(trials, fivePercentVaR, 100, .05)
...
(-0.019480970253736192,-1.4971191125093586E-4)
```

We can bootstrap the CVaR as well:

```
bootstrappedConfidenceInterval(trials, fivePercentCVaR, 100, .05)
...
(-0.10051267317397554,-0.08058996149775266)
```

The confidence interval helps us understand how confident our model is in its result, but it does little to help us understand how well our model matches reality. Backtesting on historical data is a good way to check the quality of a result. One common test for VaR is Kupiec's proportion-of-failures (POF) test. It considers how the portfolio performed at many historical time intervals and counts the number of times the losses exceeded the VaR. The null hypothesis is that the VaR is reasonable, and a sufficiently extreme test statistic means that the VaR estimate does not accurately describe the data. The test statistic—which relies on p, the confidence level parameter of the VaR calculation; x, the number of historical intervals over which the losses exceeded the VaR; and T, the total number of historical intervals considered—is computed as:

$$-2 \ln \left(\frac{(1-p)^{T-x} p^x}{\left(1-\frac{x}{T}\right)^{T-x} \left(\frac{x}{T}\right)^x} \right)$$

The following computes the test statistic on our historical data. We expand out the logs for better numerical stability:

$$-2\Big((T - x) \ln (1 - p) + x \ln (p) - (T - x) \ln \Big(1 - \frac{x}{T}\Big) - x \ln \Big(\frac{x}{T}\Big)\Big)$$

```
var failures = 0
for (i <- stocksReturns.head.indices) {
  val loss = stocksReturns.map(_(i)).sum / stocksReturns.size
  if (loss < valueAtRisk) {
    failures += 1
  }
}
failures
...
257

val total = stocksReturns.size
val confidenceLevel = 0.05
val failureRatio = failures.toDouble / total
val logNumer = ((total - failures) * math.log1p(-confidenceLevel) +
  failures * math.log(confidenceLevel))
val logDenom = ((total - failures) * math.log1p(-failureRatio) +
  failures * math.log(failureRatio))
val testStatistic = -2 * (logNumer - logDenom)
...
180.3543986286574
```

If we assume the null hypothesis that the VaR is reasonable, then this test statistic is drawn from a chi-squared distribution with a single degree of freedom. We can use the Commons Math `ChiSquaredDistribution` to find the p-value accompanying our test statistic value:

```
import org.apache.commons.math3.distribution.ChiSquaredDistribution

1 - new ChiSquaredDistribution(1.0).cumulativeProbability(testStatistic)
```

This gives us a tiny p-value, meaning we do have sufficient evidence to reject the null hypothesis that the model is reasonable. While the fairly tight confidence intervals we computed earlier indicate that our model is internally consistent, the test result indicates that it doesn't correspond well to observed reality. Looks like we need to improve it a little.

Where to Go from Here

The model laid out in this exercise is a very rough first cut of what would be used in an actual financial institution. In building an accurate VaR model, we glossed over a few very important steps. Curating the set of market factors can make or break a model, and it is not uncommon for financial institutions to incorporate hundreds of factors in their simulations. Picking these factors requires both running numerous experiments on historical data and a heavy dose of creativity. Choosing the predictive model that maps market factors to instrument returns is also important. Although we used a simple linear model, many calculations use nonlinear functions or simulate the path over time with Brownian motion.

Lastly, it is worth putting care into the distribution used to simulate the factor returns. Kolmogorov-Smirnoff tests and chi-squared tests are useful for testing an empirical distribution's normality. Q-Q plots are useful for comparing distributions visually. Usually, financial risk is better mirrored by a distribution with fatter tails than the normal distribution that we used. Mixtures of normal distributions are one good way to achieve these fatter tails. "Financial Economics, Fat-tailed Distributions" (*https://bit.ly/1ACazwy*), an article by Markus Haas and Christian Pigorsch, provides a nice reference on some of the other fat-tailed distributions out there.

Banks use Spark and large-scale data processing frameworks for calculating VaR with historical methods as well. "Evaluation of Value-at-Risk Models Using Historical Data" (*https://nyfed.org/1ACaI2O*), by Darryll Hendricks, provides a good overview and performance comparison of historical VaR methods.

Monte Carlo risk simulations can be used for more than calculating a single statistic. The results can be used to proactively reduce the risk of a portfolio by shaping invest-ment decisions. For example, if, in the trials with the poorest returns, a particular set of instruments tends to come up losing money repeatedly, we might consider drop-ping those instruments from the portfolio or adding instruments that tend to move in the opposite direction from them.

## CHAPTER 10

Analyzing Genomics Data and the BDG Project

Uri Laserson

> So we need to shoot our SCHPON [Sulfur Carbon Hydrogen Phosphorous Oxygen Nitrogen] ... into the void.
>
> —George M. Church

The advent of next-generation DNA sequencing (NGS) technology is rapidly transforming the life sciences into a data-driven field. However, making the best use of this data is butting up against a traditional computational ecosystem that builds on difficult-to-use, low-level primitives for distributed computing (e.g., DRMAA or MPI) and a jungle of semistructured text-based file formats.

This chapter will serve three primary purposes. First, we introduce the general Spark user to a set of Hadoop-friendly serialization and file formats (Avro and Parquet) that simplify many problems in data management. We broadly promote the use of these serialization technologies to achieve compact binary representations, service-oriented architectures, and language cross-compatibility. Second, we show the experienced bioinformatician how to perform typical genomics tasks in the context of Spark.

Specifically, we will use Spark to manipulate large quantities of genomics data to process and filter data, build a model that predicts transcription factor (TF) binding sites, and join ENCODE (*https://www.encodeproject.org*) genome annotations against the 1000 Genome Project (*http://www.internationalgenome.org*) variants. Finally, this chapter will serve as a tutorial to the ADAM project, which comprises a set of genomics-specific Avro schemas, Spark-based APIs, and command-line tools for large-scale genomics analysis. Among other applications, ADAM provides a natively distributed implementation of the Genome Analysis Toolkit (GATK) (*https://soft ware.broadinstitute.org/gatk/best-practices/*) best practices using Hadoop and Spark.

The genomics portions of this chapter are targeted at experienced bioinformaticians familiar with typical problems. However, the data serialization portions should be useful to anyone who is processing large amounts of data. For the interested novice, a great introduction to biology is Eric Lander's EdX course (*http://bit.ly/2qKJCcQ*). For an introduction to bioinformatics, see Arthur Lesk's *Introduction to Bioinformatics* (Oxford University Press).

Finally, because the genome implies a 1D coordinate system, many genomics operations are spatial in nature. The ADAM project provides a genomics-targeted API along with implementations for performing distributed spatial joins using the older RDD interface. Therefore, this chapter continues to use the original interface rather than the newer Dataset and DataFrame interfaces.

A Note on the Use of RDDs

In contrast to the rest of this book, this chapter and the next make use of Spark's older resilient distributed data sets (RDD) API. The primary reason is that the ADAM project has implemented a number of join operators specific for 1D geometric computations that are common in genomics processing. These operators have not yet been ported to the newer Dataset API, though this is on the roadmap. Furthermore, the DataFrame API abstracts away more details about the distributed computation; porting the ADAM join operators will require interfacing with Spark's query planner. On the other hand, this chapter can be referred to when the reader encounters uses of the RDD API, either through other Spark-based libraries or in legacy code.

Decoupling Storage from Modeling

Bioinformaticians spend a disproportionate amount of time worrying about file formats—*.fasta*, *.fastq*, *.sam*, *.bam*, *.vcf*, *.gvcf*, *.bcf*, *.bed*, *.gff*, *.gtf*, *.narrowPeak*, *.wig*, *.big-Wig*, *.bigBed*, *.ped*, and *.tped*, to name a few—not to mention the scientists who feel it is necessary to specify their own custom format for their custom tool. On top of that, many of the format specifications are incomplete or ambiguous (which makes it hard to ensure implementations are consistent or compliant) and specify ASCII-encoded data. ASCII data is very common in bioinformatics, but it is inefficient and compresses relatively poorly—this is starting to be addressed by community efforts to improve the specs (*https://github.com/samtools/hts-specs*). In addition, the data must always be parsed, necessitating additional compute cycles. This is particularly troubling because all of these file formats essentially store just a few common object types: an aligned sequence read, a called genotype, a sequence feature, and a phenotype. (The term *sequence feature* is slightly overloaded in genomics, but in this chapter we mean it in the sense of an element from a track of the UCSC Genome Browser.) Libraries like biopython (*http://biopython.org*) are popular because they are chock-

---

full-o' parsers (e.g., `Bio.SeqIO`) that attempt to read all the file formats into a small number of common in-memory models (e.g., `Bio.Seq`, `Bio.SeqRecord`, `Bio.SeqFea ture`).

We can solve all of these problems in one shot using a serialization framework like Apache Avro. The key lies in Avro's separation of the data model (i.e., an explicit schema) from the underlying storage file format and also the language's in-memory representation. Avro specifies how data of a certain type should be communicated between processes, whether that's between running processes over the Internet, or a process trying to write the data into a particular file format. For example, a Java program that uses Avro can write the data into multiple underlying file formats that are all compatible with Avro's data model. This allows each process to stop worrying about compatibility with multiple file formats: the process only needs to know how to read Avro, and the filesystem needs to know how to supply Avro.

Let's take the sequence feature as an example. We begin by specifying the desired schema for the object using the Avro interface definition language (IDL):

```
enum Strand {
  Forward,
  Reverse,
  Independent
}

record SequenceFeature {
  string featureId;
  string featureType; ❶
  string chromosome;
  long startCoord;
  long endCoord;
  Strand strand;
  double value;
  map<string> attributes;
}
```

❶ For example, "conservation," "centipede," "gene"

This data type could be used to encode, for example, conservation level, the presence of a promoter or ribosome binding site, a TF binding site, and so on at a particular location in the genome. One way to think about it is a binary version of JSON but more restricted and with higher performance. Given a particular data schema, the Avro spec then determines the precise binary encoding for the object so that it can be easily communicated between processes (even if written in different programing languages), over the network, or onto disk for storage. The Avro project includes modules for processing Avro-encoded data from many languages, including Java, C/C++, Python, and Perl; after that, the language is free to store the object in memory in whichever way is deemed most advantageous. The separation of data modeling from the storage format provides another level of flexibility/abstraction; Avro data can be stored as Avro-serialized binary objects (Avro container file), in a columnar file format for fast queries (Parquet file), or as text JSON data for maximum flexibility (minimum efficiency). Finally, Avro supports schema evolution, allowing the user to add new fields as they become necessary, while the software gracefully deals with new/old versions of the schema.

Overall, Avro is an efficient binary encoding that allows you to easily specify evolvable data schemas, process the same data from many programming languages, and store the data using many formats. Deciding to store your data using Avro schemas frees you from perpetually working with more and more custom data formats, while simultaneously increasing the performance of your computations.

Serialization/RPC Frameworks

There exist a large number of serialization frameworks in the wild. The most commonly used frameworks in the big data community are Apache Avro, Apache Thrift, and Google's Protocol Buffers (protobuf). At the core, they all provide an interface definition language for specifying the schemas of object/message types, and they all compile into a variety of programming languages. On top of IDL, Thrift also adds a way to specify RPCs. (Google's RPC framework for protobuf has been open-sourced as gRPC.) Finally, on top of IDL and RPC, Avro adds a file format specification for storing the data on-disk. Google more recently released a "serialization" framework that uses the same byte representation on-the-wire and in-memory, effectively eliminating the expensive serialization step.

It's difficult to make generalizations about which framework is appropriate in what circumstances because they all support different languages and have different performance characteristics for the various languages.

The particular `SequenceFeature` model used in the preceding example is a bit simplistic for real data, but the Big Data Genomics (BDG) project (*http://bdgenomics.org/*) has already defined Avro schemas to represent the following objects, as well as many others:

- `AlignmentRecord` for reads
- `Variant` for known genome variants and metadata
- `Genotype` for a called genotype at a particular locus
- `Feature` for a sequence feature (annotation on a genome segment)

The actual schemas can be found in the `bdg-formats` GitHub repo (*https://github.com/bigdatagenomics/bdg-formats*). The BDG formats can function as a

---

replacement of the ubiquitous "legacy" formats (like BAM and VCF), but more commonly function as high-performance "intermediate" formats. (The original goal of these BDG formats was to replace the use of BAM and VCF, but their stubborn ubiquity has proved this goal to be difficult.) The Global Alliance for Genomics and Health has also developed its own set of schemas using Protocol Buffers (*https://github.com/ga4gh/schemas*). Hopefully, this will not turn into its own situation (*https://xkcd.com/927/*), where there is a proliferation of competing schemas. Even so, Avro provides many performance and data modeling benefits over the custom ASCII status quo. In the remainder of the chapter, we'll use some of the BDG schemas to accomplish some typical genomics tasks.

Ingesting Genomics Data with the ADAM CLI

 This chapter makes heavy use of the ADAM project for genomics on Spark. The project is under heavy development, including the documentation. If you run into problems, make sure to check the latest README files on GitHub, the GitHub issue tracker, or the adam-developers mailing list.

BDG's core set of genomics tools is called ADAM. Starting from a set of mapped reads, this core includes tools that can perform mark-duplicates, base quality score recalibration, indel realignment, and variant calling, among other tasks. ADAM also contains a command-line interface that wraps the core for ease of use. In contrast to HPC, these command-line tools know about Hadoop and HDFS, and many of them can automatically parallelize across a cluster without having to split files or schedule jobs manually.

We'll start by building ADAM like the README tells us to:

```
git clone https://github.com/bigdatagenomics/adam.git && cd adam
export "MAVEN_OPTS=-Xmx512m -XX:MaxPermSize=128m"
mvn clean package -DskipTests
```

Alternatively, download one of the ADAM releases from the GitHub release page.

ADAM comes with a submission script that facilitates interfacing with Spark's spark-submit script; the easiest way to use it is probably to alias it:

```
export ADAM_HOME=path/to/adam
alias adam-submit="$ADAM_HOME/bin/adam-submit"
```

At this point, you should be able to run ADAM from the command line and get the usage message. As noted in the usage message below, Spark arguments are given before ADAM-specific arguments.

```
$ adam-submit
Using ADAM_MAIN=org.bdgenomics.adam.cli.ADAMMain
[...]


        e       888~-_         e            e    e
       d8b      888   \       d8b         d8b   d8b
      /Y88b     888    |     /Y88b       d888bdY88b
     / Y88b     888    |    / Y88b      / Y88Y Y888b
    /___Y88b    888    /   /___Y88b    /   YY   Y888b
   /     Y88b   888_-~   /     Y88b   /         Y888b

Usage: adam-submit [<spark-args> --] <adam-args>

Choose one of the following commands:

ADAM ACTIONS
           countKmers : Counts the k-mers/q-mers from a read dataset.
     countContigKmers : Counts the k-mers/q-mers from a read dataset.
            transform : Convert SAM/BAM to ADAM format and optionally perform...
     transformFeatures : Convert a file with sequence features into correspondin...
          mergeShards : Merges the shards of a file
        reads2coverage : Calculate the coverage from a given ADAM file
[...]
```

You may have to set some environment variables for this to succeed, such as
SPARK_HOME and HADOOP_CONF_DIR.

We'll start by taking a *.bam* file containing some mapped NGS reads, converting them
to the corresponding BDG format (AlignedRecord in this case), and saving them to
HDFS. First, we get our hands on a suitable *.bam* file and put it in HDFS:

```
# Note: this file is 16 GB
curl -O ftp://ftp.ncbi.nih.gov/1000genomes/ftp/phase3/data\
/HG00103/alignment/HG00103.mapped.ILLUMINA.bwa.GBR\
.low_coverage.20120522.bam

# or using Aspera instead (which is *much* faster)
ascp -i path/to/asperaweb_id_dsa.openssh -QTr -l 10G \
anonftp@ftp.ncbi.nlm.nih.gov:/1000genomes/ftp/phase3/data\
/HG00103/alignment/HG00103.mapped.ILLUMINA.bwa.GBR\
.low_coverage.20120522.bam .

hadoop fs -put HG00103.mapped.ILLUMINA.bwa.GBR\
.low_coverage.20120522.bam /user/ds/genomics
```

We can then use the ADAM transform command to convert the *.bam* file to Parquet
format (described in "Parquet Format and Columnar Storage" on page 227). This
would work both on a cluster and in local mode:

```
adam-submit \
  --master yarn \ ❶
  --deploy-mode client \
  --driver-memory 8G \
  --num-executors 6 \
  --executor-cores 4 \
  --executor-memory 12G \
  -- \
  transform \ ❷
  /user/ds/genomics/HG00103.mapped.ILLUMINA.bwa.GBR\
.low_coverage.20120522.bam \
  /user/ds/genomics/reads/HG00103
```

❶ Example Spark args for running on YARN

❷ The ADAM subcommand itself

This should kick off a pretty large amount of output to the console, including the URL to track the progress of the job. Let's see what we've generated:

```
$ hadoop fs -du -h /user/ds/genomics/reads/HG00103
0        0       ch10/reads/HG00103/_SUCCESS
8.6 K    25.7 K  ch10/reads/HG00103/_common_metadata
462.0 K  1.4 M   ch10/reads/HG00103/_metadata
1.5 K    4.4 K   ch10/reads/HG00103/_rgdict.avro
17.7 K   53.2 K  ch10/reads/HG00103/_seqdict.avro
103.1 M  309.3 M ch10/reads/HG00103/part-r-00000.gz.parquet
102.9 M  308.6 M ch10/reads/HG00103/part-r-00001.gz.parquet
102.7 M  308.2 M ch10/reads/HG00103/part-r-00002.gz.parquet
[...]
106.8 M  320.4 M ch10/reads/HG00103/part-r-00126.gz.parquet
12.4 M   37.3 M  ch10/reads/HG00103/part-r-00127.gz.parquet
```

The resulting data set is the concatenation of all the files in the */user/ds/genomics/reads/HG00103/* directory, where each *part-*.parquet* file is the output from one of the Spark tasks. You'll also notice that the data has been compressed more efficiently than the initial *.bam* file (which is gzipped underneath) thanks to the columnar storage (see "Parquet Format and Columnar Storage" on page 227).

```
$ hadoop fs -du -h "/user/ds/genomics/HG00103.*.bam"
15.9 G  /user/ds/genomics/HG00103. [...] .bam

$ hadoop fs -du -h -s /user/ds/genomics/reads/HG00103
12.8 G  /user/ds/genomics/reads/HG00103
```

Let's see what one of these objects looks like in an interactive session. First, we start up the Spark shell using the ADAM helper script. It takes the same arguments/options as the default Spark scripts, but loads all of the JARs that are necessary. In the following example, we are running Spark on YARN:

```
export SPARK_HOME=/path/to/spark
$ADAM_HOME/bin/adam-shell
```

```
[...]
Welcome to


     ____              __
    / __/__  ___ _____/ /__
   _\ \/ _ \/ _ `/ __/  '_/
  /___/ .__/\_,_/_/ /_/\_\   version 2.0.2
      /_/

Using Scala version 2.11.8 (Java HotSpot(TM) 64-Bit [...], Java 1.8.0_112)
Type in expressions to have them evaluated.
Type :help for more information.

scala>
```

Note that when you're working on YARN, the interactive Spark shell requires yarn-client deploy mode, so that the driver is executed locally. It may also be necessary to set either HADOOP_CONF_DIR or YARN_CONF_DIR appropriately. Now we'll load the aligned read data as an RDD[AlignmentRecord]:

```
import org.bdgenomics.adam.rdd.ADAMContext._

val readsRDD = sc.loadAlignments("/user/ds/genomics/reads/HG00103")
readsRDD.rdd.first()
```

This may print some logging output along with the result itself (reformatted for clarity):

```
res3: org.bdgenomics.formats.avro.AlignmentRecord = {
  "readInFragment": 0, "contigName": "1", "start": 9992,
  "oldPosition": null, "end": 10091, "mapq": 25,
  "readName": "SRR062643.12466352",
  "sequence": "CTCTTCCGATCTCCCTAACCCTAACCCTAACCCTAACCCTAACCCTAA
CCCTAACCCTAACCCTAACCCTAACCCTAACCCTAACCCTAACCCT",
  "qual": "##@@BA:36<FBGCBBD>AHHB@4DD@B;0DEF6A9EDC6>9CCC@9@IIH@I8IIC4
@GH=HGHCIHHHGAGABEGAGG@EGAFHGFFEEE?DEFDDA.",
  "cigar": "1S99M", "oldCigar": null, "basesTrimmedFromStart": 0,
  "basesTrimmedFromEnd": 0, "readPaired": true, "properPair": false,
  "readMapped": true, "mateMapped": false,
  "failedVendorQualityChecks": false, "duplicateRead": false,
  "readNegativeStrand": true, "mateNegativeStrand": true,
  "primaryAlignment": true, "secondaryAlignment": false,
  "supplementaryAlignment": false, "mis...
```

You may get a different read, because the partitioning of the data may be different on your cluster, so there is no guarantee which read will come back first.

Now we can interactively ask questions about our data set, all while executing the computations across a cluster in the background. How many reads do we have in this data set?

```
readsRDD.rdd.count()
...
res16: Long = 160397565
```

Do the reads in this data set derive from all human chromosomes?

```
val uniq_chr = (readsRDD.rdd
  .map(_.getContigName)
  .distinct()
  .collect())
uniq_chr.sorted.foreach(println)
...
1
10
11
12
[...]
GL000249.1
MT
NC_007605
X
Y
hs37d5
```

Yep, we observe reads from chromosomes 1 through 22, X and Y, along with some other chromosomal chunks that are not part of the "main" chromosomes or whose locations are unknown. Let's analyze the statement a little more closely:

```
val uniq_chr = (readsRDD ❶
  .rdd ❷
  .map(_.getContigName) ❸
  .distinct() ❹
  .collect()) ❺
```

❶ AlignedReadRDD: an ADAM type that contains the RDD that contains all our data.

❷ RDD[AlignmentRecord]: the underlying Spark RDD.

❸ RDD[String]: from each AlignmentRecord object, we extract the contig name. (A "contig" is basically equivalent to a "chromosome.")

❹ RDD[String]: this will cause a reduce/shuffle to aggregate all the distinct contig names; should be small, but still an RDD.

❺ Array[String]: this triggers the computation and brings the data in the RDD back to the client app (the shell).

For a more clinical example, say we are testing an individual's genome to check whether they carry any gene variants that put them at risk for having a child with cystic fibrosis (CF). Our genetic test uses next-generation DNA sequencing to generate reads from multiple relevant genes, such as the CFTR gene (whose mutations can cause CF). After running our data through our genotyping pipeline, we determine that the CFTR gene appears to have a premature stop codon that destroys its function. However, this mutation has never been reported before in HGMD (*http://www.hgmd.cf.ac.uk*), nor is it in the Sickkids CFTR database (*http://www.genet.sick kids.on.ca*), which aggregates CF gene variants. We want to go back to the raw sequencing data to see if the potentially deleterious genotype call is a false positive. To do so, we need to manually analyze all the reads that map to that variant locus, say, chromosome 7 at 117149189 (see Figure 10-1):

```
val cftr_reads = (readsRDD.rdd
  .filter(_.getContigName == "7")
  .filter(_.getStart <= 117149189)
  .filter(_.getEnd > 117149189)
  .collect())
cftr_reads.length // cftr_reads is a local Array[AlignmentRecord]
...
res2: Int = 9
```

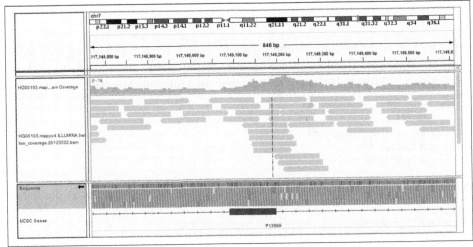

Figure 10-1. IGV visualization of the HG00103 at chr7:117149189 in the CFTR gene

It is now possible to manually inspect these nine reads, or process them through a custom aligner, for example, and check whether the reported pathogenic variant is a false positive. Exercise for the reader: what is the average coverage on chromosome 7? (It's definitely too low for reliably making a genotype call at a given position.)

Say we're running a clinical lab that is performing such carrier screening as a service to clinicians. Archiving the raw data using Hadoop ensures that the data stays relatively warm (compared with, say, tape archive). In addition to having a reliable system for actually performing the data processing, we can easily access all of the past data for quality control (QC) or for cases where there need to be manual interventions, like the CFTR example presented earlier. In addition to the rapid access to the totality of the data, the centrality also makes it easy to perform large analytical studies, like population genetics, large-scale QC analyses, and so on.

Parquet Format and Columnar Storage

In the previous section, we saw how we can manipulate a potentially large amount of sequencing data without worrying about the specifics of the underlying storage or the parallelization of the execution. However, it's worth noting that the ADAM project makes use of the Parquet file format, which confers some considerable performance advantages that we introduce here.

Parquet is an open source file format specification and a set of reader/writer implementations that we recommend for general use for data that will be used in analytical queries (write once, read many times). It is largely based on the underlying data storage format used in Google's Dremel system (see "Dremel: Interactive Analysis of Web-scale Datasets" (*http://bit.ly/2qKpnw4*) Proc. VLDB, 2010, by Melnik et al.), and has a data model that is compatible with Avro, Thrift, and Protocol Buffers. Specifically, it supports most of the common database types (int, double, string, etc.), along with arrays and records, including nested types. Significantly, it is a columnar file format, meaning that values for a particular column from many records are stored contiguously on disk (see Figure 10-2). This physical data layout allows for far more efficient data encoding/compression, and significantly reduces query times by minimizing the amount of data that must be read/deserialized (*http://bit.ly/2qKKkqG*). Parquet supports specifying different compression schemes for each column, as well as column-specific encoding schemes such as run-length encoding, dictionary encoding, and delta encoding.

Another useful feature of Parquet for increasing performance is *predicate pushdown*. A *predicate* is some expression or function that evaluates to true or false based on the data record (or equivalently, the expressions in a SQL WHERE clause). In our earlier CFTR query, Spark had to deserialize/materialize the each AlignmentRecord before deciding whether or not it passes the predicate. This leads to a significant amount of wasted I/O and CPU time. The Parquet reader implementations allow us to provide a predicate class that only deserializes the necessary columns for making the decision, before materializing the full record.

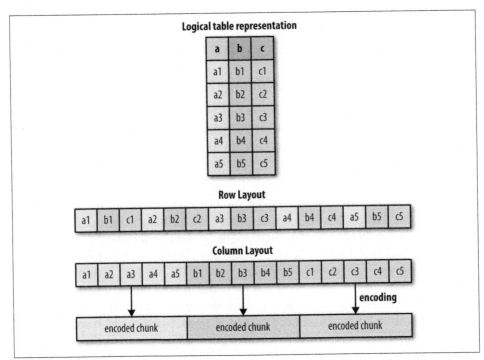

Figure 10-2. Differences between a row-major and column-major data layout

For example, to implement our CFTR query using predicate pushdown, we must first define a suitable predicate class that tests whether the `AlignmentRecord` is in the target locus:

```
import org.apache.parquet.filter2.dsl.Dsl._

val chr = BinaryColumn("contigName")
val start = LongColumn("start")
val end = LongColumn("end")

val cftrLocusPredicate = (
  chr === "7" && start <= 117149189 && end >= 117149189) ❶
```

❶ See the documentation for more info on the DSL. Note we use === instead of ==.

Because we use Parquet-specific features, we must load the data explicitly with the Parquet reader:

```
val readsRDD = sc.loadParquetAlignments(
  "/user/ds/genomics/reads/HG00103",
  Some(cftrLocusPredicate))
```

This should execute faster because it no longer must materialize all of the `AlignmentRecord` objects.

Predicting Transcription Factor Binding Sites from ENCODE Data

In this example, we will use publicly available sequence feature data to build a simple model for transcription factor binding. TFs are proteins that bind to specific DNA sequences in the genome and help control the expression of different genes. As a result, they are critical in determining the phenotype of a particular cell, and are involved in many physiological and disease processes. ChIP-seq is an NGS-based assay that allows the genome-wide characterization of binding sites for a particular TF in a particular cell/tissue type. However, in addition to ChIP-seq's cost and technical difficulty, it requires a separate experiment for each tissue/TF pair. In contrast, DNase-seq is an assay that finds regions of open-chromatin genome-wide, and only needs to be performed once per tissue type. Instead of assaying TF binding sites by performing a ChIP-seq experiment for each tissue/TF combination, we'd like to predict TF binding sites in a new tissue type assuming only the availability of DNase-seq data.

In particular, we will predict the binding sites for the CTCF TF using DNase-seq data along with known sequence motif data (from HT-SELEX (*http://bit.ly/2qjsTNL*)) and other data from the publicly available ENCODE data set (*https://www.encodepro ject.org*). We have chosen six different cell types that have available DNase-seq and CTCF ChIP-seq data for training. A training example will be a DNase hypersensitivity (HS) peak (a segment of the genome), and the binary label for whether the TF is bound/unbound will be derived from the ChIP-seq data.

To summarize the overall data flow: the main training/test examples will be derived from the DNase-seq data. Each region of open-chromatin (an interval on the genome) will be used to generate a prediction of whether a particular TF in a particular tissue type will be bound there. To do so, we spatially join the ChIP-seq data to the DNase-seq data; every overlap is a positive label for the DNase seq objects. Finally, to improve the prediction accuracy, we generate some additional features at each interval in the DNase-seq data, such as conservation scores (from the phylop data set), distance to a transcription start site (using the Gencode data set), and how well the sequence of the DNase-seq interval matches the known binding motif of the TF (using an empirically determined position weight matrix). In almost all cases, the features are added into the training examples by performing a spatial join (with a possible aggregation).

We will use data from the following cell lines:

GM12878
　　Commonly studied lymphoblastoid cell line

K562

Female chronic myelogenous leukemia

BJ

Skin fibroblast

HEK293

Embryonic kidney

H54

Glioblastoma

HepG2

Hepatocellular carcinoma

First, we download the DNase data for each cell line in *.narrowPeak* format:

```
hadoop fs -mkdir /user/ds/genomics/dnase
curl -s -L <...DNase URL...> \ ❶
  | gunzip \ ❷
  | hadoop fs -put - /user/ds/genomics/dnase/sample.DNase.narrowPeak
[...]
```

❶ See accompanying code repo for actual curl commands.

❷ Streaming decompression.

Next, we download the ChIP-seq data for the CTCF TF, also in *.narrowPeak* format, and the GENCODE data, in GTF format:

```
hadoop fs -mkdir /user/ds/genomics/chip-seq
curl -s -L <...ChIP-seq URL...> \ ❶
  | gunzip \
  | hadoop fs -put - /user/ds/genomics/chip-seq/samp.CTCF.narrowPeak
[...]
```

❶ See accompanying code repo for actual curl commands

Note how we unzip the stream of data with `gunzip` on the way to depositing it in HDFS. Now we download the actual human genome sequence, which is used to evaluate a position weight matrix to generate one of the features:

```
# the hg19 human genome reference sequence
curl -s -L -O \
  "http://hgdownload.cse.ucsc.edu/goldenPath/hg19/bigZips/hg19.2bit"
```

Finally, the conservation data is available in fixed wiggle format, which is difficult to read as a splittable file. Specifically, it is not "splittable" because it is very difficult to enter the file at an arbitrary location and start reading records. This is because the wiggle format intersperses data records with some metadata that describes the current genome location. It is not possible to predict how far back in a file a particular task must read in order to obtain the metadata about the contig coordinates. Therefore, we convert the *.wigFix* data to BED format using the BEDOPS tool on the way into HDFS as well:

```
hadoop fs -mkdir /user/ds/genomics/phylop
for i in $(seq 1 22); do
    curl -s -L <...phyloP.chr$i URL...> \ ❶
        | gunzip \
        | wig2bed -d \ ❷
        | hadoop fs -put - "/user/ds/genomics/phylop/chr$i.phyloP.bed"
done
[...]
```

❶ See accompanying code repo for actual curl commands

❷ This command is from the BEDOPS CLI. It's easy to write your own Python script as well

Finally, we perform a one-time conversion of the phyloP data from the text-based *.bed* format to Parquet in a Spark shell:

```
import org.bdgenomics.adam.rdd.ADAMContext._
(sc
  .loadBed("/user/ds/genomics/phylop_text")
  .saveAsParquet("/user/ds/genomics/phylop"))
```

From all of this raw data, we want to generate a training set with a schema like the following:

1. Chromosome
2. Start
3. End
4. Highest TF motif position weight matrix (PWM) score
5. Average phyloP conservation score
6. Minimum phyloP conservation score
7. Maximum phyloP conservation score
8. Distance to closest transcription start site (TSS)
9. TF identity (always "CTCF" in this case)
10. Cell line
11. TF binding status (boolean; the target variable)

This data set can easily be converted into an RDD[LabeledPoint] to carry into a machine learning library. Since we need to generate the data for multiple cell lines, we will define an RDD for each cell line individually and concatenate them at the end:

```
val cellLines = Vector(
  "GM12878", "K562", "BJ", "HEK293", "H54", "HepG2")
val dataByCellLine = cellLines.map(cellLine => { // For each cell line…
  // …generate an RDD suitable for conversion
  // to RDD[LabeledPoint]
})
// Concatenate the RDDs and carry through into MLlib, for example
```

Before we start, we load some data that will be used throughout the computation, including conservation, transcription start sites, the human genome reference sequence, and the CTCF PWM as derived from HT-SELEX (*http://bit.ly/2qjsTNL*). We also define a couple of utility functions that will be used to generate the PWM and TSS features:

```
val hdfsPrefix = "/user/ds/genomics"
val localPrefix = "/user/ds/genomics"

// Set up broadcast variables for computing features along with some
// utility functions

// Load the human genome reference sequence
val bHg19Data = sc.broadcast(
  new TwoBitFile(
    new LocalFileByteAccess(
      new File(Paths.get(localPrefix, "hg19.2bit").toString))))

// fn for finding closest transcription start site
// naive; exercise for reader: make this faster
def distanceToClosest(loci: Vector[Long], query: Long): Long = {
  loci.map(x => math.abs(x - query)).min
}

// CTCF PWM from https://dx.doi.org/10.1016/j.cell.2012.12.009
// generated with genomics/src/main/python/pwm.py
val bPwmData = sc.broadcast(Vector(
  Map('A'->0.4553,'C'->0.0459,'G'->0.1455,'T'->0.3533),
  Map('A'->0.1737,'C'->0.0248,'G'->0.7592,'T'->0.0423),
  Map('A'->0.0001,'C'->0.9407,'G'->0.0001,'T'->0.0591),
  Map('A'->0.0051,'C'->0.0001,'G'->0.9879,'T'->0.0069),
  Map('A'->0.0624,'C'->0.9322,'G'->0.0009,'T'->0.0046),
  Map('A'->0.0046,'C'->0.9952,'G'->0.0001,'T'->0.0001),
  Map('A'->0.5075,'C'->0.4533,'G'->0.0181,'T'->0.0211),
  Map('A'->0.0079,'C'->0.6407,'G'->0.0001,'T'->0.3513),
  Map('A'->0.0001,'C'->0.9995,'G'->0.0002,'T'->0.0001),
  Map('A'->0.0027,'C'->0.0035,'G'->0.0017,'T'->0.9921),
  Map('A'->0.7635,'C'->0.0210,'G'->0.1175,'T'->0.0980),
  Map('A'->0.0074,'C'->0.1314,'G'->0.7990,'T'->0.0622),
  Map('A'->0.0138,'C'->0.3879,'G'->0.0001,'T'->0.5981),
```

```
  Map('A'->0.0003,'C'->0.0001,'G'->0.9853,'T'->0.0142),
  Map('A'->0.0399,'C'->0.0113,'G'->0.7312,'T'->0.2177),
  Map('A'->0.1520,'C'->0.2820,'G'->0.0082,'T'->0.5578),
  Map('A'->0.3644,'C'->0.3105,'G'->0.2125,'T'->0.1127)))

// compute a motif score based on the TF PWM
def scorePWM(ref: String): Double = {
  val score1 = (ref.sliding(bPwmData.value.length)
    .map(s => {
      s.zipWithIndex.map(p => bPwmData.value(p._2)(p._1)).product})
    .max)
  val rc = Alphabet.dna.reverseComplementExact(ref)
  val score2 = (rc.sliding(bPwmData.value.length)
    .map(s => {
      s.zipWithIndex.map(p => bPwmData.value(p._2)(p._1)).product})
    .max)
  math.max(score1, score2)
}

// build in-memory structure for computing distance to TSS
// we are essentially manually implementing a broadcast join here
val tssRDD = (
  sc.loadFeatures(
    Paths.get(hdfsPrefix, "gencode.v18.annotation.gtf").toString).rdd
  .filter(_.getFeatureType == "transcript")
  .map(f => (f.getContigName, f.getStart))).rdd
  .filter(_.getFeatureType == "transcript")
  .map(f => (f.getContigName, f.getStart)))
// this broadcast variable will hold the broadcast side of the "join"
val bTssData = sc.broadcast(tssRDD
  // group by contig name
  .groupBy(_._1)
  // create Vector of TSS sites for each chromosome
  .map(p => (p._1, p._2.map(_._2.toLong).toVector))
  // collect into local in-memory structure for broadcasting
  .collect().toMap)

// load conservation data; independent of cell line
val phylopRDD = (
  sc.loadParquetFeatures(Paths.get(hdfsPrefix, "phylop").toString).rdd
  // clean up a few irregularities in the phylop data
  .filter(f => f.getStart <= f.getEnd)
  .map(f => (ReferenceRegion.unstranded(f), f))).rdd
  // clean up a few irregularities in the phylop data
  .filter(f => f.getStart <= f.getEnd)
  .map(f => (ReferenceRegion.unstranded(f), f)))
```

Now that we've loaded the data necessary for defining our training examples, we define the body of the "loop" for computing the data on each cell line. Note how we read the text representations of the ChIP-seq and DNase data, because the data sets are not so large that they will hurt performance.

To do so, we load the DNase and ChIP-seq data as RDDs:

```
val dnasePath = (
  Paths.get(hdfsPrefix, s"dnase/$cellLine.DNase.narrowPeak")
    .toString)
val dnaseRDD = (sc.loadFeatures(dnasePath).rdd
  .map(f => ReferenceRegion.unstranded(f))
  .map(r => (r, r))) ❶

val chipseqPath = (
  Paths.get(hdfsPrefix, s"chip-seq/$cellLine.ChIP-seq.CTCF.narrowPeak")
    .toString)
val chipseqRDD = (sc.loadFeatures(chipseqPath).rdd
  .map(f => ReferenceRegion.unstranded(f))
  .map(r => (r, r))) ❶
```

❶ RDD[(ReferenceRegion, ReferenceRegion)]

The core object is a DNase hypersensitivity site, as defined by a ReferenceRegion object in dnaseRDD. Sites that overlap a ChIP-seq peak, as defined by a ReferenceRegion in chipseqRDD, have TF binding sites and are therefore labeled true, while the rest of the sites are labeled false. This is accomplished using the 1D spatial join primitives provided in the ADAM API. The join functionality requires an RDD that is keyed by a ReferenceRegion, and will produce tuples that have overlapping regions, according to usual join semantics (e.g., inner versus outer).

```
val dnaseWithLabelRDD = (
  LeftOuterShuffleRegionJoin(bHg19Data.value.sequences, 1000000, sc)
    .partitionAndJoin(dnaseRDD, chipseqRDD) ❶
    .map(p => (p._1, p._2.size)) ❷
    .reduceByKey(_ + _) ❸
    .map(p => (p._1, p._2 > 0)) ❹
    .map(p => (p._1, p))) ❺
```

❶ RDD[(ReferenceRegion, Option[ReferenceRegion])]: there is an Option because we are employing a left outer join

❷ RDD[(ReferenceRegion, Int)]: 0 for None and 1 for a successful match

❸ Aggregate all possible TF binding sites overlaying DNase site

❹ Positive values indicate an overlap between the data sets and therefore a TF binding site

❺ Prepare RDD for next join by keying it with a ReferenceRegion

Separately, we compute the conservation features by joining the DNase data to the phyloP data:

```
// given phylop values on a site, compute some stats
def aggPhylop(values: Vector[Double]) = {
  val avg = values.sum / values.length
  val m = values.min
  val M = values.max
  (avg, m, M)
}
val dnaseWithPhylopRDD = (
  LeftOuterShuffleRegionJoin(bHg19Data.value.sequences, 1000000, sc)
    .partitionAndJoin(dnaseRDD, phylopRDD) ❶
    .filter(!_._2.isEmpty) ❷
    .map(p => (p._1, p._2.get.getScore.doubleValue))
    .groupByKey() ❸
    .map(p => (p._1, aggPhylop(p._2.toVector)))) ❹
```

❶ RDD[(ReferenceRegion, Option[Feature])]

❷ Filter out sites for which there is missing phylop data

❸ Aggregate together all phylop values for each site

❹ RDD[(ReferenceRegion, (Double, Double, Double))]

Now we compute the final set of features on each DNase peak by joining together the
two RDDs from above and adding a few additional features by mapping over the
sites:

```
// build final training example RDD
val examplesRDD = (
  InnerShuffleRegionJoin(bHg19Data.value.sequences, 1000000, sc) ❶
    .partitionAndJoin(dnaseWithLabelRDD, dnaseWithPhylopRDD)
    .map(tup => {
      val seq = bHg19Data.value.extract(tup._1._1) ❷
      (tup._1, tup._2, seq)})
    .filter(!_._3.contains("N")) ❸
    .map(tup => { ❹
      val region = tup._1._1
      val label = tup._1._2
      val contig = region.referenceName
      val start = region.start
      val end = region.end
      val phylopAvg = tup._2._1
      val phylopMin = tup._2._2
      val phylopMax = tup._2._3
      val seq = tup._3
      val pwmScore = scorePWM(seq)
      val closestTss = math.min(
        distanceToClosest(bTssData.value(contig), start),
        distanceToClosest(bTssData.value(contig), end))
      val tf = "CTCF"
```

```
(contig, start, end, pwmScore, phylopAvg, phylopMin, phylopMax,
    closestTss, tf, cellLine, label)}))
```

❶ Inner join to ensure we get well-defined feature vectors

❷ Extract the genome sequence corresponding to this site in the genome and attach it to the tuple

❸ Drop any site where the genome sequence is ambiguous

❹ Here we build the final feature vector

This final RDD is computed in each pass of the loop over the cell lines. Finally, we union each RDD from each cell line, and cache this data in memory in preparation for training models off of it:

```
val preTrainingData = dataByCellLine.reduce(_ ++ _)
preTrainingData.cache()

preTrainingData.count() // 802059
preTrainingData.filter(_._12 == true).count() // 220344
```

At this point, the data in `preTrainingData` can be normalized and converted into an `RDD[LabeledPoint]` for training a classifier, as described in Chapter 4. Note that you should perform cross-validation, where in each fold, you hold out the data from one of the cell lines.

Querying Genotypes from the 1000 Genomes Project

In this example, we will be ingesting the full 1000 Genomes genotype data set. First, we will download the raw data directly into HDFS, unzipping in-flight, and then run an ADAM job to convert the data to Parquet. The following example command should be executed for all chromosomes, and can be parallelized across the cluster:

```
curl -s -L ftp://.../1000genomes/.../chr1.vcf.gz \ ❶
  | gunzip \
  | hadoop fs -put - /user/ds/genomics/1kg/vcf/chr1.vcf ❷

adam/bin/adam-submit --master yarn --deploy-mode client \
  --driver-memory 8G --num-executors 192 --executor-cores 4 \
  --executor-memory 16G \
  -- \
  vcf2adam /user/ds/genomics/1kg/vcf /user/ds/genomics/1kg/parquet
```

❶ See the accompanying repo for the actual curl commands

❷ Copy the text VCF file into Hadoop

From an ADAM shell, we load and inspect an object like so:

```
import org.bdgenomics.adam.rdd.ADAMContext._

val genotypesRDD = sc.loadGenotypes("/user/ds/genomics/1kg/parquet")
val gt = genotypesRDD.rdd.first()
...
```

Say we want to compute the minor allele frequency across all our samples for each variant genome-wide that overlaps a CTCF binding site. We essentially must join our CTCF data from the previous section with the genotype data from the 1000 Genomes project. In the previous TF binding site example, we showed how to use the ADAM join machinery directly. However, when we load data through ADAM, in many cases we obtain an object that implements the GenomicRDD trait, which has some built-in methods for filtering and joining, as we show below:

```
import org.bdgenomics.adam.models.ReferenceRegion
import org.bdgenomics.adam.rdd.InnerTreeRegionJoin
val ctcfRDD = (sc.loadFeatures(
  "/user/ds/genomics/chip-seq/GM12878.ChIP-seq.CTCF.narrowPeak").rdd
  .map(f => { ❶
    f.setContigName(f.getContigName.stripPrefix("chr"))
    f
  })
  .map(f => (ReferenceRegion.unstranded(f), f)))
val keyedGenotypesRDD = genotypesRDD.rdd.map(f => (ReferenceRegion(f), f))
val filteredGenotypesRDD = ( ❷
  InnerTreeRegionJoin().partitionAndJoin(ctcfRDD, keyedGenotypesRDD)
  .map(_._2))
filteredGenotypesRDD.cache() ❸
filteredGenotypesRDD.count() // 408107700
```

❶ We must perform this mapping because the CTCF data uses "chr1" whereas the genotype data uses "1" to refer to the same chromosome.

❷ The inner join performs the filtering. We broadcast the CTCF data because it is relatively small.

❸ Because the computation is large, we cache the resulting filtered data to avoid recomputing it.

We also need a function that will take a Genotype and compute the counts of the reference/alternate alleles:

```
import scala.collection.JavaConverters._
import org.bdgenomics.formats.avro.{Genotype, Variant, GenotypeAllele}
def genotypeToAlleleCounts(gt: Genotype): (Variant, (Int, Int)) = {
  val counts = gt.getAlleles.asScala.map(allele => { allele match {
    case GenotypeAllele.REF => (1, 0)
    case GenotypeAllele.ALT => (0, 1)
    case _ => (0, 0)
  }}).reduce((x, y) => (x._1 + y._1, x._2 + y._2))
```

```
      (gt.getVariant, (counts._1, counts._2))
  }
```

Finally, we generate the RDD[(Variant, (Int, Int))] and perform the aggregation:

```
val counts = filteredGenotypesRDD.map(gt => {  ❶
  val counts = gt.getAlleles.asScala.map(allele => { allele match {
    case GenotypeAllele.REF => (1, 0)
    case GenotypeAllele.ALT => (0, 1)
    case _ => (0, 0)
  }}).reduce((x, y) => (x._1 + y._1, x._2 + y._2))
  (gt.getVariant, (counts._1, counts._2))
})
val countsByVariant = counts.reduceByKey(
  (x, y) => (x._1 + y._1, x._2 + y._2))
val mafByVariant = countsByVariant.map(tup => {
  val (v, (r, a)) = tup
  val n = r + a
  (v, math.min(r, a).toDouble / n)
})
```

❶ We write this function anonymously because of a potential problem with closure serialization when working in a shell. Spark will try to serialize everything in the shell, which can cause errors. When running as a submitted job, the named function should work fine.

The countsByVariant RDD stores objects of type (Variant, (Int, Int)), where the first member of the tuple is the specific genome variant and the second member is a pair of counts: the first is the number of reference alleles seen, while the second is the number of alternate alleles seen. The mafByVariant RDD stores objects of type (Variant, Double), where the second member is the computed minor allele frequency from the pairs in countsByVariant. As an example:

```
scala> countsByVariant.first._2
res21: (Int, Int) = (1655,4)

scala> val mafExample = mafByVariant.first
mafExample: (org.bdgenomics.formats.avro.Variant, Double) = [...]

scala> mafExample._1.getContigName -> mafExample._1.getStart
res17: (String, Long) = (X,149849811)

scala> mafExample._2
res18: Double = 0.0024110910186859553
```

Traversing the entire data set is a sizable operation. Because we're only accessing a few fields from the genotype data, it would certainly benefit from predicate pushdown and projection, which we leave as an exercise to the reader. Also try running the computation on a subset of the data files if you cannot access a suitable cluster.

Where to Go from Here

Many computations in genomics fit nicely into the Spark computational paradigm. When you're performing ad hoc analysis, the most valuable contribution that projects like ADAM provide is the set of Avro schemas that represents the underlying analytical objects (along with the conversion tools). We saw how once data is converted into the corresponding Avro schemas, many large-scale computations become relatively easy to express and distribute.

While there may still be a relative dearth of tools for performing scientific research on Hadoop/Spark, there do exist a few projects that could help avoid reinventing the wheel. We explored the core functionality implemented in ADAM, but the project already has implementations for the entire GATK best-practices pipeline, including BQSR, indel realignment, and deduplication. In addition to ADAM, many institutions have signed on to the Global Alliance for Genomics and Health, which has started to generate schemas of its own for genomics analysis. The Broad Institute is now developing major software projects using Spark, including the newest version of the GATK4 (*https://github.com/broadinstitute/gatk*) and a new project called Hail (*https://github.com/hail-is/hail*) for large-scale population genetics computations. The Hammerbacher lab at Mount Sinai School of Medicine has also developed Guacamole (*https://github.com/hammerlab/guacamole*), a suite of tools mainly aimed at somatic variant calling for cancer genomics. All of these tools are open source, so if you start using them in your own work, please consider contributing improvements!

## CHAPTER 11

Analyzing Neuroimaging Data with PySpark and Thunder

Uri Laserson

We are not interested in the fact that the brain has the consistency of cold porridge.
   —Alan Turing

Advances in imaging equipment and automation have led to a glut of data on the function of the brain. While past experiments might have generated time series data from only a handful of electrodes in the brain or a small number of static images of brain slices, technologies today can sample brain activity from a large number of neurons in a large region while organisms are actively behaving. Indeed, the BRAIN Initiative (*https://www.braininitiative.nih.gov*) is a government-funded initiative with the lofty technology development goals of enabling, for example, simultaneous recording of the electrical activity of every neuron of the mouse brain over an extended period of time. While breakthroughs in measurement technology are certainly necessary, the amount of data generated will create completely new paradigms for biology.

In this chapter, we will introduce the PySpark API (*https://spark.apache.org/docs/latest/api/python/*) for interacting with Spark through Python, as well as the Thunder project (*http://thunder-project.org*), which is developed on top of PySpark for processing large amounts of time series data in general and neuroimaging data in particular. PySpark is a particularly flexible tool for exploratory big data analysis because it integrates well with the rest of the PyData ecosystem, including matplotlib for visualization, and even IPython Notebook (Jupyter) for "executable documents."

We will marshal these tools for the task of understanding some of the structure of zebrafish brains. Using Thunder, we will cluster different regions of the brain (representing groups of neurons) to discover patterns of activity as the zebrafish behaves over time. Like the chapter, Thunder was built on the PySpark RDD API, and continues to use it.

Overview of PySpark

Python is a favorite tool for many data scientists (*https://bit.ly/186ShId*), due to its high-level syntax and extensive library of packages, among other things. The Spark ecosystem has recognized Python's importance in the data analytics milieu and has invested in a Python API for using Spark, despite Python's historical difficulties integrating with the JVM.

Python for Scientific Computing and Data Science

Python has become a favorite tool for scientific computing and data science. It is now being used for many applications that would have traditionally used MATLAB, R, or Mathematica. The reasons include the following:

- Python is a high-level language that is easy to use and learn.
- It has an extensive library system ranging from niche numerical calculations to web-scraping utilities to data visualization tools.
- It interfaces easily with C/C++ code, allowing access to high-performance libraries, including BLAS/LAPACK/ATLAS.

Some libraries to keep in mind in particular include:

`numpy/scipy/matplotlib`
These libraries recapitulate typical MATLAB functionality, including fast array operations, scientific functions, and a widely used MATLAB-inspired plotting library.

`pandas`
This library provides functionality similar to R's `data.frame`, and oftentimes with much higher performance to boot.

`scikit-learn/statsmodels`
These libraries provide high-quality implementations of machine learning algorithms (e.g., classification/regression, clustering, matrix factorization) and statistical models.

`nltk`
A popular library for natural language processing.

You can find a large list of many other available libraries curated at the awesome-python repository on GitHub (*https://github.com/vinta/awesome-python*).

Start PySpark just like Spark:

```
export PYSPARK_DRIVER_PYTHON=ipython # PySpark can use the IPython shell
export PYSPARK_PYTHON=path/to/desired/python # For the worker nodes
pyspark --master ... --num-executors ... ❶
```

❶ pyspark takes the same Spark arguments as spark-submit and spark-shell

We can submit Python scripts using spark-submit, which will detect the *.py* extension on our scripts. You can specify which version of Python to use for the driver (e.g., IPython) and for the worker nodes; their versions must match. When the Python shell starts, it creates a Python SparkContext object (named sc) through which we interact with the cluster. Once the SparkContext is available, the PySpark API is very similar to the Scala API. For example, to load some CSV data:

```
raw_data = sc.textFile('path/to/csv/data') # RDD[string]
# filter, split on comma, parse floats to get a RDD[list[float]]
data = (raw_data
    .filter(lambda x: x.startswith("#"))
    .map(lambda x: map(float, x.split(','))))
data.take(5)
```

Just like in the Scala RDD API, we load a text file, filter out rows that start with #, and parse the CSV data into a list of float values. The Python functions passed to, for example, filter and map, are very flexible. They must take a Python object and return a Python object (in the case of filter, the return value is interpreted as a boolean). The only restrictions are that the Python function objects must be serializable with cloudpickle (which includes anonymous lambda functions), and any necessary modules referenced in the closures must be available on the PYTHONPATH of the executor Python processes. To ensure the availability of referenced modules, either the modules must be installed cluster-wide and available on the PYTHONPATH of the executor Python processes, or the corresponding module ZIP/EGG files must be explicitly distributed around by Spark, which will then add them to the PYTHONPATH. This latter functionality can be accomplished by a call to sc.addPyFile().

The PySpark RDDs are just RDDs of Python objects: like Python lists, they can store objects with mixed types (because underneath, all the objects are instances of PyObject).

PySpark Internals

It is useful to understand a bit about how PySpark is implemented in order to simplify debugging and also to be conscious of possible performance pitfalls (see Figure 11-1).

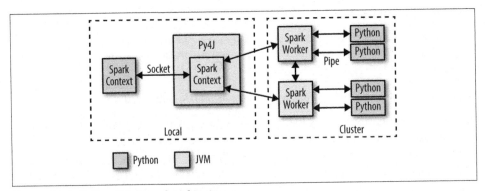

Figure 11-1. PySpark internal architecture

When PySpark's Python interpreter starts, it also starts a JVM with which it communicates through a socket. PySpark uses the Py4J project to handle this communication. The JVM functions as the actual Spark driver, and loads a JavaSparkContext that communicates with the Spark executors across the cluster. Python API calls to the SparkContext object are then translated into Java API calls to the JavaSparkContext. For example, the implementation of PySpark's sc.textFile() dispatches a call to the .textFile method of the JavaSparkContext, which ultimately communicates with the Spark executor JVMs to load the text data from HDFS.

The Spark executors on the cluster start a Python interpreter for each core, with which they communicate data through a Unix pipe (stdin and stdout) when they need to execute user code. A Python RDD in the local PySpark client corresponds to a PythonRDD object in the local JVM. The data associated with the RDD actually lives in the Spark JVMs as Java objects. For example, running sc.textFile() in the Python interpreter will call the JavaSparkContext's textFile method, which loads the data as Java String objects in the cluster. Similarly, loading a Parquet/Avro file using newAPIHadoopFile will load the objects as Java Avro objects.

When an API call is made on the Python RDD, any associated code (e.g., Python lambda function) is serialized via cloudpickle and distributed to the executors. The data is then converted from Java objects to a Python-compatible representation (e.g., pickle objects) and streamed to executor-associated Python interpreters through a pipe. Any necessary Python processing is executed in the interpreter, and the resulting data is stored back as an RDD (as pickle objects by default) in the JVMs.

Python's built-in support for serializing executable code is not as powerful as Scala's. As a result, the authors of PySpark had to use a custom module called "cloudpickle" built by the now defunct PiCloud.

Overview and Installation of the Thunder Library

Thunder Examples and Documentation

The Thunder package has excellent documentation and tutorials. The following examples draw from the documentation's data sets and tutorials.

Thunder is a Python tool set for processing large amounts of spatial/temporal data sets (i.e., large multidimensional matrices) on Spark. It makes heavy use of NumPy for matrix computations and also the MLlib library for distributed implementations of some statistical techniques. Python also makes it very flexible and accessible to a broad audience. In the following section, we introduce the Thunder API and attempt to classify some neural traces into a set of patterns using MLlib's K-means implementation as wrapped by Thunder and PySpark. Installing Thunder simply requires calling `pip install thunder-python`, though it must be installed on all worker nodes.

After installation, and setting the SPARK_HOME environment variable, we can create PySpark shell like so:

```
$ export PYSPARK_DRIVER_PYTHON=ipython # recommended as usual
$ pyspark --master ... --num-executors ...

[...some logging output...]
Welcome to


   / __/__  ___ _____/ /__
  _\ \/ _ \/ _ `/ __/  '_/
 /__ / .__/\_,_/_/ /_/\_\   version 2.0.2
    /_/

Using Python version 2.7.6 (default, Apr  9 2014 11:54:50)
SparkContext available as sc.

Running thunder version 0.5.0_dev
A thunder context is available as tsc

In [1]:
```

Loading Data with Thunder

Thunder was designed especially with neuroimaging data sets in mind. Therefore, it is geared toward analyzing data from large sets of images that are often captured over time.

Let's start by loading some images of zebrafish brains from an example data set provided by the Thunder repository in S3: s3://thunder-sample-data/images/fish/. For the purposes of demonstration, the examples presented are performed on enormously downsampled data. See the Thunder documentation for additional (and larger) data sets. The zebrafish is a commonly used model organism in biology research. It is small, reproduces quickly, and is used as a model for vertebrate development. It's also interesting because it has exceptionally fast regenerative capabilities. In the context of neuroscience, the zebrafish makes a great model because it is transparent and the brain is small enough that it is essentially possible to image it entirely at a high-enough resolution to distinguish individual neurons. Here is the code to load the data:

```
import thunder as td
data = td.images.fromtif('/user/ds/neuro/fish', engine=sc)  ❶
print data
print type(data.values)
print data.values._rdd
...
Images
mode: spark  ❷
dtype: uint8
shape: (20, 2, 76, 87)
<class 'bolt.spark.array.BoltArraySpark'>  ❸
PythonRDD[2] at RDD at PythonRDD.scala:48  ❹
```

❶ Note how we pass the SparkContext object. Thunder also supports local operations with the same API.

❷ We can see an Images object backed by Spark.

❸ The underlying data container abstraction is a BoltArray. This project abstracts over local data representation and Spark RDD representations.

❹ The underlying RDD object

This created an Images object that ultimately wraps an RDD, accessible as data.values._rdd. The Images object exposes the relevant similar functionality (like count, first, etc.) as well. The underlying objects stored in Images are key-value pairs:

```
print data.values._rdd.first()
...
((0,), array([[[26, 26, 26, ..., 26, 26, 26],
        [26, 26, 26, ..., 26, 26, 26],
        [26, 26, 26, ..., 27, 27, 26],
        ...,
        [26, 26, 26, ..., 27, 27, 26],
        [26, 26, 26, ..., 27, 26, 26],
        [25, 25, 25, ..., 26, 26, 26]],

       [[25, 25, 25, ..., 26, 26, 26],
        [25, 25, 25, ..., 26, 26, 26],
```

```
[26, 26, 26, ..., 26, 26, 26],
...,
[26, 26, 26, ..., 26, 26, 26],
[26, 26, 26, ..., 26, 26, 26],
[25, 25, 25, ..., 26, 26, 26]]], dtype=uint8))
```

The key (0,) corresponds to the zeroth image in the set (they are ordered lexicographically from the data directory), and the value is a NumPy array corresponding to the image. All of the core data types in Thunder are ultimately backed by Python RDDs of key-value pairs, where the keys are typically some kind of tuple and the values are NumPy arrays. The keys and values always have a homogeneous type across the RDD, even though PySpark generally allows RDDs of heterogeneous collections. Because of the homogeneity, the Images object exposes a .shape property describing the underlying dimensions:

```
print data.shape
...
(20, 2, 76, 87)
```

This describes 20 "images" where each image is a 2×76×87 stack.

Pixels, Voxels, and Stacks

"Pixel" is a portmanteau of "picture element." Digital images can be modeled as simple 2D matrices of intensity values, and each element in the matrix is a pixel. (A color image would require three of these matrices, one each for a red, green, and blue channel.) However, because the brain is a 3D object, a single 2D slice is not nearly enough to capture its activity. To address this, multiple techniques will either acquire multiple 2D images in different planes on top of each other (a z-stack), and some will even generate 3D information directly (e.g., light field microscopy). This ultimately produces a 3D matrix of intensity values, where each value represents a "volume element," or "voxel." Consistent with this, Thunder models all images as 2D or 3D matrices, depending on the specific data type, and can read file formats like *.tiff* that can natively represent 3D stacks.

One of the features of working in Python is that we can easily visualize our data while working with the RDDs, in this case using the venerable matplotlib library (see Figure 11-2):

```
import matplotlib.pyplot as plt
img = data.first()
plt.imshow(img[:, :, 0], interpolation='nearest', aspect='equal',
    cmap='gray')
```

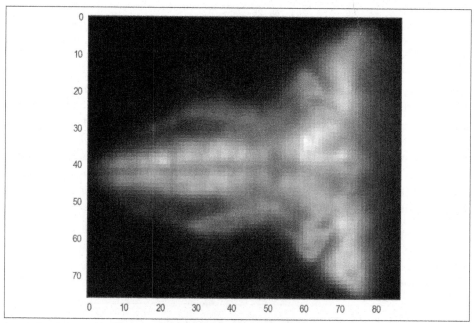

Figure 11-2. A single slice from the raw zebrafish data

The `Images` API offers useful methods for working with the image data in a distributed fashion—for example, to subsample each image down (see Figure 11-3):

```
subsampled = data.subsample((1, 5, 5)) ❶
plt.imshow(subsampled.first()[:, :, 0], interpolation='nearest',
    aspect='equal', cmap='gray')
print subsampled.shape
...
(20, 2, 16, 18)
```

❶ The stride to subsample each dimension: the first dimension is not subsampled while the second and third dimensions take every fifth value. Note that this is an RDD operation, so it returns immediately, waiting for an RDD action to trigger computation.

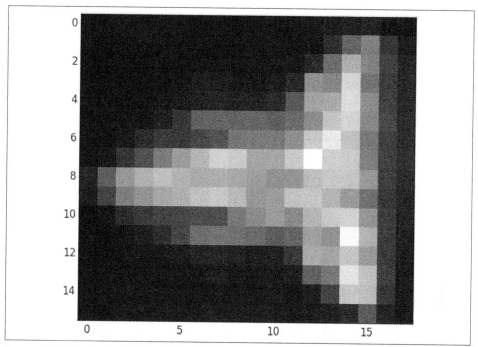

Figure 11-3. A single slice from the subsampled zebrafish data

While analyzing the collection of images may be useful for certain operations (e.g., normalizing images in certain ways), it's difficult to take the temporal relationship of the images into account. To do so, we'd rather work with the image data as a collection of pixel/voxel time series. This is exactly what the Thunder `Series` object is for, and there is an easy way to convert:

```
series = data.toseries()
```

This operation executes a large-scale reorganization of the data into a `Series` object, which is an RDD of key-value pairs where the key is a tuple of the coordinates of each image (i.e., the voxel identifier) and the value is a 1D NumPy array corresponding to the time series of values:

```
print series.shape
print series.index
print series.count()
...
(2, 76, 87, 20)
[ 0  1  2  3  4  5  6  7  8  9 10 11 12 13 14 15 16 17 18 19]
13224
```

Whereas `data` was a collection of 20 images with dimensions 76×87×2, `series` is a collection of 13,224 (76×87×2) time series of length 20. The `series.index` property is a Pandas-style index that can be used to reference each of the arrays. Because our original images were 3D, the keys are 3-tuples:

```
print series.values._rdd.takeSample(False, 1)[0]
...
((0, 50, 6), array([29, 29, 29, 29, 29, 29, 29, 29, 29, 29, 29, 29, 29,
    29, 29, 29, 29, 29, 29, 29], dtype=uint8))
```

The Series API offers many methods for performing computations across the time series, either at the per-series level or across all series. For example:

```
print series.max().values
...
[[[[158 152 145 143 142 141 140 140 139 139 140 140 142 144 153 168 179 185
    185 182]]]]
```

computes the maximum value across all voxels at each time point, while:

```
stddev = series.map(lambda s: s.std())
print stddev.values._rdd.take(3)
print stddev.shape
...
[((0, 0, 0), array([ 0.4])), ((0, 0, 1), array([ 0.35707142]))]
(2, 76, 87, 20)
```

computes the standard deviation of each time series and returns the result as an RDD, preserving all the keys.

We can also locally repack the Series into a NumPy array with the specified shape (2×76×87 in this case):

```
repacked = stddev.toarray()
plt.imshow(repacked[:,:,0], interpolation='nearest', cmap='gray',
    aspect='equal')
print type(repacked)
print repacked.shape
...
<type 'numpy.ndarray'>
(2, 76, 87)
```

This allows us to plot the standard deviation of each voxel using the same spatial relationships (see Figure 11-4). We should take care to make sure that we're not trying to return too much data to the client, because it will consume significant network and memory resources.

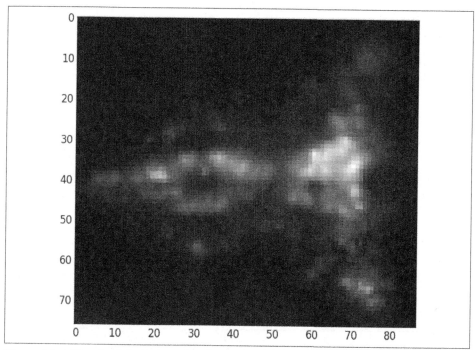

Figure 11-4. Standard deviation of each voxel in the raw zebrafish data

Alternatively, we can look at the centered time series directly, by plotting a subset of them (see Figure 11-5):

```
plt.plot(series.center().sample(50).toarray().T)
```

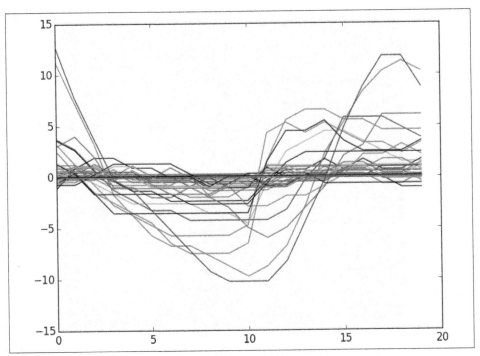

Figure 11-5. A random subset of 50 of the centered time series

It's also very easy to apply any UDFs to each series (including lambda functions), using the map method, which calls the underlying RDD's .map() method on the values in the underlying key-value pairs.

```
series.map(lambda x: x.argmin())
```

Thunder Core Data Types

More generally, the two core data types in Thunder, Series and Images, both inherit from the Data class, which ultimately contains a BoltArray that is backed by either a local NumPy array or a Spark RDD. The Data class models RDDs of key-value pairs, where the key represents some type of semantic identifier (e.g., a tuple of coordinates in space), and the value is a NumPy array of actual data. For the Images object, the key could be a time point, for example, and the value is the image at that time point formatted as a NumPy array. For the Series object, the key might be an *n*-dimensional tuple with the coordinates of the corresponding voxel, while the value is a 1D NumPy array representing the time series of measurements at that voxel. All the arrays in Series must have the same dimensions.

We can typically represent the same data set as either an `Images` or `Series` object, converting between the two through a (possibly expensive) shuffle operation (analogous to switching between row-major and column-major representations).

Data for Thunder can be persisted as a set of images, with the ordering encoded by lexicographic ordering of the individual image filenames; or the data can be persisted as a set of binary 1D arrays for `Series` objects. See the documentation (*http://docs.thunder-project.org*) for more details.

Categorizing Neuron Types with Thunder

In this example, we'll use the K-means algorithm to cluster the various fish time series into multiple clusters in an attempt to describe the classes of neural behavior. We will use data already persisted as `Series` data packaged in the repo that is larger than the image data used previously. However, the spatial resolution of this data is still too low to define individual neurons.

First, we load the data:

```
# this data set is available in the aas repo
images = td.images.frombinary(
    '/user/ds/neuro/fish-long', order='F', engine=sc)
series = images.toseries()
print series.shape
...
(76, 87, 2, 240)
[  0   1   2   3   4   5   6  ...   234 235 236 237 238 239]
```

We see this represents images with the same dimensions as earlier, but with 240 time points instead of 20. We must normalize our features to get the best clustering:

```
normalized = series.normalize(method='mean')
```

Let's plot a few of the series to see what they look like. Thunder allows us to take a random subset of the RDD and filter only collection elements that meet a certain criterion, like minimum standard deviation by default. To choose a good value for the threshold, let's first compute the standard deviation of each series and plot a histogram of a 10% sample of the values (see Figure 11-6):

```
stddevs = (normalized
    .map(lambda s: s.std())
    .sample(1000))
plt.hist(stddevs.values, bins=20)
```

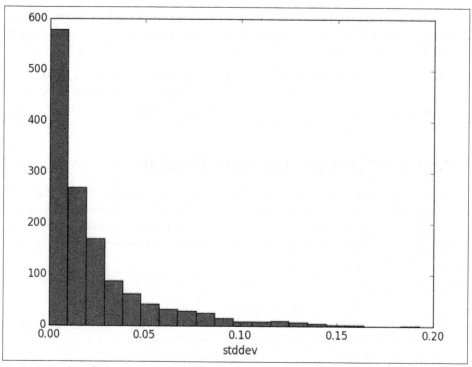

Figure 11-6. Distribution of the standard deviations of the voxels

With this in mind, we'll choose a threshold of 0.1 to look at the most "active" series (see Figure 11-7):

```
plt.plot(
    normalized
        .filter(lambda s: s.std() >= 0.1)
        .sample(50)
        .values.T)
```

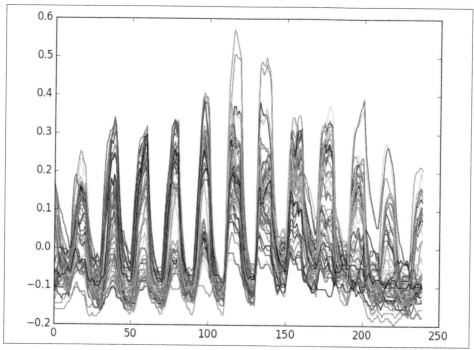

Figure 11-7. Fifty of the most active time series, based on standard deviation

Now that we have a feel for the data, let's finally cluster the voxels into the various patterns of behavior using MLlib's K-means implementation. We will perform K-means for multiple values of *k*:

```
from pyspark.mllib.clustering import KMeans
ks = [5, 10, 15, 20, 30, 50, 100, 200]
models = []
for k in ks:
    models.append(KMeans.train(normalized.values._rdd.values(), k))
```

Now we'll compute two simple error metrics on each of the clusterings. The first will simply be the sum across all time series of the Euclidean distance from the time series to its cluster center. The second will be a built-in metric of the KMeansModel object:

```
def model_error_1(model):
    def series_error(series):
        cluster_id = model.predict(series)
        center = model.centers[cluster_id]
        diff = center - series
        return diff.dot(diff) ** 0.5

    return (normalized
        .map(series_error)
        .toarray()
```

```
        .sum())

    def model_error_2(model):
        return model.computeCost(normalized.values._rdd.values())
```

We will compute both error metrics for each value of k and plot them (see Figure 11-8):

```
import numpy as np
errors_1 = np.asarray(map(model_error_1, models))
errors_2 = np.asarray(map(model_error_2, models))
plt.plot(
    ks, errors_1 / errors_1.sum(), 'k-o',
    ks, errors_2 / errors_2.sum(), 'b:v')
```

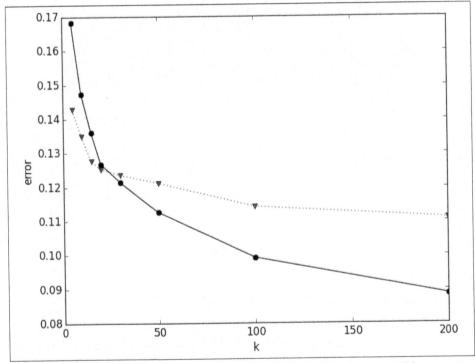

Figure 11-8. K-means error metrics as a function of k (black circles are model_error_1 and blue triangles are model_error_2)

We'd expect these metrics to generally be monotonically decreasing with k; it seems like k=20 might be a sharper elbow in the curve. Let's visualize the cluster centers that we've learned from the data (see Figure 11-9):

```
model20 = models[3]
plt.plot(np.asarray(model20.centers).T)
```

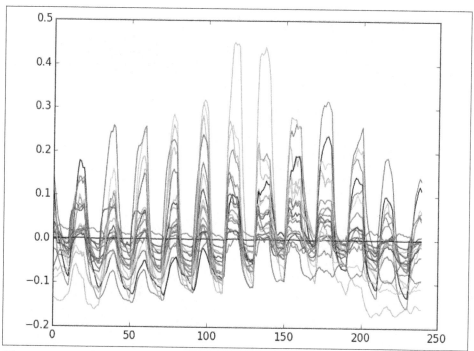

Figure 11-9. Model centers for k=20

It's also easy to plot the images themselves with the voxels colored according to their assigned cluster (see Figure 11-10):

```
import seaborn as sns
from matplotlib.colors import ListedColormap
cmap_cat = ListedColormap(sns.color_palette("hls", 10), name='from_list')
by_cluster = normalized.map(lambda s: model20.predict(s)).toarray()
plt.imshow(by_cluster[:, :, 0], interpolation='nearest',
    aspect='equal', cmap='gray')
```

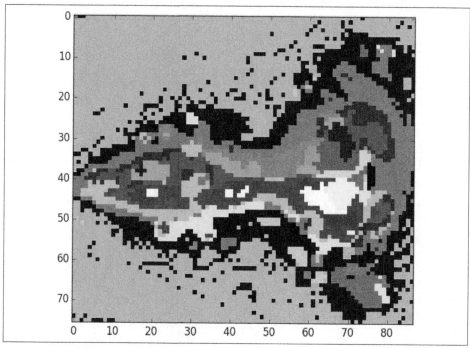

Figure 11-10. Voxels colored by cluster membership

It's clear that the learned clusters recapitulate certain elements of zebrafish brain anatomy. If the original data were high resolution enough to resolve subcellular structures, we could first perform clustering of the voxels with k equal to an estimate of the number of neurons in the imaged volume. This would allow us to effectively map out the entire neuron cell bodies. We would then define time series for each neuron, which could be used for clustering again to determine different functional categories.

Where to Go from Here

Thunder is a relatively new project, but includes a rich set of functionality. In addition to statistics on time series and clustering, it has modules for matrix factorizations, regression/classification, and tools for visualization. It has fantastic documentation and tutorials covering a large array of its functionality. To see Thunder in action, see the "Mapping brain activity at scale with cluster computing" (*https://bit.ly/186YPqi*) by Thunder authors in *Nature Methods* (July 2014).

Index

About the Authors

Sandy Ryza develops algorithms for public transit at Remix. Before that, he was a senior data scientist at Cloudera and Clover Health. He is an Apache Spark committer, Apache Hadoop PMC member, and founder of the Time Series for Spark project. He holds the Brown University computer science department's 2012 Twining award for "Most Chill."

Uri Laserson is an Assistant Professor of Genetics at the Icahn School of Medicine at Mount Sinai, where he develops scalable technology for genomics and immunology using the Hadoop ecosystem.

Sean Owen is Director of Data Science at Cloudera. He is an Apache Spark committer and PMC member, and was an Apache Mahout committer.

Josh Wills is the Head of Data Engineering at Slack, the founder of the Apache Crunch project, and wrote a tweet about data scientists once.

Colophon

The animal on the cover of *Advanced Analytics with Spark* is a peregrine falcon (*Falco peregrinus*); these falcons are among the world's most common birds of prey and live on all continents except Antarctica. They can survive in a wide variety of habitats including urban cities, the tropics, deserts, and the tundra. Some migrate long distances from their wintering areas to their summer nesting areas.

Peregrine falcons are the fastest-flying birds in the world—they are able to dive at 200 miles per hour. They eat other birds such as songbirds and ducks, as well as bats, and they catch their prey in mid-air.

Adults have blue-gray wings, dark brown backs, a buff-colored underside with brown spots, and white faces with a black tear stripe on their cheeks. They have a hooked beak and strong talons. Their name comes from the Latin word *peregrinus*, which means "to wander." Peregrines are favored by falconers, and have been used in that sport for many centuries.

Many of the animals on O'Reilly covers are endangered; all of them are important to the world. To learn more about how you can help, go to *animals.oreilly.com*.

The cover image is from Lydekker's *Royal Natural History*. The cover fonts are URW Typewriter and Guardian Sans. The text font is Adobe Minion Pro; the heading font is Adobe Myriad Condensed; and the code font is Dalton Maag's Ubuntu Mono.

Learn from experts.
Find the answers you need.

Sign up for a **10-day free trial** to get **unlimited access** to all of the content on Safari, including Learning Paths, interactive tutorials, and curated playlists that draw from thousands of ebooks and training videos on a wide range of topics, including data, design, DevOps, management, business—and much more.

Start your free trial at:
oreilly.com/safari

(No credit card required.)

CPSIA information can be obtained
at www.ICGtesting.com
Printed in the USA
BVOW08s0001200617
486784BV00012B/1/P